# IMITATION, KNOWLEDGE, AND THE TASK OF CHRISTOLOGY IN MAXIMUS THE CONFESSOR

# IMITATION, KNOWLEDGE, AND THE TASK OF CHRISTOLOGY IN MAXIMUS THE CONFESSOR

Luke Steven

CASCADE *Books* • Eugene, Oregon

IMITATION, KNOWLEDGE, AND THE TASK OF CHRISTOLOGY
IN MAXIMUS THE CONFESSOR

Cascade Books
An Imprint of Wipf and Stock Publishers
199 W. 8th Ave., Suite 3
Eugene, OR 97401

www.wipfandstock.com

PAPERBACK ISBN: 978-1-5326-7279-8
HARDCOVER ISBN: 978-1-5326-7280-4
EBOOK ISBN: 978-1-5326-7281-1

*Cataloguing-in-Publication data:*

Names: Steven, Luke, author.

Title: Imitation, knowledge, and the task of Christology in Maximus the Confessor / Luke Steven.

Description: Eugene, OR: Cascade Books, 2020 | Includes bibliographical references and index.

Identifiers: ISBN 978-1-5326-7279-8 (paperback) | ISBN 978-1-5326-7280-4 (hardcover) | ISBN 978-1-5326-7281-1 (ebook)

Subjects: LCSH: Maximus,—Confessor, Saint,—approximately 580–662. | Knowledge, Theory of (Religion). | Theology, Doctrinal—Byzantine Empire. | Jesus Christ—Person and office. | Jesus Christ—History of doctrines.

Classification: BR65.M416 S72 2020 (print) | BR65.M416 (ebook)

Manufactured in the U.S.A.                                    MARCH 2, 2020

# Table of contents

# Acknowledgements

I am grateful to my doctoral supervisor, Sarah Coakley, for all the time she gave me and for her willing and wise direction in the production of this study. I am grateful to my academic friends and colleagues in Cambridge and Durham universities for reading my work and helping me think through things, and to Hilary Goy, my guide in all things Greek. I am grateful to my family and friends for distracting me.

# Abbreviations

## Bible

Abbreviations of books of the Bible are from *The SBL Handbook of Style: for Ancient Near Eastern, Biblical, and Early Christian Studies*, edited by Patrick H. Alexander et al. Peabody, MA: Hendrickson, 1999.

## Maximus the Confessor

| | |
|---|---|
| *Ambig.* | *Ambigua ad Johannem* |
| *Ambig. Thom.* | *Ambigua ad Thomam* |
| *Bizy.* | *Disputatio Bizyae* |
| *Carit.* | *Capita de caritate* |
| *Cap. theol.* | *Capita theologica et oeconomica* |
| *Ep.* | *Epistulae* |
| *Ep. sec.* | *Epistula secunda ad Thomam* |
| *Myst.* | *Mystagogia* |
| *Op.* | *Opuscula theologica et polemica* |
| *Or. dom.* | *Expositio orationis dominicae* |
| *Pyrr.* | *Disputatio cum Pyrrho* |
| *Qu. dub.* | *Quaestiones et dubia* |
| *Qu. Thal.* | *Quaestiones ad Thalassium* |

# Other ancient authors

Abbreviations of works by Plato, Aristotle, and other classical authors are from: *The Oxford Classical Dictionary*, 3rd ed., edited by Simon Horn-blower and Antony Spawforth, xxix–liv. Oxford: Oxford University Press, 2003.

Abbreviations of Gregory of Nyssa's works are from: *The Brill Dictionary of Gregory of Nyssa*, edited by Lucas Francisco Mateo-Seco and Giulio Maspero, translated by Seth Cherney, xix–xxii. Leiden: Brill, 2010.

Abbreviations of works by other patristic authors are from: *A Patristic Greek Lexicon*, edited by G. W. H. Lampe, ix–xliii. Oxford: Clarendon, 1961.

## Series of editions and/or translations:

| | |
|---|---|
| ACO | Acta conciliorum oecumenicorum |
| ACW | Ancient Christian Writers |
| CAG | Commentaria in Aristotelem Graeca |
| CCSG | Corpus Christianorum, series graeca |
| CCT | Corpus Christianorum in Translation |
| FC | Fathers of the Church |
| GCS | Die Griechischen christlichen schriftsteller |
| GNO | Gregorii Nysseni Opera |
| LCL | Loeb Classical Library |
| PAO | Philonis Alexandrini opera quae supersunt |
| PG | Patrologia Graeca |
| PO | Patrologia Orientalis |
| PTS | Patristische Texte Und Studien |
| SC | Sources Chrétiennes |

## Journals

| | |
|---|---|
| JECS | *Journal of Early Christian Studies* |

JTS             *Journal of Theological Studies*

SP              *Studia Patristica*

VG              *Vigiliae Christianae*

# *Introduction*

## Dogma versus "spirituality":
## a problem in the thought of Maximus the Confessor

Maximus the Confessor (580–662) was a Palestinian monk whose combustive historical era, committed doctrinal reflection, and loud and influential voice took him on a turbulent career of traveling and writing around the Mediterranean. His career ended in his eighties with mutilation and death for the sake of a christological position subsequently vindicated as orthodox. Although the evidence is partial and ambiguous, the story of his life has been retold with increasing clarity in recent years.[1] The primary object of this work is not the history and details of this man's unusually influential monastic career. Rather, this work will take up the more focused task of deciphering something of his theological epistemology, by which I mean his conception of what enables knowledge of God.[2] Specifically, the aim of this work is to identify and examine the intriguing connection between *imitation* and *knowledge* that Maximus upholds throughout his written oeuvre. From his earliest to his latest works, I will suggest, Maximus proposes that knowledge of God comes about as the knower achieves a likeness to God. However, to claim, as I am, that there is any enduring characteristic of Maximus' epistemology is somewhat

---

1. The best recent summaries of Maximus' life and historical context are: Booth, *Crisis of Empire*, 143–70; Allen, "Life and Times of Maximus," 3–18; Blowers, *Maximus the Confessor*, 9–63.

2. My anachronistic use of the term "epistemology" throughout this study is intended to share none of the skeptical anxieties associated with the so-called problem of "foundationalism" in the modern period.

counter-intuitive in light of one dramatic historical shift in his career. It is worth highlighting this shift at the outset.

Changes of style in the Confessor's works are not themselves surprising because, as commentators have observed, Maximus lived a busy life of traveling and networking and his writings are, on the whole, "occasional";[3] his teaching and philosophical claims appear in action, in response to particular and varying situations or calls, rather than in summary. However, from around 633, Maximus became engaged in a particularly protracted and complicated occasion of christological conflict, in response to which he drastically and forevermore turned his communicative style and, apparently, his approach to knowledge into something much more dogmatic, polemical, and scholastic than can be found in his early works of exegesis and spirituality.[4] It was this engagement in the intensifying christological conflict of his day that earned him the posthumous title "Confessor" and that divides what I will call his "early" and "late" writings. In its nascent form, the conflict was over the question of whether Christ had one divine-and-human "activity" (ἐνέργεια), or two "activities" (ἐνεργεῖαι)—one divine and one human. In the late 630s, the terms of the debate shifted from "activities" to "wills" (θελήματα), and the issue then became whether Christ possessed one divine-and-human "will," or two "wills"—one divine and one human. Maximus became a pioneer and spokesman for the latter side of the debate, labeled by scholars the "dyoenergist" and "dyothelite" position, the opposing side being "monenergist" and "monothelite."

As Maximus engaged in this christological conflict his writings took on a new and permanent character, a character that has caused some anxiety amongst scholars, for reasons perhaps best articulated by the historian Averil Cameron. Cameron highlights a growing obsession in sixth- and seventh-century Byzantine Christianity with *disputation* and *definition* as the key modes and literary forms for ordering knowledge.[5] From this rhetorical observation she characterizes this period of Christian discourse as an "attempt to find a new systematization of knowledge,"[6] a new structure of "certainty" in the face of the insecurity and huge social

---

3. Andrew Louth was perhaps the first to characterize Maximus' writings like this. See Louth, *Maximus the Confessor*, 15, 42.

4. Louth, "Dogma and Spirituality," 199–200.

5. See Cameron, "Disputations," 91–108, and "Byzantium and the Past," 250–76.

6. Cameron, "Disputations," 100.

and political collapses caused by invading Persian and Arab armies.[7] The rhetoric of Christian writers of the period, among whom Cameron includes Maximus as a perfect example, shows that these Christians set out to produce a "total discourse,"[8] "complete systems of knowledge" in which "Christian history and Christian authority is defined . . . as consisting in the Scriptures, the Councils and the works of the approved, or select, Fathers. All necessary human knowledge is to be found and confined in that chain of authority."[9] Of Maximus' works, the late writings on Christology most clearly fit Cameron's portrait of a new Byzantine system of Christian knowledge-management.

The cause of consternation for the reader of Maximus is not the fact of discrepancy in style or content between his early and late works. As already noted, such differences are not themselves surprising or problematic. The problem is the apparent discrepancy between two approaches to knowledge and how to manage it. In Maximus' early exegetical and spiritual works, knowledge emerges through improvising, through provisional exploration, and is regulated and authenticated by ascetic practice and the language and imagery of the Bible; in the late works, by contrast, knowledge arrives as the heavily jargonized and technical product of logical argument, severe polemic, and slavish recourse to a small selection of patristic citations. The hard discrepancy is not between Maximus' early and late works *per se*, but, as Louth articulates it, between "dogma and spirituality." Although Louth aims to collapse this distinction by showing that these two modes of knowledge-management in fact harmoniously inhere, he does not quite fulfil his proposal, and instead discourses on two related but not ultimately relevant points (that "intellect" and "desire" are not opposed for Maximus, and that his early and late works share a philosophical vocabulary).[10] A more promising attempt to reconcile Maximus' diverging approaches to knowledge in his early and late works has recently been offered by Paul Blowers. Blowers attempts to qualify Cameron's thesis in a way that can hold together Maximus' early and late works. He argues that Maximus' later christological polemical works—his works of *disputation* and *definition*—rest upon his long prior monastic career of spiritual and ascetic reflection. By the time Maximus

7. Cameron, "Disputations," 107.

8. Cameron, "Byzantium and the Past," 269 (see also 255).

9. Cameron, "Disputations," 106.

10. Louth, "Dogma and Spirituality," 197–208.

turned his hand to the christological conflicts of his day, Blowers argues, he held a "charismatic authority" that was itself a crucial ingredient in the Christian validity structure of his day.[11] In essence, Maximus' earlier spiritual works and ascetic enterprise earned him the authority to adopt a dryer and more abstracted epistemological procedure in his later christological works. I find Blower's theory compelling, but he does not show how it is grounded in the texts themselves.

It is in fact Cameron herself, in a later article, who comes closest to offering the more nuanced way forward that Blowers is feeling towards, taking serious account of Maximus' identity as a monk and spiritual authority. Cameron's new suggestion is, however, no less acerbic and suspicious than her previous approach. Cameron argues that the "competitive process of system construction" and "persistent impulse towards definition" of Christian writing in Maximus' period relied upon another crucial ingredient: "ascetic discourse." By this Cameron simply means forms of discourse that express "ascetic ideas" and use ascetic "vocabulary."[12] Cameron says that Christian asceticism by "its very nature implied discipline as well as certainty," and "allowed no overt challenge, no possibility of tolerance, no uncertainty." In this way, ascetic texts were perfectly suited to the task of forging an epistemological "closure" or total discourse that Cameron says characterized early Byzantine Christianity.[13] By this analysis, Maximus' early ascetic works and his late dogmatic works would in fact share the same structure of knowledge-management, not because his late dogmatic works are ascetically grounded, but the opposite: because his early ascetic works were in fact authoritarian and dogmatic in the first place.

The present work began as an attempt to read Maximus' late christological works, which are mainly letters, with both the methods of rhetorical analysis of a Byzantinist like Cameron and with the eye of a patristics scholar like Blowers, more sensitive to theological and spiritual themes. I have found that if one listens to Maximus' late letters slowly and fully in this way—giving attention to their rhetorical form and aims as well as their spiritual integrity and purpose—a picture of Maximus' approach to knowledge emerges that is more convincing, textually based, and accurate than what Cameron and Blowers describe, an approach,

11. Blowers, *Maximus the Confessor*, 65–66; 96–98.

12. Cameron, "Ascetic Closure," 147–61; 150.

13. Cameron, "Ascetic Closure," 156–57.

moreover, that pervades Maximus' whole career and spans the disparate genres of his writings. Let me outline this picture. In amongst the scholastic argument and dogmatic intoning of his late christological letters, the careful listener can in fact hear the Confessor addressing his reader with "ascetic discourse," in Cameron's words: all the themes of imitation, desire, renunciation, battle, and spiritual ascent are present that one would expect to find in any ascetic text. But Cameron's quite bleak and reductive picture of "ascetic discourse" as a means of furnishing epistemological "closure" is completely uncharacteristic of what we find here. Instead, what Maximus offers is an epistemological method that aims at *opening* his reader to a transformation of mind and life. As Maximus and his contemporaries busily write letters to each other, in desperate attempts to clarify christological technicalities and to discern and settle upon the most faithful ways to speak and think of the mystery of the incarnation, Maximus' voice can be heard again and again sounding the same guiding advice to his colleagues: our task of discernment not only involves scriptural and argumentative reflection, and adherence to our orthodox forebears, but, first and foremost, it grows out from the hard labor of *imitating* Christ the Word. Knowing divine things and drawing towards a right confession of Christian doctrine depends on imitation, on conformation in likeness to the object of knowledge. This ascetically grounded epistemological procedure is what Maximus' late christological works frequently propound, it is what ties them to his early spiritual and ascetic works, and it is the subject-matter of the present work.

## Knowing-by-likeness

That doctrinal truth is discerned by likeness or imitation is a broad patristic truism.[14] By this model, knowers know by becoming like their object of knowledge. Indeed, this is an ancient maxim of Greek philosophy,

---

14. Perhaps the clearest earlier example comes in the conclusion of Athanasius' *On the Incarnation*, a passage that we will look at in the first chapter. In Latin Christianity, Lewis Ayres and Rowan Williams have both argued that Augustine paints a similar picture, where Christ-likeness is the condition for understanding and assenting to the mystery of the incarnation (Ayres, "Christology as Contemplative Practice," 190–211; Williams, "Augustine's Christology," 176–89). In Williams' summary, "there can be no accurate discussion of the incarnation that is not itself incarnationally modeled," that is, modeled by "humility" in particular (188).

classically summarized by Aristotle in the words "like is known by like."[15] But it is something worth studying in Maximus in particular because this epistemological approach permeates his work yet has not been identified or elucidated before. On the one hand, it is scattered through Maximus' early ascetic works, appearing in tried and tested as well as original ways. On the other hand, and even more intriguingly, Maximus puts this epistemology into action by building it into the rhetoric of many of his (early and late) letters: namely, through the rhetorical form of the epistolary praise address, whose recurring presence, consistent form, and epistemological and theological function have been ignored in Maximus scholarship until now. The aims of this project are (in order): to identify how this epistemological model entered early Christian discourse; to unpack its significance in Maximus' early works; and to highlight the crucial role it plays in the rhetoric and methodology of the Confessor's late christological letters.

I am aware that this angle of research sits somewhat strangely against the landscape of Maximus scholarship. On the one hand, there is little precedent for examining the epistemological assumption that like is known by like (from now I will simply call this a "likeness epistemology") in any early Christian thinkers, let alone in Maximus the Confessor. Classical scholars have long acknowledged a likeness epistemology amongst pre-Christian Greek thinkers. Scholars of early Christianity, however, whilst aware of it, have rarely analyzed it, despite its subtle or explicit presence in the thought of so many Christian thinkers, especially in the traditions of theology that spring from Clement and Origen of Alexandria. When it comes to Maximus, his theological epistemology has been studied in some depth, and has usually been presented as an aspect of his engulfing doctrine of "deification," whereby knowledge of God is one result of conformation to God. In this sense, by acknowledging deification as the foundation of Maximus' theological epistemology, commentators have often but obliquely acknowledged that his epistemology takes for granted something of the knowing-by-likeness model. But scholarship has shown no alertness to the shades and details of this generic epistemological pattern in Maximus, which are many and intriguing.

On the other hand, while Maximus' Christology has always drawn much attention for its *propositional content*,[16] the latter chapters of this

15. *De an.* 404B.

16. Perhaps the most detailed contemporary account of Maximus' Christology is offered by Bathrellos, *The Byzantine Christ.* For a briefer summary of Maximus'

study identify the *method* and *ascetic procedure* of his Christology.[17] I will be taking a new route into the Confessor's Christology by aiming to highlight how imitation largely constitutes, not just complements, his dogmatic christological method. This aspect of Maximus' Christology will be drawn out by treating his christological works for what they are: *letters*, and not systematic treatises, with rhetorical features and tactics that tell us a great deal about what Maximus thought he was doing in writing Christology.

In short, this work takes untrodden routes into the Confessor's thought. As a consequence, in researching and writing it I have had the pleasure of finding little to argue against and much to argue for, and I have also felt the exciting sense of finding a new object, a new aspect of the Confessor, that I hope will be a convincing addition to our current understanding of the man.

## Order of the study

The present work will unfold in six chapters. Chapter 1 is an essay on how a likeness epistemology took hold in Christian thought. It will be shown that there were at least two distinct strands of the notion that "like is known by like" in pre-Christian Greek thought, one that was developed in philosophical and scientific discussions about how perception works, and another that belonged to the assumptions of allegorical interpreters about how hidden truth can be accessed through texts. This latter strand of the knowing-by-likeness motif is the one that most heavily influenced Christian thinkers, especially Clement and Origen of Alexandria, and that was in turn bequeathed to their theological successors, including Maximus.

Readers who would like to get to Maximus himself may begin at Chapter 2. This chapter focuses on the Confessor's early works, those written before he became involved in christological conflicts. I will begin

---

developed christological position in the context of neo-Chalcedonian Christology and politics, see Hovorun, "Maximus, a Cautious Neo-Chalcedonian."

17. For a good example of a similarly ascetically grounded christological method from the Christian East, see David Michelson's recent monograph on the monophysite christologian Philoxenos of Mabbug. Michelson argues that Philoxenos presents the knowledge of God and the discernment of doctrine as achievements marked and enabled by ascetic practice—but not, however, by *imitative* ascetic practice (Michelson, *The Practical Christology of Philoxenos*).

by pointing out that Maximus witnesses to the same likeness epistemology identified in Chapter 1 in the allegorical methods of Clement and Origen, and I will take some time to show that Gregory Nazianzen in particular mediated this epistemological tradition to Maximus. The remainder of the chapter will explore three original ways that a likeness epistemology appears in the Confessor's early writings. First, I will turn to the *Centuries on Love*, in which Maximus presents love as a condition for knowledge of God, who is Love himself. Secondly, the chapter will focus on the theme of knowing by "virtue." Maximus regularly suggests that virtue is a means of attaining knowledge of God, and I will argue that this is because, for him, "virtue" is the means of restoring human "likeness" to God, or indeed is itself "Godlikeness." Thirdly, we will explore some daring passages in which Maximus paints a picture of what I will call "unknowing-by-likeness": he suggests that it is possible for the believer's desire to stretch to imitate even God's unknowable attributes, and thereby grasp them in a comprehension that is beyond knowledge.

Chapter 3 establishes Maximus' doctrine of deification as a crucial conceptual foundation that enables him to take for granted and experiment with the knowing-by-likeness motif in the ways displayed in Chapter 2. Although there is much excellent scholarship on deification in Maximus, the topic has become sprawling and confusing in the secondary literature, so my first aim in this chapter will be to offer a tidy and straightforward definition of the doctrine. I will then proceed to identify two ways that Maximus' doctrine of deification grounds his likeness epistemology. On the one hand, in Maximus' mind deification is precisely an achievement of "likeness" to God, and in this sense "knowing-by-deification" is just as valid a summary of Maximus' epistemology as is "knowing-by-likeness." On the other hand, Maximus' doctrine of deification is defined by a rule of "proportion" (ἀναλογία is the key term). Although Maximus' concept or rule of "proportion" has hitherto been largely passed over by commentators, it is in fact a very commonly recurring logical habit or thought-pattern in the Confessor's works. This will be worth unpacking in detail, at least to make up for the lack of scholarly attention, but also because Maximus' rule of "proportion"—whereby God interacts with the creature "in proportion" to the creature's likeness to God—gives a deeper framework for his likeness epistemology. The second half of this chapter will transpose the discussion slightly: just as deification, identity with God by likeness, is the theological concept that undergirds Maximus' likeness epistemology, I will argue that Maximus' notion of Christ "incarnating" himself in believers who imitate him provides the theological keystone for Maximus' later christological method, which will be the topic of the rest of the study.

The final three chapters explore how a likeness epistemology plays out in Maximus' later works of dogmatic Christology. These chapters together will assemble the single claim that, in his christological letters, Maximus consistently presents the imitation of Christ as a crucial condition for right understanding of the mystery of the incarnation. Just as in the early works "like is known by like," so in these late works christological doctrine is discerned by Christ-likeness. Chapter 4 makes the first steps towards this claim by identifying one of Maximus' favorite and unique rhetorical forms: the epistolary praise address. Maximus often begins his letters or sent works with praise of the recipient. I will explore how the form of these praise addresses, while reflecting many late-antique conventions of praise rhetoric, is unique to Maximus. I will also show that the function of these addresses is unique: Maximus often carefully composes his address to praise his recipient for imitating the very content that the letter will cover. In *Letter* 2, for example, which will be examined at length as a case study, Maximus begins by praising the addressees for the ways they display divine love in their lives, before he turns to the letter's subject: divine love itself. The rhetorical function of epistolary addresses like this is to persuade the listener of the letter's teachings, and Maximus thinks he can do so by praising his listener for already imitating and manifesting these teachings in their ascetic striving. The tactic of these praise addresses reveals something of the kind of epistemological endeavor that Maximus imagines himself and his readers to be undertaking: an endeavor in which the goal of correct understanding and confession of divine things comes nearer as one is shaped and assimilated to those divine things. "Like is known by like," in other words. The second case study considered in this chapter will be Maximus' *Second Letter to Thomas*. This letter also opens with a praise address, which exemplifies the same tactics of persuasion noted in *Letter* 2, but this time the content of the letter is christological. We will highlight how Maximus accordingly shifts his rhetorical aim, and now praises his addressee for imitating Christ and, indeed, the finer points of the christological doctrine that the letter communicates. Again, the rhetoric gives us a clue about how Maximus thinks doctrinal discernment works; Maximus prepares his reader to digest his christological teachings by first encouraging them to take up habits of Christ-like life. Here we will get our first glimpse of Maximus' methodological assumption that christological doctrine is discerned by Christ-likeness.

Having established the form and epistemological function of Maximus' praise addresses, the fifth chapter will turn to more of the Confessor's christological letter addresses in order to unearth his assumptions about doctrinal discernment more fully. This discussion will be prefaced with two short explorations into two important pieces of Maximus' doctrinal vocabulary: "dogma" and "mystery." First, I will argue that in Maximus' wider works "dogma" (or "doctrine") is a piece of *ascetic* vocabulary, and that approaching Christian doctrines is an ascetic, rather than scholastic, enterprise. This makes some sense of Maximus' claims about the importance of imitation in discerning "dogma." Secondly, Maximus characterizes the endeavor of his christological letters with the language of "mystery," and I will argue that for him, as for his predecessors going right back to the ancient texts dealt with in Chapter 1, "mystery" labels not only a reality to be known, but a reality to have one's life shaped by. Something of the "knowing-by-likeness" theme belongs to the notion of "mystery" itself, in other words. Having set the stage by exploring these two pieces of doctrinal vocabulary, the chapter will turn to the christological letters, and especially their rhetorical praise addresses. I will argue that in these texts Maximus rhetorically encourages at least two broad shapes of Christ-likeness to his readers as epistemic aids: descending and ascending. He recommends virtues of descent and humility that imitate the Word's self-emptying into humanity, and he praises his readers for achievements of ascent and exposure to what is hidden, imitating the Word's own life with the Father and his hidden divinity.

In the sixth and final chapter we will follow this same procedure with the more specific aim of discovering what kinds of imitation Maximus recommends to his readers when it comes to grasping the mystery of Christ's two *wills*, or the "dyothelite" confession, in particular. In examining some of Maximus' dyothelite letters I will argue that, alongside virtues of descending and rising, Maximus sketches a third way of imitation for his readers to adopt: willing or desiring. I will point out that Maximus often prefaces his teaching on dyothelite Christology by praising his recipients' desire. By doing so he aids his dyothelite argumentation with the following tactic: he attempts to bring his reader to understand and confess that Christ had a human will totally obedient to the divine will (as Maximus' dyothelite position maintains), by exhorting them to harmonize their own human wills with God's through a transformation of their desire.

At the heart of this study, then, is a neglected theme in Maximus' thought—that "like is known by like." This is an epistemological theme that is present throughout his early works and definitive of the method of his late works; and once we are aware of it, we can more easily read together these otherwise divergent regions of his thought. It is also a theme whose Christian origins are obscure, and the first task of this study is to cast some light on them.

All translations of Greek text in this study are my own unless otherwise indicated.

# 1

## *Knowing-by-likeness*

### *Some origins of a patristic epistemology*

According to Clement of Alexandria, a key ingredient for successful education is likeness to one's teacher:

> And just as Ischomachus will make whoever attaches himself to him a husbandman, and Lampis a sea-captain, and Charidemus a general, and Simon a horseman, and Perdix a salesman, and Crobylus a cook, and Archelaus a dancer, and Homer a poet, and Pyrrho a wrangler, and Demosthenes an orator, and Chrysippus a dialectician, and Aristotle a scientist, and Plato a philosopher, so whoever obeys the Lord . . . is perfectly perfected after the image of his Teacher, and goes about a god in flesh.[1]

Origen, Clement's slightly younger successor, agreed with him: "The goal of the teacher . . . is this: to make the disciple as [ὡς] himself." Indeed, Jesus says as much too, Origen points out: "It is sufficient for the disciple that he be as his teacher" (Matt 10:25).[2] Clement and Origen both witness to a *phenomenological* observation, or piece of common sense, that was basic to ancient Greek *paideia*: you become like what you study. But along with this observation, Clement and Origen made an additional *epistemological* claim: likeness to your object of study is not only *the result of*, but the *condition for* knowing it. First comes the movement, following the steps of your teacher, then comes the understanding; or, as Aristotle was

1. *Strom.* 7.16.101 (SC 428, 304).
2. *Jo.* 32.10.118–19 (SC 385, 238–41).

the first to put it, "like is known by like."[3] This truism of Greek thought entered Christianity when Alexandrian theologians, namely Clement and Origen, made Greek education and epistemology their own, as they forged a distinct Christian concept and practice of education. In their picture, not only might a believer hope to be conformed to the objects of Christian philosophy, but he should seek this conformation *in order* to discern these objects. This chapter tackles in detail the question of how the seeds of this epistemological model—that "like is known by like"—landed in the Christian discourse of second- and third-century Alexandria and began to flourish there (wherefrom its roots grew and eventually extended to the thought of Maximus the Confessor and nourished it, as we will see in the ensuing chapters). This is a preliminary question; my aim in asking it is to fill out the background and tradition upon which Maximus' epistemology stands. But this is also a really worthwhile question to ask for its own sake, because the principle that "like is known by like" was widespread enough in Greek thought to sit indistinctly against the early Christian landscape, hiding in the open, and has largely eluded the specification of scholars of early Christianity. To answer this difficult question with control in this chapter, it will be enough to focus on two unmistakable sources of a developing Christian likeness epistemology.

The first source to explore is ancient Greek philosophy and science. The maxim that like is perceived or known by like was an old, prevalent, but somewhat vague assumption of Greek philosophy. I will summarize how it began to be more deliberately articulated from Aristotle in the fourth century BCE onwards, and then notably attracted the scientific, or biological, elucidation of Galen in the second century CE. The product of this tradition was a version of the like-is-known-by-like maxim imagined and defined in *optical* terms, terms of "perception," "vision," "light." This product was polished and available, but, I will argue, Christians did not buy it. They seemed to consider this knowing-by-likeness model to be true, but at the same time obvious enough to earn only occasional interest. On such occasions, we will see, Christian thinkers deployed it in intriguing ways. Ultimately, however, the like-by-like maxim in its optical rendition appears sporadically and insubstantially in the writings of Greek-speaking Christians of the first centuries CE. The situation has not changed much with Maximus either: whilst, as we will see later, he was probably aware of Galen's scientific theory that like is perceived by like, it

3. *De an.* 404B.

was hardly a major inspiration of the broad brushes of the knowing-by-likeness motif that color Maximus' writings.

The second origin will be worth exploring at greater length. I will argue that a Christian likeness epistemology largely emerged not out of a philosophical or scientific heritage but out of an *exegetical* heritage: that is, a tradition of opinion about how to interpret texts. To be specific, I will claim that an *exegetical* rendition, as I will call it, of the knowing-by-likeness motif was adopted by Alexandrian Christians as a working assumption at the point that they began reading Scripture as an *enigmatic* text, a text that at first conceals its deepest meaning. Here Christians joined a long Greek tradition of "allegorical" or "figurative" reading, as it is normally called in the scholarship. This joining took place in the second and third centuries,[4] especially in the hands of Clement and Origen of Alexandria, two theologians who, working in a city of libraries and temples (and libraries in temples[5]), began wondering in detail how best to approach a *text* whose meaning is *mysterious*. The premises of the allegorical tradition that they embraced—premises given authority, they thought, by the Bible itself—offered Clement and Origen the ingredients for a model of discernment according to which readers must conform themselves to the hidden truth of the text to access it. The definitive themes of this exegetical rendition of the likeness epistemology are not "vision" and "light," but *darkness* and its demands: "enigma," "mystery," "holiness," "initiation," "purity." It is this rendition and these themes that most obviously find their way to Maximus in the seventh century. I will come at this exegetical origin of the Christian likeness epistemology in three parts. First, a selection of allegorical accounts from a one-thousand-year period (fourth century BCE to the sixth century CE) will introduce the crucial and lasting link between allegorical or enigmatic exegesis and the knowing-by-likeness motif. Then our focus will narrow to Alexandria at the turn of the millennium, to find the same link upheld by some influential figures whose practice of allegorical reading directly informed Clement and Origen's philosophical culture. Thirdly, we will turn to these two theologians themselves, and explore how their allegorical reading

---

4. However, the stirrings of Christian allegorical reading belong to the Bible itself, most obviously when Paul uses the verb ἀλληγορέω in Gal 4:24. As Alain Le Boulluec puts it: Paul gives the examples, Origen gives the theory (Boulluec, "De Paul à Origène," 415).

5. Watts, *City and School*, 149–50.

substantially furnished the thesis that "like is known by like" for the first time in Christian discourse.

## Knowing-by-likeness in Greek philosophy and science and its impact on Christian thought

Let us turn to the first origin of a Christian likeness epistemology that I mentioned: the *optical* rendition of the knowing-by-likeness motif that came out of Greek philosophy and science. Plato mentions the proverbial maxim that "like is friend [φίλον] to like." He calls it an "ancient saying" (λόγος ἀρχαῖος), with folkloric origin in Homer, and attributes it to the philosophers of nature in general.[6] In the *Eudemian Ethics*, Aristotle gives this maxim the same provenance—the poets and philosophers of nature[7]—and elsewhere identifies a similar teaching in Democritus[8] and Heraclitus.[9] As Müller says, what Plato and Aristotle pointed to was less a "theory" than "a tacit assumption . . . widespread among early Greek thought."[10] A number of famed philosophers and scientists seem to have brought this assumption to discussions about sense perception, and especially sight, discussions that were summarized by doxographers (writers describing the opinions of past thinkers) from Aristotle onwards with the formula: "like is known by like."[11] Two passages that were normally voiced in evidence of this notion were the following by Empedocles and Plato accordingly:[12]

6. *Lysis* 214A–15D. The line from Homer that Plato references is *od.* 17.218: "God always brings like and like together" (ὡς αἰεὶ τὸν ὁμοῖον ἄγει θεὸς ὡς τὸν ὁμοῖν). Plato also invokes the maxim that "like is friend to like" at *Grg.* 510B and *Leg.* 716C.

7. *Eth. Eud.* 1235A. Amongst his citations from the poets, Aristotle includes the same line from Homer.

8. *Gen. corr.* 323B.

9. *De an.* 405A; and again at *metaph.* 1000B.

10. Müller, *Gleiches zu Gleichem*, 8. Müller's work is the key piece of secondary literature on the various manifestations of this assumption among pre-Socratic philosophers.

11. Schneider clarifies that the late-antique epistemological model emerged from pre-Socratic sayings about sense perception (Schneider, "Der Gedanke der Erkenntnis," 66).

12. Some late-antique writers, like Sextus Empiricus, attributed the theory to Pythagoras and the Pythagoreans (*math.* 1.303). Schneider takes for granted that it was a Pythagorean doctrine on the basis of Sextus' attribution ("Der Gedanke Der Erkenntnis," 65–66), but Müller has shown that this attribution stems from an earlier

> For it is with earth that we see earth, with water water, with air divine air, with fire destructive fire, with love love, with grim strife strife. For all are constructed and fitted together out of these, and it is with these that we think and feel pleasure and pain.[13]

> The eyes were the first of the organs to be fashioned by the gods, to conduct light . . . Now the pure fire inside us . . . they made to flow through the eyes . . . Now whenever daylight surrounds the visual stream, like makes contact with like and coalesces with it to make up a single homogenous body aligned with the direction of the eyes . . . This brings about the sensation we call "seeing."[14]

Although in passages like these the notion that "like is known by like" appears obscurely and in passing, philosophers in the fourth century BCE began to uphold Empedocles, some other pre-Socratics, and Plato as propounders of a *theory* of knowing-by-likeness.[15] In *De Anima*, Aristotle was the first to name the thesis, citing the above passages to attribute it to Empedocles and Plato: "like is known by like" (γινώσκεσθαι τῷ ὁμοίῳ τὸ ὅμοιον).[16] In reality, this epithetical phrase collectively referred to lone and ambiguous passages, like those above, from two or three philosophers (normally Parmenides, Empedocles, and Plato),[17] rather than to the epistemological theory of any one author, or to widely shared opinions. It was, in David Sedley's words, an "over-schematised and doxographical" invention.[18] Sedley points to Theophrastus, Aristotle's student and successor, who gives us a clear glimpse not only of what the like-by-like theory was understood to comprise, but of how the

---

misinterpretation by Poseidonius (*Gleiches zu Gleichem*, 3–7).

13. Fr. 77–78 (Wright, *Empedocles: The Extant Fragments*, 123–24; trans. Sedley, "Empedocles' Theory of Vision," 28).

14. *Ti.* 45B–D (trans. Cooper and Hutchinson, *Plato: Complete Works*, 1248).

15. Neither Empedocles nor Plato were describing sense perception *per se* in these passages, and in that sense Aristotle and his students misinterpreted them. Empedocles was explaining what he thought made up blood—for him, the mediator of sense-perception (Sedley, "Empedocles' Theory of Vision," 28). And Plato was explaining how, when the fire from the eyes meets the fire from the sun, a cone-shaped visual body is formed, which acts as a quasi sense organ.

16. *De an.* 404B.

17. On the ambiguity and misinterpretation of these passages, see Sedley, "Empedocles' Theory of Vision," especially 29–31.

18. Sedley, "Empedocles' Theory of Vision," 29.

theory was used as a category to carve up and sort the philosophical land-scape. It is worth looking at the opening few sentences of Theophrastus' *De Sensibus* in full:

> The various opinions (δόξαι) concerning sense perception, when regarded broadly, fall into two groups. By some investigators it is ascribed to likeness, by others to contrast. Parmenides, Empedocles, and Plato attribute it to likeness; Anaxagoras and Heraclitus to contrast. The one party is persuaded by the thought that other things are, for the most part, best interpreted in the light of what is like them; that it is a native endowment of all creatures to know their kin; and furthermore, that sense perception takes place by means of an effluence, and like is carried towards like. The rival party assumes that perception comes to pass by an alteration; that the like is unaffected by the like, whereas opposites are affected by each other.[19]

Theophrastus' ensuing interpretation of the first group of thinkers is questionable, because his chief care is to fit each of them into the like-by-like box whatever they have to say. That he is schematizing or stereotyping becomes more obvious, Sedley notices, when he eventually admits that the latter group are not in fact opposite-by-opposite theorists, but rather simply those who do *not* hold to the like-by-like theory.[20] Theophrastus may have begun his work with these two contrary opinions (like-by-like vs. opposite-by-opposite) in imitation of Aristotle's parallel schematisation of the maxim that "like is friend to like" in *Eudemian Ethics*, but Aristotle at least admitted that "these two opinions are so widely separated [i.e., contrary] as to be too general."[21]

In short, the notion that "like is known by like" probably cropped up fitfully and ambiguously amongst Greek thinkers before it was schematized by Aristotle and others in the fourth century. Aristotle himself rejected the theory,[22] but by examining it in multiple works he lent weight to the topic, and it became something of a general or self-evident law.[23]

19. *Sens.* 1–2 (Stratton, *Theophrastus*, 66–67).

20. *Sens.* 25 (Stratton, *Theophrastus*, 88–89); Sedley, "Empedocles' Theory of Vision," 30.

21. *Eth. Eud.* 1235A (trans. modified from LCL 285, 363). For more on how the first part of Theophrastus' *De Sensibus* depends upon, crystallizes, and updates Aristotle's schematizations, especially of like-by-like theorists, see Jaap Mansfeld, "Aristote et la structure," 158–88.

22. *De an.* 409B–411A.

23. Lehoux, *What Did the Romans Know?*, 122.

Neoplatonists, for example, reaching almost into the period of Maximus himself, would analyze and defend the theory, in spite of Aristotle's own rejection of it, in their commentaries on the *De Anima*.[24] And from an early period, Christian thinkers too seem familiar with the language in which the like-by-like theory was cast by Aristotle and his students. Hippolytus of Rome cites and discusses the above-cited popular proof text from Empedocles, for example,[25] and a number of other Christian writers inherit the phrase itself, "like is known by like," appropriating it in theological discussions of vision in particular. But before turning to these discussions, it is worth getting a sense of the odd variety of other theological topics in which Christians could put the like-by-like maxim to use.

In a homily on Psalm 48, Basil of Caesarea uses the maxim to interpret the meaning of God's breathing life into Adam's "face," as the Septuagint puts it (Gen 2:7): the text depicts, says Basil, how God "stowed away a part of his own grace in the human being in order that the like recognize the like [τῷ ὁμοίῳ ἐπιγινώσκῃ τὸ ὅμοιον]." This is what distinguishes humans as being in God's image and as having authority over other creatures, Basil says.[26] Basil's friend Gregory Nazianzen occasionally fixes upon the formula as a smart tool for comprehending another theological locus: the incarnation. In the one very short passage that survives from his *Letter* 110, the key theme, variously put, is learning; Gregory uses the words "admonition," "teaching," "training," "law-giving," and "taming." And Gregory's key claim is that learning happens *by likeness*. He gives the example that silent truths are taught through silence. In just the same way, he says, God "tames" humanity through what is human, that is, through becoming a human himself. In this light, Gregory contends,

24. A good example is the Christian Neoplatonist John Philoponus, *In Aristotelis De anima libros commentaria* 73–75 (CAG 15, 73–75). Some scholars have suggested that Maximus may have been influenced by Philoponus: Lévy, *Le créé et l'incréé*, 187–91; Tollefsen, *The Christocentric Cosmology*, 42–44, 52–53, 58, 114.

25. *Haer.* 6.11.1 (PTS 25, 216).

26. *Hom. in Ps.* 48 (PG 29, 449B–C). Basil's family friend Evagrius also uses this formula when commenting on the Psalms, though the nub of his point is somewhat more cryptic: "We know like through like [διὰ τοῦ ὁμοίου τὸ ὅμοιον ἐπιγινώσκομεν], and love through love, and righteousness through righteous. For such is the great and principle commandment itself. The lover serves the beloved. He calls God his own strength, since by him he was delivered from all his enemies, sensible and intelligible" (*sel. in Ps.* XVII, [PG 12, 1224D]; this work was for a long time attributed to Origen, see Rondeau, "Le commentaire sur les Psaumes," 329–48).

"training the like with the like" (τῷ ὁμοίῳ τὸ ὅμοιον ἐκπαιδεύων) is the very "law of Christ," the law of God's "economy" of salvation.[27] Gregory uses this logic in *Oration* 38 too, saying that the Word of God "bore flesh for the sake of our flesh, and mingled himself with an intelligent soul for my soul's sake, purifying the like by the like [τῷ ὁμοίῳ τὸ ὅμοιον ἀνακαθαίρων]."[28] And then in another letter he calls upon this same "law of Christ" to insist, against his Apollinarian opponents, that, since in Adam sin came to be through human flesh, soul, *and* mind, so the Word had to assume a human flesh, soul, *and* mind—and this is because the divine Word is in the business of "sanctifying the like by the like" (τῷ ὁμοίῳ τὸ ὅμοιον ἁγιάσας).[29]

Christians could adopt the like-by-like maxim in multiple ways, then, to help answer theological questions—about the human condition, or the character of the incarnation, for example. But if one continues to explore this maxim in the writings of late-antique Greek Christian (and non-Christian) theologians, one will notice that it usually crystallizes around the themes of light and vision.[30] The claim, hinted at by Plato in the *Timaeus* passage cited above, that light is seen by light, had already taken root in theological discussions by the turn of the millennium. Philo of Alexandria, for example, suggested that the highest form of divine knowledge works exactly like the perception of light: one knows "God by God [τὸν θεὸν θεῷ]," just as one sees "light by light [φωτὶ φῶς]."[31] Along with non-Christian theological precedents like this,[32] by the time Christians began adopting the optical like-by-like model it had received greater prominence and clarification thanks to well-known scientists, who adopted it as a foundation for their optical theories, compounding the maxim in the imagination of their philosophical culture.[33] In Rome in

27. *Ep.* 110 (Gallay, *Lettres*, vol. 2, 6).

28. *Or.* 38.13 (SC 358, 132–3).

29. *Ep.* 101, 51 (SC 208, 58).

30. This is the theme that Schneider follows when he traces like-by-like epistemologies among thinkers of the first centuries CE ("Der Gedanke der Erkenntnis," 71–75).

31. *Praem.* 47 (PAO 5, 346; see also *gig.* 9). I was led to this passage by Schneider, "Der Gedanke der Erkenntnis," 71–72.

32. Plotinus makes exactly the same claim: the soul's likeness to God enables vision of God, just as the eye's sun-likeness enables vision of the sun (*enn.* 1.6.9; *enn.* 5.3.17).

33. For a fourth-century CE compilation of like-by-like optical theories, see Nemesius of Emesa on sight in Plato, Galen, Porphyry: *nat. hom.* 7 (Morani, *Nemesii Emeseni De Natura Hominis*, 58–59).

the second century CE, the physician Galen, who proved a great and lasting influence for Christians,[34] worked this maxim into a detailed scientific theory. Galen summarizes sense perception generically "in a phrase":
"like is known by like" (τὸ ὅμοιον τῷ ὁμοίῳ γνώριμον).[35] He argues that
vision occurs through lightsome or luminous *pneuma* extending from
the eyes and striking the object of sight, and the like-by-like logic animating his account is obvious:

> [T]he organ of sight must be light-like [αὐγοειδές], the or-
> gan of hearing air-like [ἀεροειδές], that of smell vapour-like
> [ἀτμοειδές], that of taste moist, that of touch earth-like [γεῶδες].
> It is impossible that they be anything else, for they need to be
> altered by what is like them, and this was what Empedocles
> wished to show when he said, "It is with earth that we see earth,
> with water water [etc.] . . ." For we do really perceive by the more
> earthy of the senses, which is touch, the earthy nature in sense
> objects, and by the most light-like, which is sight, their light-like
> nature [etc.] . . .[36]

Galen's citation of Empedocles shows clearly that he has drawn his assumption from the like-by-like tradition as it was mediated through
Aristotle. This becomes clear again immediately, as Galen invokes Plato's
discussion of seeing by fire in the *Timaeus*, and then cites the same passage from Empedocles once more, all in order to justify his position that
sight operates when "like comes to share properties with like" (τῷ γὰρ
ὁμοίῳ τὸ ὅμοιον εἰς τὴν τῶν παθημάτων ἀφικνεῖται κοινωνίαν).[37]

The writings of a number of Christian thinkers from the second
to fourth centuries bear *theological* notions of vision that often display
assumptions about how seeing works inherited from the optical theory
exemplified by Galen; and Plato's lapidary passage from *Timaeus* was also
surely in the backs of their minds. We can begin with Clement of Alexandria, perhaps the earliest of Christian philosophers to appropriate the

34. For Galen's influence on Origen see, Grant, "Paul, Galen, and Origen," 533–36.
Nemesius' *nat. hom.* is a good later example of Galen's thorough influence on Christians. Later still, in the sixth century, Cassiodorus would recommend that his monks
read Galen (*inst.* 1.31.2).

35. *UP* 8, 7 (Helmreich, *Galeni De Usu Partium Libri XVII*, vol. 1, 641).

36. *De plac.* 7.5.42–44 (De Lacy, *On the Doctrines*, vol. 2, 462).

37. *De plac.* 7.6.2–11 (De Lacy, *On the Doctrines*, vol. 2, 462–64). For a more
detailed summary of Galen's like-by-like optical theory, see Lehoux, *What Did the
Romans Know?*, 121–25; and for an analysis of its relation to Plato and Aristotle's
teachings on vision, see Cherniss, "Galen and Posidonius' Theory of Vision."

language of "like by like." In *Paedagogus* 1.6, Clement discourses on the spiritual transformation that baptism makes possible for Christians:

> [T]hose who are baptized are cleansed of the sins which like a mist overcloud their divine spirit, and then acquire a spiritual sight which is clear and unimpeded and lightsome, the sort of sight which alone enables us to behold divinity . . . This is an admixture of eternal sunlight, giving us the power to see the eternal light. Like indeed is friend of like; so it is that what is holy is friend of the Source of holiness [ἐπεὶ τὸ ὅμοιον τῷ ὁμοίῳ φίλον, φίλον δὲ τὸ ἅγιον τῷ ἐξ οὗ τὸ ἅγιον] who properly speaking is called Light.[38]

The baptizand's vision fixes upon God because it itself deals in the same light that belongs to God, the object of vision. With Galen, Clement takes for granted that seeing occurs when eye and object deal in the same light.

One important locus for Christian theological discussion of vision was Jesus' transfiguration. It has been pointed out before that Greek patristic authors often presented the disciples themselves as agents in the transfiguration; that is, the change occurs not only in Jesus but in the disciples and their perception of him.[39] And in these discussions a like-by-like theory of vision may be at work in the background. Origen's account in his *Commentary on Matthew* is a clear example:

> It does not simply say, "he was transfigured," but with this comes a certain necessary addition, which Matthew and Mark recorded; for according to both of them, "he was transfigured *before them*." And according to this you will say that Jesus is able to be transfigured before some . . . but at once not transfigured before others . . . For Jesus is transfigured before them, and not to any of those below [at the foot of the mountain]. When he is transfigured his face shines like the sun, so that he may be shown to the "children of light" [see Eph 5:8], who have put off "the works of darkness, and put on the armor of light" [Rom 13:12] and are no longer children "of darkness or night" [see 1 Thes 5:5] but become the sons of day . . .[40]

---

38. *Paed.* 1.6.28 (SC 70, 162; trans. modified from FC 23, 27–28).

39. E.g. Clement, *strom.* 6.16.140.3 (SC 446, 340–341); Gregory of Nyssa, *cant.* 1 (GNO 6, 14–15). See McGuckin, "The Patristic Exegesis," 336; Plested, *The Macarian Legacy*, 216.

40. *Comm. in Mt.* 12.37 (GCS 40, 152–4; trans. modified from Menzies, *Ante-Nicene Christian Library: additional volume*, 470).

In Origen's interpretation, Jesus appears transfigured only to those who have been "conformed to his brilliance," as one commentator puts it,[41] and this is a theme that Maximus himself will rehearse.

A century after Origen, we find the same like-by-like optical theory in Athanasius of Alexandria. At the end of *On the Incarnation*, Athanasius tells his readers that he has only offered "the rudiments and paradigm" of the Christian faith in his treatise.[42] Consequently he implores them to seek a more complete knowledge in two ways: first, by reading Scripture, and second:

> . . . in addition to the study and true knowledge of the Scriptures are needed a good life and pure soul and virtue in Christ, so that the mind, journeying in this path, may be able to obtain and apprehend what it desires, in so far as human nature is able to learn about God the Word. For without a pure mind and a life modelled on the saints, no one can apprehend the words of the saints. For just as if someone wishes to see the light of the sun he cleanses and clears his eye, and purifies it until it is like [ὅμοιον] what he desires, so that as the eye thus becomes light it may see the light of the sun . . . [,] so he who wishes to grasp the thought of the theologians must first cleanse and wash his soul by his conduct and approach the saints in the imitation of their deeds, so that, being included in their company through the manner of his life, he may understand those things which have been revealed to them by God . . .[43]

One must be like Christ to learn from God the Word, and one must imitate the saints to understand them and grasp the revelations that they did. And this theological method, Athanasius says, follows the rules of vision, whereby the eye "becomes light" in order to see light. Athanasius expressly grounds his theological epistemology on the like-by-like optical theory.

Gregory of Nyssa is another example. For him, the vocation of all human souls from birth is "looking upon God" (βλέπειν πρὸς τὸν θεόν), or "partaking of God" (τὸ τοῦ θεοῦ μετέχειν).[44] In a passage from *De Infantibus Praemture Abreptis*, Gregory clarifies how this can be the case:

41. Wright, "The Literal Sense," 255.
42. *Inc.* 56 (Thomson, *Contra Gentes*, 272–73, including trans.).
43. *Inc.* 57 (Thomson, *Contra Gentes*, 274–75, including trans.).
44. *Infant.* (GNO 3/2, 78–79).

The would-be partaker must in some degree be akin to that which is to be partaken of. The eye enjoys the light by virtue of having light within itself to seize its kindred light, and the finger or any other limb cannot effect the act of vision because none of this natural light is organized in any of them. The same necessity requires that in our partaking of God there should be some kinship in the constitution of the partaker with that which is partaken of. Therefore, as the Scripture says, man was made in the image of God; that like, I take it, might be able to see like [τῷ ὁμοίῳ βλέποι τὸ ὅμοιον]; and to see God is, as was said above, the life of the soul.[45]

As with his brother Basil, Gregory uses the like-by-like formula to characterize the calling that belongs to humans in God's image. For Gregory, being in God's image implies "partaking" in God the archetype. "Partaking" is an ambiguous concept, but fortunately Gregory pinpoints it with an analogy: he suggests that participation in God—the fundamental condition of human existence, "the life of the soul"—works like *vision*. Both participation and vision share the same "necessity"; they both are made possible by like coming together with like. It is nothing other than a like-by-like theory of vision that provides the rules for Gregory's anthropology: just as an eye sees because it shares a likeness with the object seen, so does a human soul exist because it shares a likeness with God.

It is clear that Christians adopted the optical rendition of the knowing-by-likeness model from Greek philosophy and science, and creatively introduced it to a variety of theological topics. But such explicit appropriations of the like-by-like theory appear somewhat scarcely in Christian literature. This scarcity might indicate nothing more than the theory's status as a general, uncontested, and perhaps uninteresting assumption of the time. It is my suggestion that Greek Christians adopted and cultivated this conviction, that "like is known by like," with a great deal more eagerness and consistency, and at an early date, thanks not to scientific or philosophical legacies, but rather to the world of literary assumptions inherited in their work of interpreting Scripture.

45. *Infant.* (GNO 3/2, 79–80; trans. Schaff and Wace, *Gregory of Nyssa: Dogmatic Treatises, etc.*, 375–76).

## Knowing-by-likeness and the interpretation of enigmatic texts

> And "God is love" [1 John 4:16], who is known to those who love, just like "God is faithful" [1 Cor 1:9, 10:13], who is communicated through teaching to the faithful. And we must be assimilated to him through divine love, so that we may see the like by the like [τὸ ὅμοιον τῷ ὁμοίῳ θεωρῶμεν], hanging on the word of truth honestly and purely, just as children adhere to us. And this was what he hinted at (whoever that man was) who wrote on the entrance to the temple in Epidauros: "Pure he must remain who enters in the incensed shrine; and purity is a holy mind."[46]

This passage from the beginning of *Stromateis* 5 concludes Clement of Alexandria's attempt to justify "faith" as a reliable means of knowing God.[47] Clement invokes a likeness epistemology to crown his argument. When faith listens with love, Clement says, it imitates God who is himself "faithfulness" and "love," and it thereby sees God, because "like is seen by like." However, Clement does not draw on this epistemology as a scientific or optical theory. He uses the word "see," but beyond that makes no analogies of vision, light, or sense organs. Rather, he summarizes his epistemological picture with an inscription from the temple of Asclepius in Epidauros (south of Corinth).[48] In other words, he is not summoning an optical theory but a *ritual* theory. For Clement, in this case, the like-by-like maxim evokes not the eye straining for its object, but an initiate purifying himself and treading through incense smoke towards something hidden to those outside.

The ritual connotation that Clement associates with his likeness epistemology hints at the key mode of its inception in Christian thought. While we have seen that Greek philosophy and science bequeathed some Christian thinkers with the thesis that "like is known by like," the claim of the remainder of this chapter is that this thesis took hold of the Christian imagination when, in second and third century Alexandria, Christians

---

46. *Strom.* 5, 1.13 (SC 278, 44).

47. Commentators have highlighted that Clement assigns "faith" a crucial epistemological role; as he puts it, "knowledge is not without faith, nor is faith without knowledge" (*strom.* 5.1.1.3 [SC 278, 24]). For an introduction to Clement on "faith" see Osborn, *Clement of Alexandria*, 159–78.

48. This inscription has typically been dated around the fourth century BCE (e.g., Preger, *Inscriptiones*, 164), but for arguments in favor of dating it after the turn of our millennium, see Bremmer, "How Old Is the Ideal of Holiness," 106–8.

joined a centuries-old tradition of textual interpretation that considered its texts to be enigmatic, and imagined its task in the terms of Greek mystery rites.[49] This tradition of interpretation is normally called "allegorical" or "figurative" by scholars. The foremost rule of this tradition, that the sacred text is enigmatic, concealing its teachings,[50] invested Christians with the job of theorizing for the first time the *task* of exegesis—a task whose success, they began to feel, required the exegete to cultivate his character to match the character of the hidden and holy truth of the text; in other words, it required likeness. But why, in the minds of these Christians, did reading the Bible as an enigmatic and oracular text come hand in hand with a likeness epistemology?

An answer comes in the little-acknowledged fact that, throughout its long history, the allegorical method, or the "enigmatic" method as we might more descriptively call it,[51] was two-sided, concerning the character of the practitioner's soul as much as the meaning of the text. When faced with "allegories," one must lift "the veil of the heart" to lift "the veil of the letter," as Origen put it[52]—this is "allegory as a way of life," to play on Pierre Hadot's phrase.[53] This practical, ethical aspect of

49. For a skeptical assessment of this turn in Christian exegesis, hear Porphyry's words: "In their eagerness to find, not a way to reject the depravity of the Jewish Scriptures, but a means of explaining it away, they resorted to interpretations which cannot be reconciled or harmonized with those scriptures, and which provide not so much a defense of the original authors as a fulsome advertisement for the interpreters. 'Enigmas' is the pompous name they give to the perfectly plain statements of Moses, glorifying them as oracles full of hidden mysteries" (*Against the Christians*, preserved in Eusebius, *EH* 6.19.4; trans Williamson, in Eusebius, *The History of the Church*, 195–96).

50. Buffière, *Les mythes d'Homère*, 32–44; Lamberton, *Homer the Theologian*, 20.

51. "The most common and enduring conceptual category within allegorical reading is not ἀλληγορία, which Plutarch says is a neologism in his time [*de aud. poet.* 19E–F] . . . Rather, αἴνιγμα terms are the real conceptual engines of allegorism" (Struck, *Birth of the Symbol*, 30). "[T]he verb αἰνίττομαι ('hint at,' 'indicate by means of symbols') . . . from the time of Plato and before had been the principal verb used to designate the secondary meanings of texts and myths" (Lamberton, *Homer the Theologian*, 48). For the same point made by other scholars, see Buffière, *Mythes d'Homère*, 45, 48–54; Brisson, *How Philosophers Saved Myths*, 58–59; and Ayres, "'There's Fire in That Rain,'" 616–20. Similarly, in Christian hands, "mystery" became the crucial synonym of "allegory," as de Lubac argues, *Medieval Exegesis. Vol.* 2, 19–25.

52. *Hom. in Gen.* 6.1 (SC 7, 184).

53. Hadot is well known for convincingly characterizing ancient philosophy as a "manière de vivre." See, e.g., his collection of essays, *Philosophy as a Way of Life*. Despite a huge amount of scholarship on the nature and practice of pagan, Jewish, and

allegorical exegesis is not very surprising if one keeps in mind two points noted by Hadot: first, there was a wide late-antique assumption—typified in early Alexandrian Christianity—that moral formation is inherent to philosophy;[54] and secondly, from the fourth century BCE "philosophy" chiefly comprised textual exegesis.[55] In other words, moral formation was assumed to be inherent to the task of textual exegesis. And pre-Christian *allegorical* (or *enigmatic*) exegesis promoted a specific pattern of character formation: namely, exegesis was considered a task that required the reader to shape himself into the likeness of his subject-matter in order to access it. Like an initiate, the discerning exegete must be *pure* so that his character matches the purity of the hidden truth on offer. Therefore, we will continue to see, if there was one maxim for allegorical interpreters, it was not that light sees light, but that *pure knows pure;* and the following Platonic rule was often voiced in summary: "for the impure is not allowed to touch the pure" (*Phaedo* 67B: γὰρ καθαροῦ ἐφάπτεσθαι μὴ οὐ θεμιτὸν ᾖ).[56] Building on these assumptions, Alexandrian Christians came to consider that the Bible's hidden "pure" or "spiritual" doctrines, authored by Christ the Word, could be grasped only by those who labored to become pure, spiritual, or Christ-like themselves. Origen summarizes this assumption with great clarity:

> I think that all of the [words of the] Scriptures, even when perceived very accurately, are only very elementary rudiments of and very brief introductions to all knowledge . . . Now all are not permitted to examine the things that are "beyond what is written" [1 Cor 4:6], *unless the one who investigates has become like* [ἐξομοιωθῇ] *the things he examines.* Otherwise he will be reproved and hear the word: "Seek not the things that are too high for you, and search not into things beyond your ability" [Sir 3:21].[57]

---

Christian allegory, this abiding ethical or ascetic feature of allegorical accounts has rarely been addressed. A notable exception is Martens, *Origen and Scripture*, especially 161–92.

54. For an introduction to this theme see Wilken, "Alexandria: A School," 15–30.

55. Hadot, *Philosophy as a Way of Life*, 71–77.

56. As Festugière says, *Phaedo*'s appeal to purity as the condition for knowledge is a rendition of the wider model that "*le semblable plaît au semblable,*" a rendition, moreover, that undoubtedly finds its origin and force in the assumption of Greek religion that purity was the ritual condition for approaching what is sacred and inaccessible (Festugière, *Contemplation et vie contemplative*, 123–28).

57. *Jo.* 13.30 and 32 (SC 222, 48; trans. modified from FC 89, 74–75 [my italics]).

## Enigma, exegetical character, and knowing-by-likeness

Before turning in more detail to early Christian visions of enigmatic interpretation and their accompanying likeness epistemology, it is worth
outlining the centuries-old tradition of Greek enigmatic reading of
which these Christians became a part. This tradition of reading originally
revolved around Homer's poems. It is possible that the poems were interpreted by their very first readers as holding hidden meanings[58]—indeed,
a model of perception in which hiddenness abounds from the mortal
perspective belongs to Homer's poems themselves, and, arguably, so does
the notion that the poem's author possessed secret divine knowledge.[59]
Whatever the details of its earliest history, from the earliest surviving
texts that witness to enigmatic interpretation one can see that the tradition of Homeric interpretation quickly came to specify requisite characteristics for the expert and initiated interpreter of enigma. Readers of
Homer, and the tradition of enigmatic interpretation since, drew on the
language and logic of ritual initiations and mysteries, presenting "purity"
as the key condition for fruitful reading. As Lamberton says, the "imposi-
tion on the poetry of Homer of a structure of meaning analogous to that
of the oracles" must reach back to his earliest readers.[60] Peter Struck has
also demonstrated convincingly how ancient Greek enigmatic exegesis in
general pictured itself as something akin to ritual or oracular enigma and
its interpretation,[61] and this association has been pointed out by other
scholars too.[62] The sophist Protagorus, in Plato's dialogue, provides an

58. Homer's earliest allegorical readers probably lived in the sixth century BCE
(Brisson, *How Philosophers Saved Myths*, 32–36). They were also, perhaps, the first
Pythagoreans, in Southern Italy. Lamberton summarizes this latter contention and the
relevant scholarly convictions relating to it in *Homer the Theologian*, 31–33.

59. As Lamberton argues in detail, in *Homer the Theologian*, 2–12.

60. Lamberton, *Homer the Theologian*, 12.

61. Struck, *Birth of the Symbol*, 162–203. Struck argues that the most widespread
and generic model of enigma for the Greeks was *oracular* enigma, and that it was
understood as of a single kind with exegetical—that is, *allegorical*—enigma (see especially 165–73, 180–82).

62. For another detailed elaboration of this semantic connection, and the consequent requirement of "pure" readers, see Buffière, *Les mythes d'Homère*, 36–41. For
a comparison of allegorical reading and the Eleusian mysteries see Brisson, *How
Philosophers Saved Myths*, 58–61. For a case study of the conflation of enigma with
textual exegesis in later, Stoic philosophy, see Boys-Stones, "The Stoics' Two Types,"
205–10. For the same point made with regard to gnostic theology, see Stroumsa,
*Hidden Wisdom*, 56 and n. 34. Lamberton points out that some ancient Pythagorean

early and neat witness to this connection, when he mentions both oracles *and* poetry as methods for concealing wisdom.[63] Importantly, the assumption that "purity" is a condition for knowledge is part and parcel of this enigmatic religious tradition with which allegory became conflated. As Brisson summarizes, when a text was approached allegorically, "[i]t was the task of philosophers to unveil the text's true meaning, after an initiation in which purification and teaching were inextricably intertwined, just as they were in the mysteries."[64] To demonstrate the enduring links between enigmatic reading, the language and logic of mystery rites, and the conviction that pure is known by pure, I am going to take a spread of evidence: one very early allegorical text from the fourth century BCE, then some examples from the first century CE, and finally I will turn to the end of the Greek tradition of enigmatic reading in the sixth century CE.

As a preliminary to this, it is interesting to note that the earliest conceivable point of the tradition of enigmatic interpretation, that is, the inception of the word αἴνιγμα itself, shows how the enigmatic tradition was rooted not only in textual interpretation, but also in assumptions about what makes a good interpreter. Gregory Nagy points out that αἴνιγμα and its verb form αἰνίσσομαι/αἰνίζομαι germinate from the genre of the epinicion praise poem (sixth to fifth century), known as an αἶνος. But specifically, and intriguingly, the defining connotation of αἶνος literature was not hiddenness or obscurity as such, but rather a particular contract of expertise, an "ideology of exclusiveness" in Nagy's words.[65] The genre was intended to work as a cipher, "'understandable' . . . only for the man who is 'aware' . . . [,] a code bearing one message to its intended audience; aside from those exclusive listeners 'who can understand,' it is apt to be misunderstood, garbled."[66] No wonder, Nagy concludes, that from αἶνος

---

interpretations of Homer suggest that his poems had "a ritual use . . . to 'tranquilize' (καθημεροῦν) the soul," and were used as "magical incantations" (*Homer the Theologian*, 35; citing Porphyry, *Life of Pythagoras* 32).

63. *Prt.* 316D. Brisson suggests that this passage exemplifies the Sophist penchant for allegory or enigmatic reading: "'The Sophists thought of the poets' works as the condensed sums of all technical and ethical knowledge. By interpreting these allegorically, the Sophists were simply revealing the doctrine that the poets had purposely hidden in them" (Brisson, *How Philosophers Saved Myths*, 37).

64. Brisson, *How Philosophers Saved Myths*, 56.

65. Nagy, *The Best of the Achaeans*, 239.

66. Nagy, *The Best of the Achaeans*, 240–41. Nagy is citing the words of Bacchylides and Pindar.

there should develop a batch of words designating what is hidden and oracular, accessible to the few. This is all to say that, enshrined in the very story of its vocabulary, the Greek enigmatic tradition is a textual tradition that concerns the character of the interpreter as much as the enigma itself.

Let me turn to my first text. Although enigmatic reading (mainly of Homer) was probably carried on amongst many different and interlinking schools of thought—by Sophists and by Cynics,[67] amongst the Stoics,[68] and within Platonized Pythagoreanism, which especially compounded the emphasis on secrecy and enigma[69]—the fourth-century BCE Derveni Papyrus is the most ancient surviving witness to the allegorical/enigmatic method.[70] And the next extant witnesses emerge only around turn of the millennium. The Derveni Papyrus exemplifies an intimate concurrence of ritual and exegetical enigma, and, crucially, presents purity as the requisite condition for discerning it. Amongst the author's opinions on methods of ritual initiation into the mysteries,[71] the papyrus includes a commentary on the beginning of an Orphic poem that takes the poem to be enigmatic (αἰνιγματώδης), an approach that seems to be licensed by one of the opening lines of the poem itself: "put doors to their ears." The author interprets this opening line as follows: "he [Orpheus] says that he is not legislating for the many [but addressing himself to those] who are pure [ἀγνεύοντας] in hearing."[72] The enigmatic nature of the text demands the purification of those wishing to discern its meaning.[73] The assumption behind this link between knowledge and purity is that the object of enigma is itself sacred and pure, and thus demands that the initiate himself be purified. There is a latent likeness epistemology in Greek mystery religion and exegesis, in other words. As far as I am aware, Plato

67. Brisson, *How Philosophers Saved Myths*, 37.

68. For a summary of Stoic allegorical interpretation and the centrality of hiddenness and enigma, see De Lacy, "Stoic Views of Poetry," 259–63. See also Brisson, *How Philosophers Saved Myths*, 41–55.

69. Lamberton, *Homer the Theologian*, 32–43; Brisson, *How Philosophers Saved Myths*, 56–61.

70. For a summary of the allegorical commentary in the Derveni papyrus, see Brisson, *How Philosophers Saved Myths*, 32–35.

71. E.g. cols. V–VI, XX (Tsantsanoglou et al., *The Derveni Papyrus*, 70–73, 100–101; trans. 130, 136).

72. Col. VII (Tsantsanoglou et al., *The Derveni Papyrus*, 74–75; trans. 130–31).

73. For more on Derveni and its enigmatic themes see Obbink, "Allegory and Exegesis," 177–88; West, "Hocus-Pocus in East and West," 81–90.

was the first to identify it (*Phaedo* 67B), and it is drawn out with clarity in writers from the turn of the millennium.

Plutarch is one example. He rejected the Stoic approach to allegory, which interpreted poetry for its hidden teaching on the physical cosmos. Instead, he recommended reading enigmatic texts for the (Platonic/Pythagorean) doctrine they contain on the gods, metaphysics, and morality.[74] In his *On Isis and Osiris*, Plutarch relays to his friend Clea some of the mysteries and mythology of the Egyptians, who were regarded as the foundational human culture and thus whose doctrines Plutarch feels can be harmonized or translated into the doctrines of Greek mythology and philosophy. Before detailing the myth of Isis and Osiris, Plutarch describes the secretive and enigmatic nature of Egyptian teaching and symbolism,[75] and warns Clea, therefore, not to take their myths in a literal or materialistic sense. Instead, Plutarch says that there are conditions for approaching the myth sensibly and profitably. These are: thinking "reverently and philosophically" (ὁσίως καὶ φιλοσόφως), "always performing and keeping the established holy rites," and holding the conviction that the gods are "true."[76] In other words, proper reading of the mythic text comes of partaking in the religious life practically and intellectually. Plutarch had hinted at the details of this religious life at the beginning of his work: Isis entrusts "the sacred writings" (ὁ ἱερὸς λόγος), he says, to "those that are initiated into the sacred rites," like abstinence from certain foods, services at shrines, and virtues of patience and self-denial;[77] or again, those who wear the sacred garments, the symbols of secrecy, are those who will "within their own soul, as though within a casket, bear the sacred writings," and keep them secret.[78] Why is this roster of rituals needful in the face of an enigmatic text? Because, Plutarch thinks, there is a single methodology for tackling enigma, summarized by Plato: "for all this," Plutarch says, "there is only one true reason, which is to be found in the words of Plato: 'for the impure to touch the pure is contrary to divine ordinance' [*Phd.* 67B]."[79] Purity is the condition for deciphering the pure truth hidden in the myth; in other words, "like is known by like."

74. Brisson, *How Philosophers Saved Myths*, 63–71.

75. *De Is. et Os.* 9–10, *Mor.* 354B–355A (LCL 306, 22–29).

76. *De Is. et Os.* 11, *Mor.* 355D (LCL 306, 30–31, including trans.).

77. *De Is. et Os.* 2, *Mor.* 351F–352A (LCL 306, 8–9, including trans.).

78. *De Is. et Os.* 3, *Mor.* 352B (LCL 306, 10–11, including trans.).

79. *De Is. et Os.* 4, *Mor.* 352D (LCL 306, 12–13, including trans.).

A parallel example comes in the first-century CE *Homeric Problems* by Heraclitus, who begins his work defending Homer's poetry from the charge of being myth—"sacrilegious fables, loaded with blasphemous folly."[80] Heraclitus says that Homer does not write myth but "allegory." This is the genre that "says one thing but signifies something other."[81] Indeed, "if he [Homer] meant nothing allegorically, he was impious through and through."[82] But since he *was* an allegorist, Heraclitus says, "it is, I think, perfectly plain and evident to all that no stain of abominable myth disfigures his poems. They are pure [καθαρά] and purified [ἀγνεύουσα] of all pollution." There follows a passage in which Heraclitus clarifies that consequently only those who are themselves "purified" may properly read Homer's poems. Here Heraclitus' assumed likeness epistemology comes to the fore, and he bases it upon the analogy of ritual initiation into mysteries:

> Such is Homer's pious plan, that he honors all divinities with exceptional expressions of feeling, because he is divine himself. If some ignorant people fail to recognize Homeric allegory and have not descended into the innermost caverns of his wisdom but instead have risked a hasty judgement of the truth without proper consideration, and if then they seize hastily on what they take to be his mythical invention, because they do not know what is said in a philosophical sense—well, off with them and good riddance! But let us, who have been purified [ἡγνίσμεθα] within the sacred enclosure, methodically track down the grand truth of the poems.[83]

Homer writes about divine things by virtue of being divine himself and, Heraclitus says, this logic is mirrored in the way one should interpret his writings: Homer's readers "track down" his text's "purified" meanings, hidden in the inmost places, by virtue of themselves being "purified," themselves being "within." For Heraclitus, in other words, Homer's allegory should be met with a model of exegesis that demands a likeness between the reader's character and the text's character.

This same model would last until the ends of the Greek tradition of enigmatic interpretation, in late Neoplatonic exegetical literature. Ilsetraut Hadot has pointed out how, when composing their introductions

80. *All.* 1.1–2 (Russell and Konstan, *Heraclitus*, 2–3, including trans.).

81. *All.* 5.1 (Russell and Konstan, *Heraclitus*, 8–9, including trans.).

82. *All.* 1.1–2 (Russell and Konstan, *Heraclitus*, 2–3, including trans.).

83. *All.* 3.1–3 (Russell and Konstan, *Heraclitus*, 6–7; modified trans.).

to commentaries on Aristotle, it became a convention for Neoplatonists after Proclus to include notices about (among other things) the obscurity of the text at hand and the consequent preparation required of the reader.[84] We can take Ammonius Hermiae's introduction to his commentary *On Aristotle's Categories* for an example:

> [L]et us ask how one should prepare oneself to listen to what is to come in Aristotle's writings. We reply that one must be educated in character and pure of soul. "For the impure is not allowed to attain the pure," as Plato said [*Phd.* 67B].[85]

Ammonius exposes his assumption that "like is known by like." But what is it about Aristotle's writings that tells us they are "pure" and thus demand the purifying of the soul who wills to understand them? The answer is: they are enigmatic. The classic "pure by pure" line from Plato offers a clue: as we have seen, Plato's rule was read as a rule for approaching *enigma*, whether textual or ritual. Ammonius goes on to spell this out in his conventional introductory note on the text's obscurity:

> [L]et us ask why on earth the philosopher is contended with obscure teaching. We reply that it is just as in the temples, where curtains are used for the purpose of preventing everyone, and especially the impure, from encountering things they are not worthy of meeting.[86]

It is precisely the obscurity of Aristotle's writings that indicates their purity, and thus limits the readership to the pure. And as with Derveni, Plutarch, and Heraclitus, Ammonius uses an analogy of *ritual* obscurity to express this.

Let me cite George Boys-Stones' words to summarize what we have seen in this spread of texts: "a common theme in allegorical commentaries—from Derveni to the latest Neoplatonist writers—is the value of concealment. Allegory, by making obscure the wisdom communicated, is a way of restricting that wisdom to a particular audience, to those initiates . . . who have the 'key' to its decoding."[87] Having looked at some examples ourselves, we can add to Boys-Stones' evaluation that, more often than

---

84. Hadot, "Les introductions aux commentaires," 102–6.

85. *In Aristotelis Categorias commentarius* prol. (CAG 4.4, 6.21–24; trans. Cohen and Matthews, *On Aristotle's Categories*, 14).

86. *In Aristotelis Categorias commentarius* prol. (CAG 4.4, 7.6–14; trans. Cohen and Matthews, *On Aristotle's Categories*, 15).

87. Boys-Stones, "The Stoics' Two Types," 210.

not, the interpretive "key" that decodes the hidden meanings is "purity," the virtue that imitates the character of the hidden truth itself.

### Versions of enigmatic exegesis and models of knowing-by-likeness influencing Alexandria

The above examples indicate in a cursory way that the long tradition of enigmatic exegesis was always concerned that the interpreter's character imitate the purity of the text. I wish now to highlight this same concern amongst enigmatic exegetes who directly influenced Christian enigmatic reading in second- and third-century Alexandria (when and where Neoplatonic and Christian enigmatic reading were incubated). As Ayres summarizes, second-century Christian exegesis in Alexandria, among both catholic and Gnostic Christians, "flourished alongside other hermeneutical visions that saw particular texts as [1.] intentionally enigmatic, hinting at truths about the divine that [2.] the expert and initiated could uncover."[88] The hermeneutical visions that Ayres says influenced Alexandrian Christian exegesis all resembled and influenced each other enough to be members of one tradition, normally called "allegorical," but which I have been calling "enigmatic," after its more common vocabulary. We can note a few of the influential figures here, all of whom claimed that the truth of their texts is hidden and pure, and requires an interpreter whose character bears semblance to that truth.

One figure whose influence loomed large was Philo, a Jewish Platonist and exegete in Alexandria in the first century BCE. Much could be said about Philo's exegesis and his influence on second- and third-century exegetes,[89] but let me be content to summarize that for Philo, the text or "flesh" of the Bible in every place "hints at" (αἰνίσσεσθαι)[90] a concealed "soul" of meaning to the capable reader, leading the reader in an ethical and spiritual progression towards perfection and the vision of God:[91]

---

88. Ayres, "Irenaeus vs. the Valentinians," 159.

89. See in particular the work of van den Hoek: "Assessing Philo's Legacy," 223–39; "The 'Catechetical' School," 59–87; "Philo and Origen," 44–121; "How Alexandrian Was Clement," 179–94; *Clement of Alexandria and His Use of Philo*.

90. E.g. *spec.* 1.23, 206, 260; *mut.* 7; *her.* 128; *opif.* 154; *cher.* 21; *det.* 155; *post.* 18; *agr.* 110; *ebr.* 96–100; *somn.* 1.218; *Mos.* 2.128, 150, 180–81; *exsecr.* 63.

91. Sandmel, *Philo's Place in Judaism*, xx–xxiii.

> The interpretations of the Holy Scripture are made in accordance with the deeper meanings conveyed in allegory. For the whole of the Law seems . . . to resemble a living being with the literal commandments for its body, and for its soul the invisible meanings [ἀόρατον νοῦν] stored away in its words. It is in the latter that the rational soul begins especially to contemplate things akin to itself [τὰ οἰκεῖα] and, beholding the extraordinary beauty of the concepts as through the mirror of the words, unfolds and removes the covers of [διαπτύξασα καὶ διακαλύψασα] the symbols and brings forth the thoughts bared into the light for those who are able [τοῖς δυναμένοις] by a slight jog to their memory to view the invisible through the visible.[92]

The basic like-by-like logic here is by now becoming familiar. An invisible or obscure meaning requires a reader with a special interpretative facility,[93] a facility set astir so far as he is "akin" to his hidden object of study.

After Philo, in the first two centuries CE, there is evidence of a number of exegetes carrying on the tradition of enigmatic interpretation in Alexandria. Let me take two examples of pagan thinkers, who both transmitted the traditional picture of enigmatic interpretation as an exercise akin to ritual activity, an exercise for an initiated and purified readership. In the first century CE, there lived an influential Alexandrian Stoic called Chaeremon, who, along with other Stoic allegorists, no doubt influenced Valentinian and catholic Christian exegetes in the next centuries.[94] For example, Origen says he is familiar with Chaeremon's texts,[95] and Porphyry testifies that Origen "made use . . . of the books of Chaeremon the Stoic . . . , which taught him the allegorical method of interpreting the Greek mysteries, a method he applied to the Jewish Scriptures."[96] All we know of Chaeremon's work is secondhand and fragmentary. From the little we do know, however, Chaeremon considered concealment the mark of allegory,[97] and, as Boys-Stones points out, he also witnessed to the traditional concern over allegory's suitable

92. *Contempl.* 78 (PAO 6, 67; trans. modified from Winston, *The Contemplative Life,* 55).

93. For other examples, see *cher.* 48 and *somn.* 2.3.

94. Ramelli, "Origen and the Stoic," 195–98, 207.

95. *Cels.* 1.59 (SC 132, 236).

96. From Porphyry, *C. Christ.* 3, preserved in Eusebius, *HE* 6.19; trans. Williamson, *The History of the Church,* 196).

97. Fr. 12 (van der Horst, *Chaeremon,* 24).

readership: allegory, for Chaeremon, is a genre that makes "discrimina-tions in its audience, revealing more to those capable of understanding it."[98] According to one testimony, Chaeremon believed the aim of allegor-ical writing was "to teach the great and lofty things to the uninitiated."[99] If those who can deal with the surface of the allegorical account are "uninitiated" (ἀτελεστέροι), we can presume that, for Chaeremon, those who do see beyond allegory's veil are the "initiated." This much seems clear in Chaeremon's characterization of the esoteric Egyptian religion with which he was familiar and perhaps partook: in his presentation, those who penetrate the depths of hidden knowledge through study and reading are those (priests, along with others including "sacred scribes"[100]) who practice an "esoteric asceticism" (ἄσκησις κεκρουμμένη), marked by outlandish acts of "purification" from material concerns.[101] Although it is only outlined or intimated in the surviving evidence, Chaeremon seems to have propounded a traditional picture of allegory as a sacred genre that, on the one hand, hides holy secrets under its surface, and on the other, demands holy readers who are purified of all their surface attach-ments. Inherent in his suggestions lies the same like-by-like model that we have seen other allegorists spell out.

Similar assumptions are at work in the equally ill-preserved teaching of a thinker from the latter half of the second century CE who shaped the reading habits of Alexandria. Numenius was a Platonist, a Neopythago-rean, and prominent exegete who might have spent a good deal of time in Alexandria,[102] or at the least greatly influenced Alexandrians of the period.[103] Numenius interpreted both Homer and the Jewish scriptures in a mode that Origen recognized and approved as "allegorical,"[104] from which we can infer that Numenius considered these texts to be enigmatic,

---

98. Boys-Stones, "The Stoics' Two Types," 210–11.

99. Test. 12 (van der Horst, *Chaeremon*, 6–7).

100. Fr. 10 (van der Horst, *Chaeremon*, 22).

101. Fr. 10 (van der Horst, *Chaeremon*, 16, 18.).

102. Some scholars suggest that Numenius spent time in Alexandria: Guthrie, *Nu-menius of Apamea*, 99–101; des Places, "Notice," in Numenius, *Fragments*, 7; Ramelli, "Philo as Origen's Declared Model," 5.

103. Porphyry tells of Origen's great familiarity with Numenius (*c. Christ.* 3, pre-served in Eusebius, *HE* 6.19). This is corroborated by Origen's fourfold citing of him in *Cels.* (1.15; 4.51; 5.38; 5.57), as Ramelli points out in, "Origen and the Stoic," 199. See also Ramelli, "Philo as Origen's Declared Model," 5–6.

104. *Cels.* 4.51.

requiring interpretative expertise. This is further suggested in a polemical passage by Macrobius, who says that Numenius was such an indomitable seeker of "hidden things" (*occultorum*) that he broke their seal and let their truth spill from the divine "sanctuary" into the "brothel," available for any passersby.[105] By holding Numenius accountable as an interpreter indentured in a contract of expertise, Macrobius places him within the traditional context of enigmatic interpretation.[106] Turning to Numenius' own fragmented writings, it seems that he was the first interpreter to consider Plato's dialogues allegorical, cryptic—an understanding that would come to define Neoplatonic allegorical reading.[107] Plato conveyed his teaching, Numenius says, "by concealing [ἐπικρυψάμενος] it between clarity and lack of clarity," a method Numenius thinks elicited the confused variety, disagreement, and novelty that he watched plague readers of Plato in his day.[108] We also know, thanks to Eusebius, that Numenius in fact wrote a whole work *On the Secrets of Plato* (Περὶ τῶν παρὰ Πλάτονι ἀπορρήτων). In the single preserved passage from *On the Secrets of Plato*, Numenius reasons that Plato obscured his teaching (which he takes for granted) to avoid provoking any profane listeners and putting his life at risk.[109] As Lamberton summarizes, for Numenius, truth presents itself in an "enigmatic coded picture" in texts.[110] From the fragments mentioned, then, Numenius seemed to believe that interpreting enigmas belongs to a select few, and is potentially disastrous in the wrong hands.[111]

Another important resource for Christian allegory in Alexandria and perhaps "the earliest witness to Christian considerations of the obscurity of Scripture"[112] was the *Epistle of Barnabas*, an early second-century Alexandrian text[113] that Clement and Origen seem to have considered canonical.[114] Clement, moreover, commends the epistle specifically for its

105. Fr. 55 (Numenius, *Fragments*, 100). On polemical responses to Numenius, see Athanassiadi, *La Lutte pour l'orthodoxie*, 80–82.

106. Boys-Stones, "The Stoics' Two Types," 210.

107. Lamberton, *Homer the Theologian*, 62–63.

108. Fr. 24 (Numenius, *Fragments*, 64–65).

109. Fr. 23 (Numenius, *Fragments*, 61).

110. Lamberton, *Homer the Theologian*, 70.

111. For more on Numenius on the obscurity of Plato, see Athanassiadi, *La Lutte pour l'orthodoxie*, 96–99.

112. Harl, "Origène et les interprétations," 342.

113. Most scholars agree on this. See e.g. Loman, "The *Letter of Barnabas*," 260–63.

114. Clement is the text's earliest witness (Loman, "The *Letter of Barnabas*," 248).

understanding and interpretation of scriptural enigma.[115] In its exegetical passages, *Barnabas* intends to display "the glory of Jesus" everywhere foreshadowed in the Old Testament[116] and thereby to prove that Christians ("this people") and not Jews ("the former people") are the heirs of God's covenant.[117] To make this polemical point, *Barnabas* highlights both Scripture's obscurity and, unsurprisingly by now, the kind of reader before whom it unveils. There are two exemplary passages:

> What, therefore, does "into the good land, a land flowing with milk and honey" [Exod 33:3] mean? Blessed is our Lord, brothers and sisters, who endowed us with wisdom and understanding of his secrets [κρυφίων]. For the prophet speaks a parable [παραβολήν] concerning the Lord; who can understand it, except one who is wise and discerning and loves his Lord?[118]

> Now what type do you think was intended when he commanded Israel that men who are utterly sinful should offer a heifer, and slaughter it and burn it [Num 19] . . . ? Grasp how plainly he is speaking to you: the calf is Jesus; the sinful men who offer it are those who brought him to the slaughter . . . So, therefore, the things that happened in this way are clear to us but to them [Jews] are quite obscure [σκοτεινά], because they did not listen to the voice of the Lord.[119]

The author declares that the proper condition for demystifying the Bible is loving acceptance of "the Lord," Christ, who is himself the meaning of all Scripture. In other words, one must be in harmony with what one seeks to know, a model suggested again in the tenth chapter, where the author insists that those who are "fleshly" understand the Bible in a fleshly way and cannot comprehend the "spiritual" truth spoken by Moses.[120]

---

According to Eusebius (*HE* 6.14), Clement included Barnabus within "canonical scripture"; see Niehoff, "A Jewish Critique," 153. And Origen calls it a "catholic epistle" (*Cels.* 1.63); see Metzger, *The Canon of the New* Testament, 140.

115. *Strom.* 5.10.63 (SC 278, 128).

116. *Barn.* 12.7 (LCL 25, 58; trans. Holmes, *The Apostolic Fathers*, 191).

117. *Barn.* 13.1 (LCL 25, 60; trans. Holmes, *The Apostolic Fathers*, 191).

118. *Barn.* 6.10 (LCL 25, 32; trans. Holmes, *The Apostolic Fathers*, 183). This is the passage that Clement commends at *Strom.* 5.10.63 (SC 278, 128).

119. *Barn.* 8.1–2, 7 (LCL 25, 40–42; trans. Holmes, *The Apostolic Fathers*, 185–86).

120. *Barn.* 10.2, 9 (LCL 25, 46–48).

### Alexandrian Christian enigmatic exegesis
### and accounts of knowing-by-likeness

The assortment of witnesses considered so far serves to show that, by the second century in Alexandria, allegorical or enigmatic exegeses—exegeses thematized with ritual, initiatory language, and accompanied by notices of the sacred text's obscurity and the readership's required purity—were standard enough to dominate the imaginations of exegetes from varying philosophical and religious traditions.[121] Interpreting the Bible, in particular, became the context in which Alexandrian theologians practiced enigmatic reading and worked out its implications; after all, enigma was a self-proclaimed characteristic of the Bible.[122] We know from Irenaeus' testimony that by the 170s or 180s the Valentinian Christian school of exegesis—against whom Clement and Origen sharpened their own exegetical habits in Alexandria[123]—had begun approaching Scripture as enigmatic,[124] and Droge has emphasized the great debt Valentinian exegetes owed to the tradition of allegorical interpretation of Homer, whom Irenaeus called their "prophet."[125] The Valentinians claim, Irenaeus says, that their doctrines on cosmogony "were not declared openly [φανερῶς], because not all have the capacity for this knowledge," but "were pointed out mystically by the Savior through parables to those who were able to understand them,"[126] and not only by the Savior, but by

---

121. It is worth noting that contemporary theologians without any Alexandrian influence could hold the opposite opinion about Scripture's ambiguity. Irenaeus of Lyon is the best example: "the whole of Scripture—the prophets and the Gospels," he says, "can be clearly, unambiguously, and harmoniously understood by all" (*haer.* 2.27.2 [SC 294, 266]). When one does find "ambiguity" and "enigmas" in Scripture, these passages can simply "be solved by what [in Scripture] is manifest, and consistent, and clear" (*haer.* 2.10.1 [SC 294, 88]).

122. Clement, for example, lists some instances where Scripture witnesses to its own obscurity at *strom.* 5.10.63–66 (SC 278, 128–35); for similar passages in Origen, see *Cels.* 4.49–50 and *princ.* 4.3.11, 14. For more details on the biblical passages often used by early Christians to justify Scripture's obscurity see Harl, "Origène et les interprétations," 338–40.

123. Thomassen (*The Spiritual Seed*, 495) thinks it likely that admirers of Heracleon the Valentinian in particular were active in Alexandria in Clement and Origen's day.

124. Ayres, "Irenaeus vs. the Valentinians," 155.

125. *Haer.* 4.33.3 (SC 100, 810–1). See Droge, "Homeric Exegesis among the Gnostics," 313–21.

126. *Haer.* 1.3.1 (SC 264, 50–51; trans. ACW 55, 28).

"the law and the prophets" too.[127] Because the knowledge that Scripture contains is hidden, it is available only to the "capable." But who are the capable? It is tempting here to neatly assume that the Valentinian model of three natural human classes—"material," "soulish," and "spiritual"[128]— worked, too, as a breakdown of exegetical capabilities,[129] but the texts do not suggest this link. At the most, we can guess that the Valentinians considered "capable" interpreters to be "spiritual" or "gnostic" Christians.[130]

Clement and Origen, however, would clearly make this kind of link: Scripture avails its hidden meaning in proportion to the exegete's moral and spiritual stature. Their understanding of spiritual stature, however, was very different from the Valentinians.' As noted above, according to their catholic Christian detractors, Valentinian Christians believed humans to be cast congenitally into three classes, "material," "soulish," and "spiritual." A person's capacity for spiritual growth and even their capacity or incapacity for salvation were fixed by their natural class.[131] Kovaks has demonstrated how Clement turned the Valentinians' categories, presenting them as progressive *stages* rather than exclusive natural classes.[132] Origen follows him in this.[133] He took it further, however, proposing that these stages might structure not only Christian life in general, but the task of biblical reading in particular. He suggests that there are at least three levels of Scripture, "body," "soul," and "spirit," authored by God to fit three corresponding levels of human spiritual maturity; and here he must

127. *Haer.* 1.3.6 (SC 264, 60–61; trans. ACW 55, 29).

128. For a quick and careful summary of the origins of, witnesses to, and ambiguities of this threefold anthropology, see Thomassen, *The Spiritual Seed*, 478–79, nn. 119 and 120.

129. I am thinking of the conclusions of Pagels, *The Johannine Gospel*. Indeed, from 23–35, she even argues that Valentinian cosmology is also threefold (*pleroma*, *kenoma*, and *cosmos*) and was as a basis for their exegesis. This conclusion seems simplistic. For an incredibly detailed account of Valentinian doctrine whose attention to the subtlety and variety of the evidence resists and obscures this threefold model, see Thomassen, *The Spiritual Seed*.

130. This latter option is supported by *haer.* 3.2.1 (SC 211, 24–27) where the apt interpreter is the one initiated into the knowledge of the παράδοσις, the secret handed-down tradition.

131. For one interpretation that tentatively suggests a more fluid or progressive relation between these classes see Pagels, *The Johannine Gospel*, 57, 91–97.

132. Kovacs, "Concealment and Gnostic Exegesis," 414–37.

133. See *comm. in. Rom.* 2.4.2 (SC 532, 292), where Origen hijacks the three Valentinian categories and presents them as different levels of spiritual maturity.

be playing off and subverting the Valentinians three-tier anthropology,[134] morphing it from a congenital catalogue into a spiritual progression.[135] Both Clement and Origen subverted the Valentinian scheme with the language of Scripture, and especially Paul, on whose authority the Valentinians claimed to base their anthropology. Two favorite passages were 1 Corinthians 3:1–3 and Hebrews 5:12–14, which both express the contours of the maturing spiritual life with images of different kinds of food: milk for infants, or the "fleshly," and meat or solid food for the more mature, or "spiritual."[136] Origen, again, could understand these images as stages of accomplishment in *scriptural interpretation*. He numerously used Paul's metaphor of milk and solid food to describe not only a Christian's spiritual progress, but also their exegetical progress.[137] A clear instance comes in the prologue to his *Commentary on the Song of Songs*:

> But first we must understand that just as children are not moved to the passion of love, so neither is the age of the inner man, if it is that of a little one and an infant, allowed to grasp these words. I am referring to those who are nourished in Christ by "milk" and not by "solid food" [see Heb 5:12] and who now for the first time long for the milk that is spiritual and without deceit [see 1 Pet 2:2]. Indeed, in the words of the Song of Songs may be found that food of which the Apostle says, "But solid food is for the perfect" and requires such people as listeners who "have their

134. *Princ.* 4.2.4 (GCS 22, 312–13). Origen almost certainly refers to the sect of Valentinius, along with those of Marcion and Basilides, when he introduces the untenable exegesis of his opponents, the "heretical sects," at *princ.* 4.2.1 (GCS 22, 307). See Martens, "Why Does Origen Introduce," 5).

135. Scholars have noticed that Origen's threefold model seems too neat, matching neither his own exegesis nor his much more common *twofold* account of scriptural reading, e.g. De Lange, *Origen and the Jews*, 109. For a summary of debate on this point, see the introduction to Dively Lauro, *The Soul and Spirit of Scripture*. However, reading on until the end of chapter 3 of *Princ.* 4, we find that Origen himself was happily aware of the subtleties and even inapplicability of this theory, which is for him, it seems, heuristic rather than prescriptive.

136. E.g., Clement, *strom.* 5.4.26.1–2 (SC 278, 64–66); *strom.* 5.10.62.2–4 (SC 278, 128); Origen, *comm. in Mt.* 12.31 (GCS 40, 137–38); *hom. in Gen.* 14.4 (SC 7, 344–47); *hom. in Lev.* 4, 6 (SC 286, 184–85); *Jo.* 13.203–25 (SC 222, 144–52). Judith Kovacs is the authority on this biblical motif in Clement and Origen, and its anti-Valentinian polemical context: "Echoes of Valentinian Exegesis," 317–29; "Clement of Alexandria and Valentinian Exegesis," 187–200; "The Language of Grace," 69–85; "Grace and Works," 191–210.

137. Some examples are provided and analyzed by Kovacs, "Echoes of Valentinian Exegesis," 325–27.

faculties trained by practice to distinguish good from evil" [Heb
5:14]. Thus, if those we have called "little ones" come to these
places in Scripture, it can happen that they receive no profit at
all from this book or even that they are badly injured . . . [138]

The Song of Songs is a text that will only be grasped by readers who have
attained an appropriate level of ethical and spiritual maturity. Origen
goes on to clarify that he follows the rule of the "Hebrews," for whom this
book ranks alongside three other parts of the Bible—the beginning of
Genesis, the first chapters of Ezekiel, and the end of Ezekiel—that must
be kept until last, for the most mature readers alone.[139]

Clement and Origen both clarify that spiritual maturity proves the
fruitful condition for interpretation not in and of itself, but because the
spiritually mature reader is more closely akin to the text's hidden meaning. In doing so they witness to a more specific exegetical premise, inherited from the tradition of enigmatic exegesis: to understand an obscure
text's meaning a reader must become *like* it. We begin with Clement. For
him the divine "enigmas" are the object and goal of Christian or *gnostic*
practice in general, and he unabashedly includes them in the long tradition of pagan enigmatic interpretation:[140] "Practically everyone who has
theologized, then, Barbarians and Greeks, have hidden the principles of
things, and have delivered the truth in enigmas and symbols, in allegories
and metaphors and other such [literary] modes."[141] As a self-proclaimed
gnostic, conversant in the enigmatic tradition and the Christian enigmas,
Clement even composes enigmatic literature of his own in his *Stromateis*.
The work comprises veiled reminders of secret truths, restricted to those
who are capable and worthy of them.[142] Clement clarifies elsewhere that
those worthy of the *Stromateis'* secret truths are precisely those who are
*like* them:

138. *Cant.* prol. (GCS 33, 62; trans. Greer, *Origen*, 217–18).

139. *Cant.* prol. (GCS 33, 62).

140. See the whole of *strom.* 5.4–9 (SC 278, 56–125), in which Clement demonstrates his familiarity with the enigmatic tradition. For a summary of Clement's understanding of the enigmatic nature of Scripture, see Kovacs, "Divine Pedagogy," 17–25.

141. *Strom.* 5.4.21 (SC 278, 60).

142. *Strom.* 1.1.11–18 (SC 30, 51–57). On the deliberate obscurity of the *Stromateis*, see Fortin, "Clement and the Esoteric Tradition," 41–56. For summaries and re-
views of scholarship on this point see Itter, *Esoteric Teaching in the* Stromateis, 15–32;
and Osborn, *Clement of Alexandria*, 5–15.

> Let these my notes—as I have said many times for those who
> read them carelessly and inexpertly—be of varied character,
> ... hinting [μηνύοντα] at one thing in the sequence of the dis-
> courses while displaying something else on the surface. "For
> those who seek gold," says Heraclitus, "dig lots and find little."
> But those who are actually of golden stock, who mine for what is
> akin to them [τὸ συγγενές], will find much in the little.[143]

We see here how seamlessly a notion of textual obscurity and its contract
of expertise give rise to a like-by-like model of exegesis. And for Clement,
this notion belonged first and foremost to Scripture, whose enigmatic
ways he attempts to imitate in his *Stromateis*.[144] Scripture is obscure, he
clarifies in *Stromateis* 6, to protect the unworthy from being harmed by
misapprehending its most difficult meanings,[145] and conversely to preserve these meanings for the worthy—here, the "chosen men, selected
to knowledge in consequence of their faith."[146] Clement elsewhere clarifies that Scripture's "worthy" readers are those who are *like* Scripture's
hidden truth. In a passage from *Stromateis* 5, he grounds this like-by-
like model both in Plato's maxim in the *Phaedo* and in a biblical source
that we will see Origen latch onto with great enthusiasm: 1 Corinthians
2:13–14: "And we speak of these things in words not taught by human
wisdom but taught by the Spirit, interpreting spiritual things to those
who are spiritual [πνευματικοῖς πνευματικὰ συνκρίνοντες]. Those who
are unspiritual do not receive the gifts of God's Spirit, for they are fool-
ishness to them, and they are unable to understand them because they
are discerned spiritually."[147] Clement takes Paul's like-by-like logic as
an exegetical model for approaching enigma or obscurity,[148] and this is
quite a faithful appropriation, since Paul's words here concern precisely
the communication of "God's hidden wisdom in secret" (θεοῦ σοφίαν ἐν
μυστηρίῳ, τὴν ἀποκεκρυμμένην [1 Cor 2:7]). We can look at the passage

143. *Strom.* 4.2.4.1–2 (SC 463, 60–62).

144. "Clement sees his own practice of concealment as an imitation of the parabol-
ic, enigmatic character of Scripture" (Kovacs, "Divine Pedagogy," 20). See also Fortin,
"Clement and the Esoteric Tradition," 47.

145. For more on concealment as a means of preventing danger to those unpre-
pared for truth, see Hägg, *Clement of Alexandria*, 143–47.

146. *Strom.* 6.15.126.1–4 (SC 446, 310–12). For an analysis of this passage and the
various arguments contained in it, see Harl, "Origène et les interprétations," 349–50.

147. Trans. NRSV.

148. See also *strom.* 1.12.56.1–2 (SC 30, 89), where Clement presents the second
part of this passage (1 Cor 2:14) as a model for interpreting enigma.

in full, and observe how Clement intimately associates the themes of interpreting what is hidden, ritual initiation, and the like-by-like logic of Plato and Paul:

> The crowd is delighted not with what differs from it but with what is like it. For he who is still blind and deaf, who lacks understanding and has no love of contemplating . . . is like one uninitiated at the mystery rites, or unmusical at the dances, not yet pure or worthy of the holy truth; he is out-of-tune, disordered, material, and must "stand outside the divine dance" [*Phdr.* 247A]. For we "interpret spiritual things to those who are spiritual" [1 Cor 2:13]. It was because of this that the Egyptians, by "the innermost sanctuaries" as they say, and the Hebrews with the term "the veil," alluded to a method of concealment—a discourse completely holy, truly divine, and supremely necessary, laid down for us in the innermost sanctuary. It was only available to those of them who were made holy, I mean, who had been dedicated to God, having circumcised the lusts of the passions through love for what is divine alone. "For it is not permitted for the impure to touch what is pure" [*Phd.* 67B], as Plato himself thought. This is why the prophets and the oracles speak through enigmas, and why the mystery rites are not shown freely to just anyone, but rather are accompanied by rites of purification and warnings.[149]

At the beginning of the *Stromateis* Clement had said that the task of interpreting "what is hidden" (τὸ κρυπτόν) must be undergone in a way that resembles it: that is, "hiddenly" (κρυπτῶς).[150] Here he fills out what he meant. He draws out the association between hiddenness, holiness, and purity that runs deep in the religious imagination of the ancient Greek mind, now adding Paul's category of "spiritual" to the mix. With the help of Paul and Plato, Clement irons out this bundle of themes with a model of knowing-by-likeness that is at once exegetical and ascetic: what is hidden is pure or spiritual, therefore what is hidden can be accessed by becoming pure or spiritual oneself. It is important to note that although "pure is known by pure" was a maxim derived from the language and logic of Greek mystery religion that allegory always adopted, it was also a maxim present in Scripture that could inform Christian reflections on knowing more generally. Perhaps the best example is Matthew 5:8: "Blessed are the pure in heart for they shall see God," a passage that

149. *Strom* 5.4.19–20 (SC 278, 56–59).
150. *Strom.* 1.1.13.2–3 (SC 30, 52–53).

infiltrated the epistemological reasoning of Clement[151] and Origen,[152] and whose like-by-like logic they pinpointed.[153]

Turning now to Origen, Torjesen has shown in great detail that, in Origen's mind, the fundamental trajectory of reading Scripture is the soul's increasing purification, conformation to God, and consequent knowledge.[154] This encompassing trajectory is something of a large-scale version of the knowing-by-likeness model that one finds clarified in many smaller instances in Origen's allegorical reading practice. It is worth highlighting some of these instances. Origen's thought shares a great deal with Clement's, his slightly older contemporary in Alexandria,[155] including a conviction of Scripture's obscurity.[156] As we might expect by now, it is the theme of obscurity and hiddenness around which his claims about knowing-by-likeness crystalize. At the beginning of *On First Principles* he makes this link clear: "the entire church agrees that while the whole law is spiritual, the spirited meaning is not recognized by all, but only by those who are gifted with the grace of the Holy Spirit."[157] No doubt recalling the same passage from 1 Corinthians 2 that we saw Clement use, and which we will see more of shortly, Origen says that all Christians know that readers grasp Scripture's hidden meanings by becoming like Scripture's author, in this case, the Spirit; only the spiritual recognize the spiritual, like is discerned by like. Brian Daley has argued that the whole of *On First Principles* is structured as an itinerary that caters to this rule: first the treatise lengthily trains its reader in the church's fundamental doctrines, or "first principles," and then only in the fourth and final book, when the reader is mature, ready for spiritual things, does Origen address the nature and interpretation of Scripture.[158]

151. E.g. *strom* 1.19.94.6 (SC 30, 120); *strom* 2.20.114.6 (SC 38, 121); *strom* 4.6.39.1 (SC 463, 122); *strom.* 5.1.7.7 (SC 278, 34); *strom.* 6.12.102.1–2 (SC 446, 264–65).

152. Origen cites this passage numerously, e.g. *princ.* 1.1.9 (GCS 22, 26–27); *Jo.* 19.17 (SC 290, 54–57); *Jo.* 19.146 (SC 290, 134–35); *hom. in Luc.* 3.3 (SC 87, 122–23).

153. "They will see God, . . . having become capable of pure divinity through the purity of their heart" (*hom. in Num.* 21.1.4 [SC 461, 66]; trans. Scheck, *Homilies on Numbers*, 132).

154. Torjesen, *Hermeneutical Procedure*, 70–107.

155. For an introduction to Clement's influence on Origen, see Trigg, *Origen*, 9–10.

156. On Origen's understand of Scripture's enigmatic nature, see Torjesen, *Hermeneutical Procedure*, 110.

157. *Princ.* 1, pref. 8 (GCS 22, 14; trans. modified from Butterworth, *On First Principles*, 5).

158. Daley, "Origen's *De Principiis*," 3–21.

A clear iteration of this exegetical model of knowing-by-likeness comes at the beginning of Origen's *Commentary on John*. He stresses that only the reader who is like John will grasp the truth of John's Gospel, because of its obscurity: its "meaning no one can understand who has not leaned on Jesus' breast nor received Mary from Jesus to be his mother also."[159] As Peter Martens summarizes, Origen "argued that interpreters needed . . . to mirror the lives and ideals of the authors they were examining," and that "[t]hose who underwent such a moral formation were well conditioned to anticipate the true sense of the Scriptures." Martens highlights a number of other passages that demonstrate this.[160] In the passage above from the *Commentary on John*, however, Origen goes on to say that John's life was so perfect that Christ lived in him (Gal 2:20), so that Christ was the real author of his gospel. Therefore, to understand John's words, the exegete ultimately must be conformed not to John but to Christ.[161]

Origen reaches the same conclusion elsewhere—that Scripture's reliable interpreter is the one who is like Christ, Scripture's author. Towards the beginning of *On First Principles* 4, Origen recommends this exegetical protocol precisely as a means for tackling the enigmatic character of Scripture:

> And what must we say about the prophecies, which we all know are filled with enigmas and dark sayings [αἰνιγμάτων καὶ σκοτεινῶν]? Or if we come to the Gospels, even their accurate meaning [νοῦς], since it is the mind [νοῦς] of Christ, requires that grace that was given to the one who said, "We have the mind of Christ, so that we may know the things that were freely given to us by God, which things we also speak not in words which man's wisdom teaches, but which the Spirit teaches" [1 Cor 2:12–13].[162]

Origen argues that the qualified interpreter of "enigmas" becomes what he is trying to interpret, the νοῦς of Christ, which is the hidden meaning of Scripture. As Blossom Stefaniw clarifies, there is here an "assumed need for unity or harmony between the knower and the known."[163] And one of Origen's students, perhaps Gregory Thaumaturgus, in fact attests to his

159. *Jo.* 1.23 (SC 120, 70; trans. FC 80, 38).

160. Martens, *Origen and Scripture*, 166.

161. *Jo.* 1.23 (SC 120, 70–72).

162. *Princ.* 4.2.3 (SC 268, 305–6; trans. modified from Butterworth, *On First Principles*, 273–74).

163. Stefaniw, *Mind, Text, and Commentary*, 258.

master's own inimitable ability to himself fulfil this difficult exegetical standard, that is, to elucidate Scripture's "enigmas" out of a great friendship with and likeness to the author of Scripture, Christ the Word.[164]

In the above passage, Origen supports his argument with citations from 1 Corinthians 2, a crucial passage that we have already seen Clement reference, in which Paul explicitly presents a like-by-like, or spiritual-by-spiritual, logic as the key to interpreting the "hidden" things of God. When Origen cites this passage, and particularly verses 13–14, he offers some of his most limpid assertions of the necessity of a like-by-like exegetical practice for tackling Scripture's obscurities:[165]

> It would be the task of a wise man, capable of skillfully plumbing the depths even of Scripture, to speak of each of these matters, by examining . . . the entirety of the things written about Abraham, "which things are allegorical" [Gal 4:24], which we, as spiritual persons, shall attempt to do spiritually [see 1 Cor 2:12–15].[166]

> [K]nowing that now we do not have to wage physical wars, but that the struggles of the soul have to be exerted against spiritual adversaries . . . [, a]nd in order for us to have examples of these spiritual wars from deeds of old, he [Paul] wanted those narratives of exploits to be recited to us in church, so that, if we are spiritual . . . "we may bring together spiritual things with spiritual" [1 Cor 2:13] in the things we hear.[167]

> To be sure, if someone can, at leisure, bring together and compare divine Scripture with itself, and fit together "spiritual things with spiritual" [1 Cor 2:13], we are not unmindful that he will

---

164. *Pan. Or.* 15.174–79 (SC 148, 168–71). Joseph Trigg offers a longer analysis of this student's assessment of his master's spiritual advancement and ability to access what is "hidden." Trigg suggests, moreover, that the way that the student portrays Origen's excellence accurately reflects Origen's own portrayal of the successful spiritual exegete ("God's Marvellous *Oikonomia*," 39–42). Regarding the authorship of this text, in his landmark study *Origène: Sa vie*, Pierre Nautin argued that the text's traditional attribution to Gregory Thaumaturgus had been made in error (83–86, 182–97). For an attempt to refute his arguments, see Crouzel, "Faut-il voir trois personnages."

165. Alongside the following citations, there are a number of other parallel passages, e.g. *hom. in Ex.* 1.2 (SC 321, 46); *comm. in Rom.* 9.36.2 (SC 555, 206).

166. *Jo.* 20.74 (SC 290, 194–96; trans. modified from FC 89, 222).

167. *Hom. in Jos.* 15.1 (SC 71, 340; trans. FC 105, 138).

discover in this passage many secrets of a profound and hidden
mystery . . . [168]

The spiritual meaning of the Bible is "allegorical," "hidden," and often conveyed in unpalatable tales. The reader can only hope to plumb its strange depths through the labor of becoming spiritual himself. In the final passage above, Origen associates Paul's words in 1 Corinthians 2:13 with another interesting exegetical injunction: interpret Scripture with Scripture, or "compare Scripture with itself." Origen is here playing on the traditional *Homerum ex Homero* principle: interpret a difficulty in Homer with another passage from Homer,[169] which he associates with 1 Corinthians 2:13 elsewhere too.[170] Although this is not quite the same as the ascetical knowing-by-likeness model we have been tracing, it is nonetheless a parallel approach, in that *likeness* is the crucial deciphering tool.

## Conclusion

This chapter has presented two origins of the epistemological model, popular among Greek patristic writers, that "like is known by like." First there was the *optical* rendition of this model, mediated through Aristotle, which appeared especially in Christian theological discussions of light and vision. However, my main suggestion in this chapter has been that the real catalyst for this epistemology in early Christianity was the adoption by Alexandrian Christians of allegorical or enigmatic exegesis—an exegetical tradition that, we saw at length, took for granted that textual interpretation, like the rites of Greek mystery religion, was a task for individuals who labored to liken themselves to the truth they sought. This meant becoming "pure," as the text's hidden truth is pure. I have taken Clement and Origen as the best examples of Christians who inherited this *exegetical* rendition of the "like-by-like" epistemology. As these theologians faced the inevitable practical concerns, concerns about character, that I have suggested always attended enigmatic exegesis, they adopted and developed a conviction that Scripture's hidden truths may be discerned by readers who labor to become like them.

168. *Hom. in Gen.* 2.6 (SC 7, 112; trans. FC 71, 88).

169. Schäublin, "Homerum Ex Homero," 221–27.

170. E.g. *hom. in Jos.* 15.3 (SC 71, 334).

# 2

## Knowing-by-likeness in Maximus the Confessor

In the first chapter we identified two distinct strands of a likeness epistemology in early Greek Christian discourse, one "optical," the other "exegetical." The first was a theologically applied optical theory which dealt
in the themes of vision, light, and the knowledge of God. "Light is seen
by light" is the founding logic here. The second strand arrived when, in
second- and third-century Alexandria, Christians honed practices of allegorical reading: an exegetical approach that considered the text's meaning hidden, and that was cast in the vocabulary of Greek mystery rites.
The recurring themes of this epistemology were "purification," "holiness,"
becoming "spiritual," "initiation," "enigma" and "mystery." The maxims
that "pure knows pure" and "spiritual knows spiritual" summarized this
exegetical model of knowing by likeness, but we also witnessed more
specific claims: "the John-like person comprehends John's Gospel," for
example, or "the Christ-like person perceives the Christ-authored meanings of Scripture."

Centuries later, Maximus himself inherited a likeness epistemology
from his forebears, reproduced it, and developed it. The task of this chapter and the next is to identify how models of knowing-by-likeness present themselves in Maximus' early writings, before he became embroiled
in christological conflict from around 633. In these works, his approach
to knowledge and interpretation is strongly redolent of the exegetical,
rather than optical, strand of Christian likeness epistemology—characterized by concepts of "purity," "initiation," "enigma," etc.—and this chapter will begin by exploring how Maximus applied this epistemology, and

how he largely inherited it from Gregory Nazianzen. Maximus bears no substantial witness to the optical version of this epistemology, but, just as the earliest Jewish and Christian allegorists, like Philo, Clement, and Origen, could in different places promulgate both the exegetical and the optical strands, so sometimes Maximus' epistemological claims are also attended by images of light and vision that are more suggestive of the optical strand. I will note these instances as we come across them. After examining how Maximus inherits an exegetical likeness epistemology, we will turn to some of Maximus' explorations with the knowing-by-likeness motif that neatly fit neither the exegetical nor optical characterization. For example, Maximus suggests that God, who is "Love," is known by those who love; that God is known by those who achieve likeness to God through "virtue"; and, finally and most remarkably, Maximus proposes that God can be "unknowingly" comprehended through a conformation of desire to God's attributes. We will explore these ideas in turn: knowing-by-love, knowing-by-virtue, and unknowing-by-likeness.

Before embarking on these explorations, it is important to define our key term and clarify what Maximus understands by "likeness" to God. The answer is reasonably straightforward and Maximus expresses it straightforwardly: a person "chooses to add to his beautiful nature, which is in the image [of God], the exact likeness [of God] by means of the virtues."[1] In other words, "likeness" is a grace-enabled addition to (but not change of) human nature. Maximus, then, follows many before him in understanding the two terms from Genesis 1:26—the "image" and "likeness" of God—as two different aspects of a theological anthropology: that is, of what humans are in relation to God their creator. The "image" refers to a relationship and kinship with God that belongs unerringly and invariably to human nature; the "likeness" refers to a closeness to God that has erred, that was lost at the fall, and that is variable and can be restored in degrees. Lars Thunberg has amply elucidated this feature of the Confessor's thought and its precedents,[2] and draws attention to the following neat summary that Maximus offers in one of his *Centuries on Love*: "The one [image] is by nature, the other [likeness] by grace. Every rational nature is made to the image of God, but only the good and wise to His likeness."[3] Jean-Claude Larchet offers his own helpful summary

1. *Ambig.* 7.21 (DOML 28, 104).
2. Thunberg, *Microcosm and Mediator*, 120–29.
3. *Carit.* 3.25 (PG 90, 1024C; trans. ACW 21, 177).

by paralleling "image" and "likeness" with Maximus' favorite distinction between a creature's *logos* ("principle") of being and *tropos* ("mode") of being: that is, respectively, what is natural and fixed in a creature and what is malleable and transformable.[4]

It is also important to make two caveats at the outset about the theme of "likeness" in Maximus. The first is that, while, for Maximus, likeness to God belongs not to nature or *logos* but to way of being or *tropos*, this does not mean that likeness to God is superficial, a kind of copying or mimicking of God that in fact has nothing to do with what it means to be human. For Maximus, a creature's "way" of being is the very change that a creature undergoes,[5] the things that happen to it that make it what it is. To take some of Maximus' examples: Elijah's ascent to heaven was a change in his "way" of being; the burning bush was an innovation in the bush's "way" of being; Abraham and Sarah's elderly pregnancy was an innovation in their "way" of being.[6] For Maximus, and indeed for the biblical authors themselves, these changes are not arbitrary, they have integrity. It would be misapprehended to deem these changes superficial or irrelevant to the natures involved, and it would be similarly misapprehended, according to Maximus, to think of likeness to God as superficial to human nature in the image of God. Moreover, as already mentioned, likeness to God is a restoration of a closeness to God that, although squandered by humans, is nonetheless humanity's vocation by nature. It goes with the grain of human nature, not against it or apart from it. As much is clear when Maximus says above that "likeness" to God is something achieved "by means of the virtues," which are, for Maximus, natural.[7]

The second caveat is to point out that in this chapter we will come across many passages in which Maximus does not use the term "likeness," but rather infers the phenomenon of likeness, of having been conformed to God. He asserts, for example, that the spiritual person understands the spiritual meanings of Scripture, or that the person with simple desire comprehends the simple God. As well as this, we will come across the cognate language of "imitation" of God.[8] In all such cases, the same defi-

---

4. Larchet, *La divinisation*, 156.

5. *Ambig.* 42.26 (DOML 29, 172).

6. *Ambig.* 42.27 (DOML 29, 174).

7. Louth clarifies this point in "Virtue Ethics," 333–50.

8. Blowers points out that "imitation" is a widespread concept in Maximus, including not only the imitation of God or Christ, but the imitation of biblical *exempla* and fellow Christians past and present (*Maximus the Confessor*, 280–83).

nition of likeness must be kept in mind: first, likeness is a change in the creature's mode or way of existence, rather than a change of a creature's nature; and secondly, it is a change that is integral—not superficial—to the creature's nature, a change that makes it *more itself*, rather than copying some other standard of being.

## Maximus' inheritance of models of knowing-by-likeness

Maximus was a distant inheritor of the Alexandrian allegorical tradition, or "enigmatic" tradition as I have characterized it. Although a good interpretation of Scripture[9] "can accommodate everyone," Maximus says that Scripture conceals a "more mystical" meaning reserved for "the mystics";[10] it contains "enigmas"[11] to which it "darkly hints."[12] Together with this notion of Scripture's obscurity, Maximus inherits what we have seen was always its product: an exacting epistemology that considers *likeness* the key condition for discerning Scripture's hidden meaning. Consider the following passages in which Maximus speaks in a single breath of both the obscurity of Scripture and the need for interpreters who can read with the grain of Scripture in virtue of themselves being *like* Scripture's hidden teachings—namely, in virtue of being "spiritual" and "pure."

---

9. Good interpretation, for Maximus, is "anagogical" interpretation (see especially *qu. dub.*: 8 [CCSG 10, 7], 29 [CCSG 10, 24], 38 [CCSG 10, 31], 44 [CCSG 10, 37], 77 [CCSG 10, 48], 162 [CCSG 10, 113], 178 [CCSG 10, 122], I.35 [CCSG 10, 151]), or "spiritual contemplation" (πνευματικὴ θεωρία, *qu. dub.* 28 [CCSG 10, 23]), "spiritual interpretation" (πνευματικὴ ἑρμηνεία, *qu. Thal* intr. [CCSG 7, 21.92]), or simply "contemplation" (θεωρία, as opposed to ἱστορία, *qu. dub.* 78 [CCSG 10, 59], *qu. dub.* 112 [CCSG 10, 83]). Rather than being a technical term, in Maximus' works the "anagogical" mode and its synonyms simply designate the interpretative method that Maximus always uses in his works: that is, an interpretation that translates every word and detail of a passage into the terms of Maximus' spiritual scheme, or "anagogy," of being drawn and conformed to Christ the *Logos* through *praxis, natural contemplation*, and *theology*. Blowers emphasizes that an essential part of anagogical interpretation (again, in reality, simply Maximus' ubiquitous method of interpretation) is its ability to hold together many and diverse interpretations at once, in part to address the diverse needs and abilities of readers (*Exegesis and Spiritual Pedagogy*, 185–90).

10. *Qu. Thal.* intr. (CCSG 7, 38).

11. E.g. *qu. Thal.* 55 (CCSG 22, 483); *qu. Thal.* 17 (CCSG 7, 111).

12. *Cap. theol* 2.60 (PG 90, 1149D–1152A); *qu. dub.* 43 (CCSG 10, 36); *qu. dub.* 80 (CCSG 10, 61); *qu. dub.* I.33 (CCSG 10, 150); *qu. dub.* I.35 (CCSG 10, 151); *qu. Thal.* 44 (CCSG 22, 299); *qu. Thal.* 63 (CCSG 22, 177); *qu. Thal.* 64 (CCSG 22, 193).

> You [Thalassius] examine with the Spirit the depths of the Spirit [see 1 Cor 2:10]; and you receive from this Spirit the manifestation of hidden mysteries [τῶν κεκρυμμένων μυστηρίων] . . . [13]

> The highest and true comprehension [of Scripture] . . . is the work of the fullness of heart of those who enter upon the spiritual knowledge of hidden things [ἀπορηθέντων] [see Matt 5:8].[14]

> Or the meaning could be hinting [αἰνίττεται] by means of the letter in which the story is told at something else which is more spiritual than these, understandable only to those who are pure of mind.[15]

Maximus portrays the best conditions for discerning the enigmatic depths of Scripture in a way that is now familiar, suggesting that the reader whose character harmonizes with Scripture—that is, the reader who is "spiritual" or "pure"—will be the one to understand Scripture's hidden meanings. He makes the same move as his Alexandrian predecessors, even evoking the same passage from 1 Corinthians 2 as they did, and brings to the difficulty or obscurity of Scripture the solution of knowing-by-likeness.

Maximus expands this epistemology beyond scriptural interpretation to the task of textual interpretation in general. For example, in one of his *Difficulties* he addresses an apparent incoherence in a text of Gregory Nazianzen by suggesting that the answer will appear completely to "a person who is more or less his [Gregory's] equal in virtue."[16] Imitation is the key to understanding. Moreover, Maximus begins a later *Difficulty* by suggesting, together with the ancient allegorists we met in Chapter 1, that the problem of *obscurity* in particular necessitates this approach: "What the great teacher [Gregory] hiddenly [κρυφίως] reveals through these words is known, I believe, only to those who have received his same gift of wisdom and knowledge."[17] Following Clement centuries before him, Maximus even recommends this model of interpretation for approaching his own works; for example, he says of his *Four Centuries on Love* that

13. *Qu. Thal.* intr. (CCSG 7, 19).
14. *Qu. Thal.* intr. (CCSG 7, 23).
15. *Myst.* 24 (CCSG 69, 72–73; trans. Bethold, *Maximus Confessor*, 214).
16. *Ambig.* 42.3 (DOML 29, 124–5, including trans.).
17. *Ambig.* 45.2 (DOML 29, 192–3; modified trans.).

only the reader who reads "with love" will find in its words "something useful for the soul."[18] We will see Maximus consistently encourage this like-by-like model of discernment amongst readers of his own writings when we turn to his christological letters in the final chapters.

The interpretation of texts is not the only locus in which this Alexandrian, exegetical, likeness epistemology plays out in Maximus. Long before his time, this model of *textual* discernment came to define the task of theology in general for many thinkers in the heritage of Origen. Maximus was one of them, and in his works this epistemological assumption spreads beyond questions of textual exegesis. The easiest way of tracing this epistemology beyond the exegetical context is by looking out for the language of its definitive Platonic and biblical slogan: "pure is known by pure." This language and logic survive unchanged in Maximus' thought.[19] One "eagerly sets oneself on divine knowledge by means of purification," he says.[20] Or again, "The one who keeps the commandments is purified. The one who is purified is illumined. And the one who is illumined is judged worthy to sleep with the Word-Spouse in the inner chamber of the mysteries."[21] There are two notable features of this last passage. First, Maximus hints, in a way redolent of the Song commentary tradition, that by deepening into divine knowledge the knower undergoes an erotic encounter. Throughout this study we will continue to see Maximus press this theme that love or desire is the supreme means of conformation to and comprehension of one's object of knowledge. Secondly, Maximus makes the classic link between purity and enigma, or "mystery." In the following passage he sees this relationship of purity and mystery displayed vividly in Jesus' transfiguration:

> [C]ertain of Christ's disciples, through diligence in virtue, ascended and were raised aloft with Him on the mountain of His manifestation, where they beheld Him transfigured, "unapproachable" by reason of the "light" of His face [1 Tim 6:16] . . . [T]hey crossed over from the flesh to the spirit . . . through the substitution of their powers of sense perception by the activity of the Spirit, who removed the veils of the passions that had

18. *Carit.* prol. (PG 90, 960B).

19. It is particularly prevalent in his *carit.*: 1.83 (PG 90, 1117A–C); 2.61 (PG 90, 1152A–B); 2.70 (PG 90, 1156C); 2.80–82 (PG 90, 1161D–1163A); 2.100 (PG 90, 1173A).

20. *Cap. theol.* 1.30 (PG 91, 1093C).

21. *Cap. theol.* 1.16 (PG 91, 1089A; trans. Berthold, *Maximus Confessor*, 131).

covered the intellective capacity within them. With the sensory
organs of their souls and bodies purified through the Spirit, they
were taught the spiritual principles of the mysteries that had
been disclosed to them.[22]

Here Maximus clearly stands within the epistemological tradition of Origen that we addressed in the first chapter. As with Origen, for Maximus it is the case that "[t]he Transfiguration takes place as much in the disciples as it does in the garments of Christ."[23] Maximus presents this transformation with the language of "purity" and "mystery," characteristic of the ancient exegetical strand of the likeness epistemology. But he also conceptualizes it in terms of vision or sense-perception, which recalls the philosophical and scientific roots of this epistemology in its optical rendition.[24] In this passage, the mix of the oracular and the optical produces the following version of the knowing-by-likeness motif: the senses are purified, and this purity provides the sure condition for seeing what is secret, veiled, or mysterious. Maximus appears here to be a distant inheritor of both the exegetical *and* optical renditions of the like-by-like theory.

However, Maximus rarely chooses these optical themes of vision and light to express his assumption that "like is known by like." He prefers, we have already seen, to present the knowing-by-likeness motif in the traditional terms of Alexandrian exegesis. If this is the case, from whom did he learn it? Gregory Nazianzen was one theologian who expanded the originally exegetical theory that "like is known by like" into a general rule of theological discernment. And Gregory's *Orations* were certainly one means by which this rule of discernment reached Maximus. The *Orations* witness to how the exegetical likeness epistemology traced in the first chapter developed; and, moreover, Maximus was devoted to these texts and spent almost the entirety of his *Difficulties*, his largest work, scrutinizing and explaining them.[25]

22. *Ambig.* 10.28 (DOML 28, 190–91, including trans.).

23. Lollar, *To See into the Life of Things*, 256. See also McFarland, "Developing an Apophatic Christocentrism," 207. Maximus expresses this elsewhere: "by the transfiguration of the Word in them they [who are like Peter, James, and John], with unveiled face, behold as in a mirror the Lord's glory" (*cap. theol.* 1.97 [PG 90, 1124A]).

24. For a summary of Maximus and the "spiritual senses," which focuses especially on the role of virtue in transformed sensing, but not on Maximus' Alexandrian heritage, see Aquino, "Maximus the Confessor," 104–20.

25. On Maximus as a reader and interpreter of Gregory, see Louth, "St Gregory the Theologian," 117–30.

Christopher Beeley has emphasized that "a cardinal principle" of Gregory's "theological system is his repeated insistence that the knowledge of God is inseparably related to the condition of the human knower—that theology both demands and causes a change in the state of the theologian."[26] The same could be said of Gregory's Alexandrian predecessors like Clement and Origen, and of his successor Maximus. Moreover, for Gregory the specific "condition" of knowledge is often *likeness*. As Jospeh Trigg summarizes, the knowledge of God unfolds "though a gradual process of assimilation to the divine."[27] Gregory can put this daringly. As he navigates the doctrine of the Trinity in *Oration* 25, he exhorts his reader as follows: "First get to be one of things that we have talked about [the Father, Son, and Holy Spirit], or someone of like sort, and then you will come to know in the same measure as they are known by one another."[28] In other words, Gregory seems to say that creaturely minds can hope to join the Trinity's life of mutual knowing precisely by imitating the persons of the Trinity.

Gregory presents this likeness epistemology as a cornerstone of theological discernment. In a sequence of twenty-eight of his *Difficulties*,[29] Maximus tackles passages from Gregory's *Orations* 27–30, which, along with *Oration* 31, are known by modern readers as the "Theological" orations. In them, Gregory is concerned with the immanent rather than the economic life of God, that is, with "theology," and especially how to talk of God as Father, Son, and Spirit distinctly, without introducing a subordination in substances within God, as did Gregory's adversaries the Eunomians.[30] Gregory knows that this is a difficult subject with plenty of pitfalls, and a subject whose depths are only open to a few. Therefore, *Oration* 27 introduces the subject by identifying the apt conditions for doing theology safely, which include, importantly, *likeness* to theology's objects:

> Discussion of theology is not for everyone . . . Nor, I would
> add, is it for every occasion, or every audience . . . It must be

26. Beeley, *Gregory of Nazianzus*, 63.

27. Trigg, "Knowing God," 86.

28. *Or.* 25.17 (SC 284, 198; trans. FC 107, 172).

29. *Ambig.* 13–30. See the very useful "Summary of the Works of Gregory Nazianzen Treated in the *Difficulties to John*" in the "Appendix" to Lollar, *To See into the Life of Things*, 333–34.

30. For a summary of the teaching of Aetius and Eunomius, the two key "Eunomian" or "heterousian" theologians, see Ayres, *Nicaea and Its Legacy*, 144–49.

> reserved for certain occasions, for certain audiences, and cer-
> tain limits must be observed. It is not for all people, but only for
> those who have been tested and have found a sound footing in
> contemplation, and, more importantly, have undergone, or at
> the very least are undergoing, purification of body and soul. For
> one who is not pure to lay hold of pure things is dangerous [see
> *Phd.* 67B] . . .[31]

Purification, for Gregory, is the key to knowledge of God, as Beeley has
highlighted.[32] But more exactly, what makes purity work as an epistemic
aid is the fact that it *matches* the knowledge of God, which is itself a "pure
thing." It is not difficult to see in this passage how the model of textual interpretation that we saw in Chapter 1 has been transposed to the context
of "theology" in general. Just as in older Alexandrian enigmatic exegesis,
stamped by the *Phaedo*'s pure-by-pure maxim, here the "purity" of the
object of knowledge demands the purification of the knower. Gregory
makes this clear in other passages from the *Orations* discussed by Maximus: "God is seen and known according to one's proportion of purity";[33]
"he [the Word] is purity, so that what is pure may be filled with his
pureness";[34] and finally, as Gregory says on two occasions, "one must first
purify oneself, then associate oneself with what is pure."[35] For Gregory,
purification is the key condition for knowing God, and this is because
purity imitates God.

As Gregory continues his train of thought in *Oration* 27, and specifies the proper audience of theology, he offers a vivid example of his underlying like-by-like, or pure-by-pure, epistemology:

> Why do we allow audiences hostile to our subject-matter to lis-
> ten to discussion of the "generation" and "creation" of God, or
> of God's "production from non-being" . . . ? How, I ask you, will
> such a discussion be interpreted by the man who subscribes to a
> creed of adulteries and infanticides, who worships the passions,
> who is incapable of conceiving anything higher than the body

31. *Or.* 27.3 (SC 250, 76–77; trans. Williams and Wickham, *On God and Christ*,
26–27).

32. Beeley, *Gregory of Nazianzus*, 64–90.

33. *Or.* 40.45 (SC 358, 306). In the next chapter we will examine how Maximus
uses this language of "proportion" and how it links with his epistemology.

34. *Or.* 30.20 (SC 250, 270–71; trans. Williams and Wickham, *On God and Christ*,
110).

35. *Or.* 39.9 (SC 358, 164–65; trans. Daley, *Gregory of Nazianzus*, 131). The same
phrase comes in an identical passage at *or.* 20.4 (SC 270, 62–63).

...? What sort of construction will he put on it? Is he not certain
to take it in a crude, obscene, material sense, as is his wont? Will
he not appropriate your theology to defend his own gods and
passions?[36]

There is no doubt, Gregory thinks, that people will interpret as much
as they can in terms that suit them and that do not transgress their own
settled mental and bodily predilections. Theology has no special defense
from these blundering attempts at knowing, and should therefore be reserved for those that labor to bring their mind and body into harmony
with the objects of theology, and not the other way around. Just as simili-
tude is the condition for understanding, so is dissimilitude the depend-
able condition for misunderstanding.

Although the language of "purity" dominates these discussions,
Gregory can also express his epistemological approach with the optical
like-by-like theory discussed in Chapter 1. For example, our first passage from *Oration* 27 cited above continues like this: "For one who is
not pure to lay hold of pure things is dangerous [see *Phd.* 67B], just as it
is for weak eyes to look at the sun's brightness."[37] And at the beginning
of the next *Oration*, number 28 (which provides the subject matter for
Maximus' *Difficulties* 15–22), Gregory says that the theologian should
become "as pure as possible, making for a perception of light by light."[38]
Later on in the same *Oration*, he makes the similar point that one might
hope to know God "in his nature and essence" only "when this God-like
[θεοειδές], divine thing, I mean our mind and reason, mingles with its
kin [τῷ οἰκείῳ]."[39] Gregory's language of a "God-like" faculty recalls Galen's like-by-like theory of perception, outlined in Chapter 1, where the
"light-like" [αὐγοειδές] organ perceives light, the "air-like" [ἀεροειδές]
organ perceives sound, the "earth-like" [γεῶδες] organ perceives touch,
and so on.[40] Even if Gregory's language only hints at this theory of perception, Maximus would certainly have been familiar with Galen's

36. *Or.* 27.6 (SC 250, 84–85; trans. Williams and Wickham, *On God and Christ*,
29–30).

37. *Or.* 27.3 (SC 250, 76–77; trans. Williams and Wickham, *On God and Christ*,
27).

38. *Or* 28.1 (SC 250, 100–101; trans. modified from Williams and Wickham, *On
God and Christ*, 37).

39. *Or.* 28.17 (SC 250, 134–35; trans. Williams and Wickham, *On God and Christ*,
49–51).

40. *De plac.* 7.5.42–44 (De Lacy, *On the Doctrines*, vol. 2, 462).

doctrine of sense perception and its vocabulary thanks to his familiarity with Nemesius of Emesa's *De Natura Hominis*, which presents Galen's theory of perception "by likeness" (καθ' ὁμοιότητα) as scientific fact.[41] Indeed, Maximus himself seems to echo this optical theory in his use of the term "light-like" (φωτοειδής), especially as all six occurrences of this term in Maximus' corpus belong to discussions of knowledge or perception. Two of them describe the divine "brilliance" that dazzles the mind.[42] Two instances identify "light-likeness" as the effect upon the mind when it looks at God,[43] which resembles Nemesius' single use of the term "light-likeness" to describe the sun's effect upon air.[44] In the two remaining instances, which occur together, Maximus takes "light-likeness" as a *condition* for perception, and here we are closest to Galen's theory. However, Maximus is clear that this light-likeness, "they say," belongs to the vision of "the ox" in particular, rather than of animals and humans in general. Nonetheless, for Maximus the ox's peculiar mode of perception reminds us of something true about the theological perception yielded by ascetic practice: Maximus swaps the category of light for that of "virtue" or "righteousness," so that having "light-like" eyes like an ox means contemplating knowledge from the "sun of righteousness" through "virtues."[45] There is some cause, then, to believe that Maximus had adopted the language and logic of an optical like-by-like theory—perhaps through Gregory, more likely through Nemesius—and considered it a valid theological tool.

Staying with the *Orations*, Gregory not only demands *that* students of theology purify themselves into the likeness of their object of study. He also suggests *how* they can go about it. In *Oration* 27, again, Gregory says that theological discourse itself can become excessive and distracting, a kind of amusement to gratify oneself or pass the time.[46] Discussion of theology, Gregory says, must have its own "due season" (καιρός, Eccl 3:1) and fitting employment, for which the theologian gets a feel not by continuously thinking about theology, but by continuous contemplation, or "remembrance of God":

41. *Nat. hom.* 11 (Morani, *Nemesii Emeseni*, 67). Galen's theory is summarized in more detail at *nat. hom.* 6 (Morani, *Nemesii Emeseni*, 56).

42. *Ambig.* 10.64 (DOML 28, 254–55); *qu. Thal.* intr. (CCSG 7, 41).

43. *Carit.* 2.48 (PG 90, 1000C–D); *carit.* 3.97 (PG 90, 1045D).

44. *Nat. hom.* 3 (Morani, *Nemesii Emeseni*, 40–41).

45. *Qu. dub.* 17 (CCSG 10, 14–15).

46. *Or.* 27.3 (SC 250, 76–79).

It is more important that we should remember God than that we should breathe: indeed, if one may say so, we should do nothing else besides. I am one of those who approve the precept that commands us to "meditate day and night" [Ps 1:2, LXX; Josh 1:8], to tell of the Lord "evening, and morning, and at noon" [Ps 54:17, LXX], and to "bless the Lord at all times" [Ps 33:1, LXX], or in the words of Moses, "when we lie down, when we rise up, when we walk by the way" [Deut 6:7], or when we do anything else whatever, and by this mindfulness [μνήμη] be molded to purity. So it is not continual remembrance of God I seek to discourage, but continual discussion of theology.[47]

This lasting prayer or contemplation, Gregory thinks, is the fixed earth from which theology springs, since it is the source of "purity," likeness to God. In short, the *how* of knowing-by-likeness is contemplation.

In *Oration* 38, Gregory offers a second answer to this *how* question. In a passage that would become the stimulus for Maximus' *Difficulty* 34, Gregory arrives at the conclusion that although God is completely ungraspable by human minds, one may yet come to know God by becoming like God—"like is known by like," or "God by gods" [Θεὸς θεοῖς], Gregory says. Interestingly, Gregory reaches this conclusion by thinking about "desire" or "yearning" (πόθος): the human activity that God's incomprehensibility excites and from which good theological reflection springs:

[God] is known not directly but indirectly, as one image is derived from another to form a single representation of the truth: fleeing before it is grasped, escaping before it is fully known, shining on our guiding reason—provided we have been purified—as a swift, fleeting flash of lightening shines in our eyes. And he does this, it seems to me, so that, insofar as it can be comprehended, the Divine might draw us to itself—for what is completely beyond our grasp is also beyond hope, beyond attainment—but that insofar as it is incomprehensible, it might stir up our wonder, and through wonder might be yearned for all the more, and through our yearning might purify us, and in purifying us might make us like God; and when we have become this, that he might then associate with us intimately as friends—my words here are rash and daring!—uniting himself

47. *Or.* 27.4 (SC 250, 78–81; trans. Williams and Wickham, *On God and Christ,* 27–28).

with us, making himself known to us, as God to gods [Θεὸς
θεοῖς ἑνούμενός τε καὶ γνωριζόμενος] . . .⁴⁸

Human cognition and imagination are too weak to comprehend the tran-
scendent God. But it is precisely this human frailty and this ungraspable
nature of theology's object that Gregory thinks offers hope, because, in
the face of the small glimpses and flashes of God's abundance with which
the mind can cope, "wonder" and consequent "yearning" or "desire"
grow and build momentum. And these impulses constitute theology's
basic activity and the best condition for knowing God, since they in turn
cultivate purity, Godlikeness. In short, "desire" is another means, a *how*,
of knowing God by likeness.

Maximus was completely familiar with Gregory's theoretical reflections on knowing God and the task of theology in his *Orations*, and they
are one obvious source of his own picture of discernment and knowledge
as dependent on assimilation to God. As we have seen, Maximus follows
Gregory in presenting a likeness epistemology largely in the terms of "purity," and occasionally of vision. And as we will see when we turn now to
Maximus' other renditions of this epistemology, he also follows Gregory
in conceptualizing it in the terms of love or desire.

## Maximus' own voice on knowing-by-likeness

Maximus adventures with the logic of knowing-by-likeness in ways that
are his own. I am going to trace three such ventures here: knowing-by-
love, knowing-by-virtue, and unknowing-by-likeness.

### Knowing by love

Maximus devotes a whole work, his *Four Centuries on Love*, to one version of the knowing-by-likeness motif. Despite its title, the work is in
great part a treatise on knowing. Unswervingly, chapter by chapter, the
*Centuries* press the claim that knowing God depends upon loving God⁴⁹
or desiring God,⁵⁰ that "divine knowledge" is "activated [ἐνεργουμένης]

---

48. *Or.* 38.7 (SC 358, 116–17; trans. Daley, *Gregory of Nazianzus*, 120).

49. *Carit.* 1.1 (PG 90, 961A); 1.4 (PG 90, 961B–C); 1.31 (PG 90, 967A); 1.46 (PG
90, 969A); 2.26 (PG 90, 992C); 4.60 (PG 90, 1061A–B).

50. *Carit.* 1.4 (PG 90, 961B–C); 2.48 (PG 90, 1000C–D).

by love";[51] and the treatise as a whole takes the reader through the details and struggles of this "way of peace that leads the lovers [ἐραστάς] of the knowledge of God through love to that knowledge."[52] This knowledge growing out from love makes up the whole "life of the mind" (ἡ ζωὴ τοῦ νοῦ), Maximus says.[53] For this reason, when the nourishment of love departs, the mind distracts itself with smaller objects,[54] becomes arrogant and presumptive with its possession and yet envies more,[55] until the mind's eye has been so blotted by resentment and sorrow and hate that it knows no more.[56] On the other hand, when the mind remains steadfast in love, it "becomes wise, good, powerful, benevolent, merciful, long-suffering; in a word, it contains in itself practically all the divine attributes [τὰ θεῖα ἰδιώματα]."[57] In this extraordinary sentence Maximus hints at an undergirding likeness epistemology coursing through his *Centuries*: love brings knowledge of God because love renders one Godlike, an imitator of "all the divine attributes."

Apart from hints like this one, the reader must wait until the very last chapter of the *Centuries* for Maximus to uncover with clarity the foundation of the relationship between love and knowledge of God:

> Many have said much about love. Looking for it only among the disciples of Christ will you find it, for they alone held the true Love, the Teacher of love, of which it is said: "If I should have prophecy and should know all mysteries, and all knowledge . . . , and have not love, it profits me nothing" [1 Cor 13:3]. He then that possesses love, possesses God Himself, for "God is love" [1 John 4:8].[58]

Love lends so much to knowing, and to knowing God especially, because God *is* love, or at the very least love is the resource than which "there is nothing is more Godlike [θεοειδέστερον]," as Maximus says in another text from this early period of his writing.[59] This claim, that Love is known

---

51. *Carit.* 1.47 (PG 90, 969B).

52. *Carit.* 1.69 (PG 90, 976A; trans. modified from ACW 21, 146).

53. *Carit.* 1.9 (PG 90, 964A).

54. *Carit.* 3.67 (PG 90, 1037A–B).

55. *Carit.* 4.59–61 (PG 90, 1061A–B).

56. *Carit.* 4.62 (PG 90, 1061C–1064A).

57. *Carit.* 2.52 (PG 90, 1001B; trans. ACW 21, 163).

58. *Carit.* 4.100 (PG 90 1073A, trans. modified from ACW 21, 208).

59. *Ep.* 2 (PG 91, 393B).

by love, surely explains the epistemological power that Maximus assigns to love in the *Centuries*.

## Knowing by virtue

Looking to Maximus' other early works, there is another like-by-like logic that runs in the veins, supplying all the places of his thought: this is the common pair—or even the *single* "principle"[60]—of "virtue and knowledge" (ἀρετὴ καὶ γνῶσις). Doubtless, as Völker suggests, this coupling is the product of Maximus' long ascetic heritage, which intimately linked two parallel notions: "practice" (πρᾶξις) and "contemplation" (θεωρία).[61] But there are also precedents for the coupling of "virtue" and "knowledge" themselves: "the knowledge of the Good," Gregory of Nyssa says, "that transcends every intellect comes to us through the virtues, even as it is possible through some image to get a glimpse of the archetypal Beauty." Paul exemplified this, Gregory thought, when he "imitated" the Word "by his virtues" and thus "inscribed within himself the unapproachable Beauty."[62] As well as habitually speaking of the spiritual life in these dual terms of "virtue and knowledge," Maximus seems to have thought quite deeply about the link between the two, opening up the workings, seeing the kind of relationship they hold; and his conclusion is the same as Gregory's:

> To put it briefly: virtue is the form in which knowledge appears to us, but knowledge is the power that holds virtue together.[63]

> The Word journeys forward through each person and, like a voice running on ahead, preparing each person for his presence, he gives grace in advance: in some comes repentance as a forerunner of justice to come, in others comes virtue as preparation for awaited knowledge . . .[64]

---

60. *Cap. theol.* 1.72 (PG 91, 1109B: τὸν λόγον τῆς ἀρετῆς καὶ τῆς γνώσεως).

61. Völker outlines this tradition, and also gives a list of passages in Maximus where the couplet "virtue and knowledge" appear (*Maximus Confessor als Meister*, 232–35).

62. *Cant.* 3 (GNO 6, 91; trans. Norris, *Homilies*, 101).

63. *Qu. Thal.* 63 (CCSG 22, 171; trans. modified from von Balthasar, *Cosmic Liturgy*, 332).

64. *Qu. Thal.* 47 (CCSG 7, 325).

The Word of God is a "door" [John 10:9], because he leads on to knowledge those who have rightly accomplished the way of the virtues in a blameless course of asceticism . . .[65]

The one who has given himself over to the pleasures of the body is neither active in virtue nor does he properly move toward knowledge . . . [A]s soon as the water moves he throws himself into the pool [see John 5:1–9], that is, into virtue which receives knowledge . . .[66]

We take the ladder [that Jacob sees, Gen 28:12] to be reverence for God. Regarding the angels who descend and ascend, those who ascend are the *logoi* of the virtues being elevated through us, and those who descend are the *logoi* of knowledge that come down because of the elevation of our virtues.[67]

Those who comprehend divine mysteries say that where there is purification of the soul by the virtues, there is also illumination by knowledge, subsequent to pious reflection on beings. This illumination raises up the soul to the understanding of God, and unites its desire with the ultimate object of its desire, which is God . . .[68]

In each of these instances, the relationship between virtue and knowledge is the same that Gregory of Nyssa outlined: virtue yields knowledge of God.[69] Virtue fashions the knower after the object of knowledge.

Virtue possesses this fashioning power because, in Maximus' mind, virtue itself is nothing other than likeness to God, and, as we are continuing to see, Maximus believes likeness to be a crucial epistemic condition. That virtue is a form of Godlikeness is apparent if one explores the context of the final quotation above. The passage by Gregory Nazianzen that Maximus is interpreting here reads as follows: "where there is purification there is also illumination, and illumination is the fulfilment of desire for those who desire [God] . . . For this reason, one must first purify

65. *Cap. theol.* 1.69 (PG 90, 1156B; trans. Berthold, *Maximus Confessor*, 162).

66. *Cap. theol.* 1.80 (PG 91, 1113B–C; trans. Berthold, *Maximus Confessor*, 142–43).

67. *Qu. dub.* 88 (CCSG 10, 68, trans. Prassas, *Questions and Doubts*, 91).

68. *Ambig.* 40.2 (DOML 29, 98–99, including trans.).

69. This is also the conclusion of Aquino, "Maximus the Confessor," 113–16.

oneself, then associate oneself with what is pure."[70] Maximus interprets Gregory's likeness epistemology by reconfiguring it: onto Gregory's claim that pure-knows-pure Maximus maps the claim that virtue-knows-God, thereby showing that he understands the relationship between virtue and the knowledge of God to be a relationship of like to like. But more and ample evidence of Maximus' conviction that virtue consists in likeness to or imitation of God can be found elsewhere in his works, so much so that Larchet has suggested that the generic "power" behind virtue, the motor that makes it move and work at all in Maximus' theological scheme (the scheme of "deification" as Larchet presents it), comes down to this: "virtue achieves an assimilation, a conformation of the faithful to Christ and to God."[71] Perhaps the simplest expression of this comes in *Difficulty* 7, when Maximus clarifies that creaturely virtues arise "limitedly" (προσδιωρισμένως), as expressions of God's life where they exist "absolutely" [ἀπολύτως].[72] This means that the one who practices the virtues shares in God, or Christ, who is the archetype and "essence [οὐσία] of all the virtues,"[73] as Origen too had held.[74] Such a person, Maximus clarifies, "becomes like [God] by means of the virtues."[75] Maximus can also reverse this formula, so that through virtue, God becomes "like" humans:[76]

> Maybe what is meant by what was spoken from the face of
> the Lord, "I have been likened [ὡμοιώθην] in the hands of the

70. *Or.* 39.8–9 (SC 358, 164–65; trans. modified from Daley, *Gregory of Nazianzus*, 131).

71. Larchet, *La divinisation*, 471. Louth has also highlighted the foundational role that achieving God's likeness plays, for Maximus, in the notion of virtue ("Virtue Ethics," 355). See also the verdict of, Aquino: "the virtues are crucial for moving humans towards their proper end—likeness to God" ("Maximus the Confessor," 111). The same point is made by Salés, "Divine Incarnation,"164.

72. At *cap. theol.* 1.48 (PG 91, 1100D–1101A), Maximus says that virtue, along with simplicity and immutability, belongs to God from eternity.

73. *Ambig.* 7.21 (DOML 28, 102–3, including trans.). On this point see Larchet, *La divinisation*, 462, 474–76.

74. Crouzel, *Théologie de l'image*, 227–32.

75. *Ambig.* 7.21 (DOML 28, 104).

76. Maximus has a predilection for emphasizing the palpable reality of divine encounter with a logic of reciprocity, or exchange: as far as someone becomes God or is deified, thus far does God become "humanified" in them. Deification and incarnation are two sides of the same coin. See, e.g., *ambig.* 60.4 (DOML 29, 264–65); *or. dom.* (CCSG 23, 32–33). This recurring theme has received much scholarly attention: von Balthasar, *Cosmic Liturgy*, 280–81; Larchet, *La divinisation*, 221–25; 376–82; Cooper, *The Body in St Maximus*, 46–47; Thunberg, *Microcosm and Mediator*, 325–26.

prophets" [Hos 12:11], is this: through his great love of humanity, God takes form in each person out of the virtue that is present in them through practice. For the "hand" of every just person means his practice of virtue, in which and through which God receives likeness [ὁμοίωσιν] to human beings.[77]

Larchet notices that Maximus sometimes elaborates the irresistible mutual likening that virtue performs with the vocabulary of color and light.[78] A passage from *Letter* 1 is a good example. Maximus comments on God's command to Israel, "prepare to invoke your God" (Amos 4:12). Preparation, Maximus says, is necessary "in order that we may receive, through the virtues, as if through certain divine colors [τινων θείων χρωμάτων], the exact assimilation to God [τὴν ἀκριβῆ πρὸς Θεὸν ἐξομοίωσιν]."[79] The analogy itself and its particular vocabulary strongly suggest that Maximus is repeating an image offered by Gregory of Nyssa (an image also adopted by at least one other monastic writer who influenced Maximus, Diadochus of Photike[80]): in *On the Making of Man*, Gregory had explained, in the same language that Maximus would use, that God bestows his "likeness" (ὁμοίωσις) upon humans through "virtues" as if he were a "painter," lavishing a canvas with "colors" (χρώματα), so that "the archetype's beauty would be exactly [δι' ἀκριβείας] transferred to the likeness."[81] Maximus seems to play on Gregory's image elsewhere too: God is a continuously more brilliant light, dappling the believer through the virtues with ever "more divine patterns" (θειοτέρων διατυπώσεων);[82] or again, the believer who enters into the divine darkness "paints in himself the beauty of the divine virtues just as a drawing is a good imitation of its archetype";[83] and as a last example, Maximus says that "God who is truly light according to essence is in those who walk in him by the

77. *Ep.* 2 (PG 91, 401B). On reciprocity in *ep.* 2 see Thunberg, *Microcosm and Mediator*, 329–30.

78. Larchet, *La divinisation*, 467–69.

79. *Ep.* 1 (PG 91, 377D–380A).

80. As Andrew Louth notices, for Diadochus "likeness" to God is something that God "paints"; but Louth does not mention the possible connection with Gregory of Nyssa (*The Origins*, 126). On Diadochus' influence on Maximus, see Louth, *Maximus the Confessor*, 25.

81. *Hom. opif.* 5 (PG 44, 137A–B).

82. *Cap. theol.* 1.35 (PG 91, 1096C–D).

83. *Cap. theol.* 1.85 (PG 90, 1120A; trans. modified from Berthold, *Maximus Confessor*, 144).

virtues, becoming themselves truly light."[84] The virtues yield knowledge of God because they share in God's color and luminosity; light is seen by light. This recurring imaginative formula, in which Maximus expresses the Godlike character of the virtues in terms of color and light, recalls the optical "like-by-like" theory that Maximus' Alexandrian predecessors employed in their theology.

That Maximus considered virtues to be the stuff of Godlikeness explains why the bond of "virtue" and "knowledge" of God adheres so strongly in his thought. Likeness is the link. And the way the couplet "virtue and knowledge, virtue and knowledge" riffs so unceasingly through the Confessor's works points to the fact that he considered this task of imitating and thus knowing God to be an endemic vocation of human existence. Humans are created to the "likeness" of God (Gen 1:27), and their natural task of attaining this divine likeness, Maximus says, God "left for our voluntary disposition, anticipating the perfection of the human being, in the case that someone might establish him or herself 'like' [ὅμοιον] God through imitation of the God-befitting characteristics of virtue."[85] More fundamentally still, Maximus occasionally seems to suggest that the move from virtue to knowledge, and the like-by-like logic that binds them, in fact belongs to the principles and structures not only of human nature, but of the created order itself in which humans find themselves. Consider the following passage from *Difficulty* 10:

> [T]he saints made distinctions within the created order, and reverently gathered together its hidden principles, dividing them into being, motion, difference, mixture, and position. On the one hand they affirmed that three of these have priority in leading us to the knowledge of God . . . , namely, the [principles] according to being, motion, and difference. Through these God becomes known to us, insofar as we gather from the things that exist the reflections of God's attributes, as creator, provider, and judge. On the other hand they said that the two remaining principles educate one towards virtue and assimilation [οἰκείωσιν] to God, since through mixture and position, man is molded and shaped into God, and from the things that exist he passively undergoes [παθὼν] becoming God. The seeing [ὁρῶν], as it were, of his mind beholds the whole reflection of God in his goodness, and he reasonably gives this reflection a clear and unmixed form

84. *Qu. thal.* 8 (CCSG 7, 77).

85. *Qu. dub.* III.1 (CCSG 10, 170; trans. modified from Prassas, *Questions and Doubts*, 157).

within himself. So they say that what the pure mind sees [ὁρᾷν] naturally through reverent knowledge it can also passively undergo [παθεῖν], becoming through its habit of virtue the very thing it sees.[86]

This passage is cryptic and it is unclear what Maximus' sources are. It is clear, at least, that Maximus is making a distinction between a cognitive knowledge of God, a "seeing," deduced from the realm of existing things, and a more intimate comprehension of God, a comprehension that is a matter of "undergoing" (παθὼν) rather than of "seeing" or figuring out. Maximus says that these two ways of knowing (for the latter is certainly an epistemic as well as an experiential category, as has been highlighted before[87]) are progressive. First comes positive, cognitive knowledge, then this gives way to undergoing, or even "becoming" (γινόμενος), the object of knowledge through the practice of virtue—and virtue, again, is a form of imitation of and "assimilation [οἰκείωσιν] to God." In short, likeness to God perfects the knowing process, moving the mind from affirmative knowledge to experiential understanding. Less straightforwardly, Maximus seems to suggest that the knowledge of God and its two aspects, cognitive and passive, simply result from the way it is for humans in the universe. Cognitive knowledge of God is made possible by "being," "motion," and "difference," principles that structure the created order and tell of its divine source. On the other hand, "mixture" and "position," Maximus says, point to an aspect of the created order that opens up to and accommodates the transformative activity of its divine source, that lets rational creatures know God through encountering and undergoing God. These latter, arcane, terms—"mixture" (κρᾶσις) and "position" (θέσις)— make a little more sense once one notices that they are two notions with which Maximus habitually describes deification. Maximus can say that through desiring God a human "mixes" with God in deification;[88] and he also often clarifies that a human may become God by θέσις (which can mean "position" or "adoption") rather than by nature.[89]

In summary of this complicated passage, let me specify two points. Maximus suggests that knowing-by-likeness—that is, knowing by

86. *Ambig.* 10.35 (DOML 28, 202–5; modified trans.)

87. Miquel, "Πεῖρα," 358–61; Aquino, "Maximus the Confessor," 116–18. The crucial passage in which Maximus articulates the epistemological power of "experience" is *qu. Thal.* 60 (CCSG 22, 77).

88. We will discuss the theme of "mixture" with the divine in Chapter 4.

89. Larchet, *La divinisation*, 601–3.

undergoing—is the acme of knowing God, and emerges when rational or cognitive knowledge of God receives the complement of virtue. Secondly, this process of comprehending God by likeness is the proper vocation opened for humans by the structuring principles of the created order in which they find themselves.

### Unknowing by likeness

In *Difficulty* 20, Maximus comes to a parallel conclusion, suggesting that the pattern of knowing-by-likeness is naturally connected to and fixed within the hierarchy of rational creatures. Here, however, this connection brings us to Maximus' third and apophatic improvisation on the knowing-by-likeness motif:

> Again, when the Scripture speaks of the "third heaven" [2 Cor 12:2], it may perhaps be referring to the three successive orders of holy angels that are immediately above us, which Saint Paul may have reached, being initiated into their positive affirmations through the negation of his own cognitions [τῶν κατ' αὐτόν γνώσεων] and imitating [μιμούμενος] their permanent states through the elevating negations of what was his own [τῶν οἰκείων]. For every nature of rational beings, in accordance with its order and potential, is initiated into and imitates [μιμεῖται] the cognitive states [γνωστικὰς ἕξεις], propositions, and affirmations of the order and essence above it . . . , through apophatically negating what is its own [κατ' αὐτήν].[90]

Maximus describes a structure of progressive "imitation" built into the ascending "ranks" (τάξεις) of rational creation, and with this imitation come new ways of knowing, new "cognitions" (γνώσεις).[91] One surpasses one's own "cognitions" and is "initiated" into new and higher "habits of knowing" (γνωστικὰς ἕξεις), Maximus repeats, precisely through a practice of "imitating" the higher ranks of creation. Knowing transforms and advances as the knower progresses in imitation of higher and higher creaturely orders. Elsewhere Maximus opens another clear window onto

90. *Ambig.* 20.5 (DOML 28, 414–15; modified trans.)

91. Similarly, Maximus elsewhere paints a picture of the cosmos in which God is always "bringing about the assimilation [ἐξομοίωσιν] of particulars to universals until he might unite creatures' own voluntary inclination to the more universal natural principle of rational being" (*qu. Thal.* 2 [CCSG 7, 51]; trans. Blowers and Wilken, *On the Cosmic Mystery*, 100).

this angelic flow of Godlikeness, expressed, again, in the currency of "virtue": "In sharing with one another their illumination, the holy Powers share also with humankind either their virtue or their knowledge. Thus, by their virtue—an imitation of the divine goodness—they work good for themselves, for one another, and for those below them, rendering them Godlike [θεοειδεῖς]."[92] In the passage from *Difficulty* 20, however, Maximus is clear that this imitation of the angelic orders and the transformation in Godlikeness and knowledge through virtue that the angels bequeath, take shape by a process of apophasis and kataphasis: denying what is familiar (κατ᾽ αὐτόν, or οἰκεῖος) and affirming what exceeds one's familiarity. Maximus is playing intriguingly with his Dionysian heritage. First he takes Dionysius' linguistic and spiritual scheme of advance to God and inverts it. Instead of picturing, with Dionysius, affirmative praise of God that gives way to negations, Maximus says that knowledge of God goes by a pattern of self-negation followed by affirmation of what is above oneself.[93] Secondly, Maximus applies this transformative pattern of apophasis surpassed by kataphasis to Dionysius' celestial hierarchy. For Dionysius, each creature in the cosmic hierarchy is ordered according to the degree to which it naturally "imitates" God. This is a static hierarchy: the order does not change. Maximus, however, suggests that rational creatures can ascend the ranks of this hierarchy, by imitating what is above them through a process of negation and affirmation.

Despite transforming Dionysius' teachings in this way, Maximus ends where Dionysius ends. Eventually, the task of knowing by imitation draws the knower near creation's bounds, and then beyond them, to God, the source of creation, of whom it is impossible to affirm or deny anything. *Difficulty* 20 continues: "after all the orders and powers have been transcended there follows the immediate negation of knowledge concerning God, a negation beyond any positive affirmation by absolutely any being, since there is no longer any boundary or limit that could define or frame the negation."[94] Knowing ceases here, and von Balthasar says that "the only word that remains for this encounter is 'unity.'"[95] This is surely true for Maximus more broadly, but it is not the language of

92. *Carit.* 3.33 (PG 90, 1028B; trans. modified from ACW 21, 179).

93. At least two scholars have noticed that Maximus also inverts Dionysius' scheme in his interpretation of the transfiguration in *ambig.* 10: de Andia, "Transfiguration," 308–9; McFarland, "Developing an Apophatic Christocentrism," 208–11.

94. *Ambig.* 20.5 (DOML 28, 416–17; modified trans.).

95. von Balthasar, *Cosmic Liturgy*, 93.

this passage—on Maximus' own terms, here the only word left in this infinite unknowing is "imitation." And it is with this in mind that we can consider how Maximus stretches the knowing-by-likeness theory to breaking point, and makes of it a new, apophatic principle.

My claim here is twofold. First, Maximus sometimes presses the logic of knowing-by-likeness out from its own limits by suggesting that the soul can really, but "unknowingly," grasp precisely those attributes of God that make God unknowable—like simplicity, singularity, and immutability—by means of *imitating* them. Recalling the distinction Maximus made above in *Difficulty* 10 between cognitive and experiential knowledge, this grasp of the unknowable God by likeness falls under the latter category: comprehension through "undergoing." Secondly, Maximus suggests that the soul's *desire* in particular is the faculty that can be trained to imitate the divine attributes and thereby undergo the unknowable God. In the *Four Centuries on Love*, we have already seen Maximus identify love, or desire, as an important ingredient in the task of knowing God by likeness, and the same is true in this parallel picture of unknowing-by-likeness.

Let us consider another passage from *The Four Centuries on Love* that lays the foundations for this theme, in which Maximus makes a rare detailed claim about how he thinks knowing works:

> The mind, in receiving the concepts [νοήματα] of things, is naturally patterned after [μετασχηματίζεσθαι] each concept; in contemplating them spiritually, it is diversely conformed [μεταμορφοῦσθαι] to each object of contemplation. When it comes to be in God, it is entirely without form [ἄμορφος] and without pattern [ἀσχημάτιστος]. For in contemplating Him who is simple [μονοειδῆ], it becomes simple and wholly transfused with light.[96]

Knowing an object "contemplatively" or "spiritually" conforms the knower to the known. The same is still true when the object of knowledge is God: the knower is conformed to the divine simplicity. But how could any knowledge or contemplative vision possibly obtain between bounded and complex creatures and God, who is infinite and simple? After all, Maximus is elsewhere explicit that any "simple" object is by definition unthinkable and unknowable.[97] A couple of lines later Maximus

---

96. *Carit.* 3.97 (PG 90, 1045D; trans. modified from ACW 21, 191).

97. *Cap. theol.* 1.82 (PG 90, 1116B–1117A). See also *cap. theol.* 2.2 (PG 90, 1125C).

attempts to express this seemingly impossible epistemological situation with the help of some Dionysian hyperbole: the mind "supremely knows, in a way beyond unknowing, that which is beyond unknowing [τὸν ὑπεράγνωστον ὑπεραγνώστως ὑπερεγνωκώς]."[98] Whether Maximus aims to clarify or baffle here, it is obvious that he wishes to express a superabundance, rather than a lack: the activity in play reaches totally "above" and "beyond" (ὑπερ-) the transactions, safeties, and certainties involved in "knowledge" and "ignorance." But "knowing" is nonetheless still the fundamental vocabulary. In the next chapter, Maximus comple-ments this picture, identifying a second creaturely activity that lasts this ὑπερ-encounter and remains fundamental to it: "love remains for infinite ages, ever increasing beyond measure [ὑπεραύξουσα], being super-unit-ed with what is beyond infinity [τῷ ὑπεραπείρῳ ὑπερηνωμένη]."[99] It is "love" (ἀγάπη) (or "desire" [πόθος] in the language of the next chapter[100]) that brings the mind to a grasp of God, as it is conformed to God's sim-plicity and infinity. In other words, when God is the object of knowledge, Maximus' logic of knowing-by-likeness transforms into super-knowing or unknowing by love.[101] As I have already hinted, the weight bending the knowing-by-likeness principle into this apophatic and erotic contortion surely comes from the influence of Dionysius. For the pseudo-Areopagite, the highest encounter with God is an "ecstasy" into "beyond-unknowing" (ὑπεράγνωστος);[102] and this is a lover's (ἐραστής) ecstasy, fueled by a "de-sire" (ἔρος) capable of grasping and attaining the very "life of its object" (ἡ τοῦ ἐραστοῦ ζωή).[103]

Maximus clarifies his own picture and at once sharpens Dionysius' with the suggestion that desire does not simply drive the soul's confor-mation to God, but that desire itself is the human activity or faculty that becomes *like* God. Although Maximus is clear that human desire

---

98. *Carit.* 3.99 (PG 90, 1048A).

99. *Carit* 3.100 (PG 90, 1048A).

100. *Carit.* 4.1 (PG 90, 1048B).

101. *Cap. theol.* 2.86 (PG 90, 1165B) is a parallel passage: Maximus says that through "desire" (ἔφεσις) for God, "the ultimate object of desire" (τὸ ἔσχατον ὀρεκτόν), the soul attains a "repose" beyond time and movement precisely because this object—God—is itself beyond time.

102. *Myst.* 1.1 (PG 3, 997A–1000A).

103. *D.n.* 4.13 (PG 3, 712A). For a summary of these themes see Louth, *The Origins*, 169–70.

can never attain to or grasp God's "essence" (οὐσία) or nature,[104] he allows that it might nonetheless imitate God's attributes in such a way as to "dwell" with God, even with God's "nature": the one who has calmed and ordered his desires, Maximus says, "is simple in his desire [ἔφεσιν] and uncomplicated in his will [γνώμην], and makes his dwelling with the one who is simple by nature."[105] In short, desire can be assimilated to God's attributes. Maximus unpacks the consequences of this claim in terms of knowledge, suggesting that human desire's ability to imitate the unattainable divine attributes brings about an unknowing comprehension of God. At least three passages are worth looking at here. The first comes in *Difficulty* 10:

> God is absolutely and infinitely beyond all beings . . . It follows then, that the one who has wisely understood how he ought to desire [ἐρᾷν] the God who is beyond all reason and knowledge, and who singly and absolutely transcends every kind of relation and nature, will pass by all sensible and intelligible objects, and all time, age, and place without establishing any relation to them . . . [H]e will attain, ineffably and unknowably, the divine delight, which is beyond reason and intellect, and he shall attain this in a mode and principle known to God who gives such grace, and to those who are worthy to receive it.[106]

God's absolute transcendence does not leave human effort toward God hopeless or human encounter with God empty. Rather, what Maximus recommends in response to divine transcendence is a special kind of "desiring," a desiring that captures something of the sought-after object in imitation. Since God is beyond "reason" and "knowledge," and beyond "relation" and "nature," desire for God ought to imitate all three of these unknowable aspects of God: it ought, Maximus thinks, to surpass sensible and intelligible things—which are the objects of "reason" and "knowledge"—and to surpass "time, age, and place"—the objects of "relation" and "nature." Once desire has achieved these likenesses to God, it will unknowably delight in God just as God is.

The second passage that exemplifies Maximus' novel apophatic and erotic expression of the knowing-by-likeness motif comes later on in the

---

104. *Carit.* 1.100 (PG 90, 981D–984A).

105. *Or. dom.* (CCSG 23, 48–49). Maximus makes exactly the same point—that simplicity of will and love leads to an apprehension of the simple God—in *ep.* 2 (PG 91, 400D–401A).

106. *Ambig.* 10.58 (DOML 28, 242–45; modified trans.).

same *Difficulty*. Maximus ruminates upon a claim of Gregory Nazianzen that the saints "passed beyond the material dyad on account of the unity perceived in the Trinity."[107] He gives a preliminary elucidation: this "passing beyond" means that the saints "swept aside sense perception," after which:

> . . . by means of the intellect alone they ineffably assimilated [προσῳκείωσαν] the soul to God, and seeing the whole soul united to God unknowingly [ἀγνώστως] . . . , they were secretly [μυστικῶς] taught "the unity perceived in the Trinity."[108]

The saints unknowingly apprehend, or are "taught," the secret unity of the Trinity precisely by assimilation to God the Trinity; they unknowingly know God by an ineffable likeness to God. Maximus then draws over this picture a second time, detailing it intriguingly: believers can hope to cease obsessing with matter and attain this unknowing comprehension of God by likeness, if they let their *desire* imitate God's attributes:

> If someone is able to . . . surrender solely to that knowledgeable delight [γνωστικῆς θέλξεως] which remains unwavering in love [ἀγάπην], and from the many confine himself to one, single, pure, simple, and indivisible movement of the most virile power of desire [ἔφεσιν], by which he might philosophically ground his permanence in an unbroken relation to God through the identity of perpetually moving desire [ἔφεσιν]—such a person, I say, is truly happy, since he has attained not only the true and blessed union with the Holy Trinity, but also the "unity perceived in the Holy Trinity," insofar as he has become simple, indivisible, and of a single form as much as is possible in relation to simple and indivisible being, imitating the simple and indivisible Goodness through habitual exercise of the virtues, and laying aside the condition of his naturally divided faculties thanks to the grace of God, with whom he has become one.[109]

As one commentator has put it, in this passage the soul's desire attains not only "union *with* God" but "the unity *of* God."[110] An unknowing grasp of the ungraspable mystery of the Trinity forms in the soul when desire (πόθος) and the habits of virtue attending it inflame into the very shapes

---

107. *Or.* 21.2 (SC 270, 114), cited in *ambig.* 10.106 (DOML 28, 320–21, including trans.).

108. *Ambig.* 10.106 (DOML 28, 320–23; modified trans.).

109. *Ambig.* 10.107 (DOML 29, 322–23; modified trans.).

110. Lollar, *To See Into the Life of Things*, 228.

of that mystery, becoming like it, becoming "one, single, pure, indivisible." Maximus seems to consider the power of human desire to be supremely, if not infinitely, malleable, capable of searching out and taking shapes that totally elude knowledge's grip and creation's limit.

The very clearest presentation of this conviction comes at the beginning of *Letter* 1, to George, a governor in North Africa:

> When someone attaches himself by inclination [γνωμικῶς] and by desire [ἔφεσιν] to what is divine—what is one and single and passionless, what is from eternity subject to absolutely no view or inspection in the terms of some other existing thing, since nothing can reach him which was made by him—they themselves are one and single and passionless; by ascetic gravitation towards the One, they become one and single and immutable . . . So then also the lover [ἐραστής] himself, being the sorts of things that the One is, has fittingly become one and single and unchanging, since he altogether produced his unmoving inclination [γνώμην] from the One. But as for someone who has by his own inclination [γνώμην] bound his soul's desire [ἔρωτα] to ignorance of what is better—to material things that are mutable and changeable by nature, and completely incapable of remaining whole—he is of necessity mutable and passionate and fitful . . .[111]

To a powerful degree, and even "of necessity," Maximus says, you resemble what you desire. This means that, depending on the object sought, "desire" and "inclination" hold the power either to distort the soul, leaving it stuck imitating its material delights, or to perfect the soul, lifting it out of "ignorance" by assimilating it to God. As Maximus summarizes elsewhere: "it is the most perfect work of love and the goal of its activity, to contrive . . . that the names and properties of those that have been united through love should be fitting to each other."[112] When one's love is directed towards God, desire can take on the very properties of God that make God unknowable, apprehending God unknowably by a unique and ineffable form of likeness.

---

111. *Ep.* 1 (PG 91, 364B–365A).

112. *Ep.* 2 (PG 91, 401B; trans. Louth, *Maximus the Confessor*, 86).

## Conclusion

This chapter has explored some familiar and then some more original ways in which Maximus works out a likeness epistemology. Maximus often exemplified the Alexandrian exegetical version of this epistemology, according to which pure knows pure or spiritual knows spiritual, and we saw that Gregory Nazianzen was key in mediating this tradition to him. Maximus also adapted this epistemology in his own ways. God is known by the mind, we have seen Maximus suggest, because Love is known by love, or again, because Virtue is known by virtue. Finally, Maximus transformed this epistemology most daringly in his claims that one may unknowingly comprehend God by shaping one's desire into an exalted and ineffable likeness to the divine attributes. It now falls, in the next chapter, to explore why Maximus' theological vision was so variously and creatively accommodating of a likeness epistemology.

# 3

## *Deification, Christ's incarnation in the believer, and knowing-by-likeness*

We have learned that, in his early works, Maximus diversely appropriated an epistemological assumption, engrained in the Alexandrian Christian tradition of exegesis and theology that was passed down to him: an assumption that likeness, or imitation, is the key to knowledge of divine things. Now it falls to explore what conceptual resources internal to Maximus' *own* thinking made him so accommodating and creatively receptive of this likeness epistemology.

The first part of this chapter will argue that Maximus' doctrine of "deification" conceptually grounds his likeness epistemology. I will come at this encompassing and prolifically commented upon aspect of the Confessor's thought with a basic definition to guide our discussion: deification is a "tropological" reality. That is, for Maximus, it means becoming God not by "essence" or "nature" but by "way" or "mode" (*tropos*). Then I will proceed to clarify how his doctrine of deification undergirds his likeness epistemology in at least two respects. First, one way that Maximus articulates deification as a "tropological," as opposed to "essential," reality is with the notion of "likeness" to God. "Likeness" is itself a genuine form of deification. It means sharing in God's identity by having one's *tropos* of existence restored and transformed. "Likeness" to God thus makes for the theologian's ideal epistemological situation, there being little distinction in Maximus' mind between knowing God by likeness and knowing God by deification. When Maximus speaks of deification as a likeness to God, a parallel notion of sharing in God's "activity" (ἐνέργεια) is often close at hand, and we will explore its meaning to flesh out Maximus' picture of knowing God by likeness/deification. Secondly, we will consider another of Maximus' key articulations of deification as "tropological": deification, he says, occurs "in proportion" (κατὰ τὴν ἀναλογίαν) to the creature's progressing likeness to God. This rule of "proportion" is one of the Confessor's favorite logical and imaginative tools for grappling with theological problems, but it has barely been identified in the scholarship. I will demonstrate how Maximus' likeness epistemology is a product of his rule of "proportion," and will elucidate it at length.

The second part of the chapter will explore how Maximus translates these same two features of his doctrine of deification—"likeness" as a genuine form of identity with God, and the rule of "proportion"—to the closely linked theme of "Christofication," or Christ's "incarnation" and "embodiment" in the believer. This early teaching on the imitative and transformative character of the believer's relationship with Christ, I will suggest, conceptually anticipates—or makes possible and comprehensible—Maximus' later like-by-like model of christological discernment, which will be examined in our final three chapters.

## Deification

### Thinking about "deification" with Maximus

One scholar has summarized that "Maximus's religious epistemology . . . is grounded in the larger projects of ascetic theology and deification."[1] I wish to propose something similar: Maximus naturally developed a theological epistemology centered on likeness to God because, for him, likeness to God is a genuine form of deification. In other words, his conviction that one knows God by likeness boils down to a claim that one knows God by deification. It might seem that this conclusion promises more complication than clarification, since the topic of deification can feel overwhelming both in light of the diversity of ways in which the Confessor discourses on the theme, and in light of the sprawling scholarship available. So, the first thing I want to do is highlight that in fact Maximus' understanding of deification can be grasped quite painlessly.

In Maximus' works "deification" (θέωσις) is a wide concept: it is the goal and progress to which all of God's work with creatures contributes, and it is the reality towards which the themes and turns of the Confessor's

1. Aquino, "Maximus the Confessor," 104.

thought normally end up pointing.[2] Consequently, Maximus gives no single positive definition of deification. However, he is singularly clear about what deification is *not*, and this is where we can begin. Maximus always comes at the doctrine of deification by means of *qualification* or *caveat*, ever reminding his readers what *not* to imagine. And from this preoccupation of his we can construct a minimal, negative definition of his doctrine of deification: namely, *deification means a creature achieving identity with God not on the level of "essence"* (οὐσία) *or "nature"* (φύσις).[3] This caveat follows on from two of Maximus' sure presumptions: first, there is an ontological gap between finite created natures and the infinite uncreated divine nature,[4] and secondly, any alteration of an essence or nature would equate to its "destruction."[5]

From this, negative, definition, it is clear that for Maximus deification is fundamentally a difficult, paradoxical, or "apophatic" reality.[6] In the face of this, Maximus thinks hard about the least misleading ways to talk about deification *positively*. His resolution is to speak of deification in a way that, as Larchet has acutely spotted, follows the rules of one his most industrious distinctions, between *logos* and *tropos*.[7] Let me spell this out: Maximus settles on a select number of consistent illustrations of deification—of varying biblical heritage, philosophical heritage, or imaginative purchase—all of which qualify that deification means a

2. The enormous range of theological themes that "deification" entails in Maximus' writings have been elucidated by Larchet, *La divinisation*. Larchet breaks down the variety of "deification" words that Maximus uses, and records how often they occur. The noun θέωσις (seventy-seven times) and the verb θεόω (forty-four times) are the most common terms by far (*La divinisation*, 60, n. 334). As Carl Mosser points out, it was Maximus who popularized this particular vocabulary of deification, first coined by Gregory Nazianzen (Mosser, "Deification," 11).

3. *Qu. Thal.* 22 (CCSG 7, 139, 141); *carit.* 3.25 (PG 90, 1024B–C); *qu. dub.* 61 (CCSG 10, 48); *ambig.* 7.26 (DOML 28, 112–13), *ambig.* 20.2 (DOML 28, 408–9); *ambig.* 41 (DOML 29, 108–9). Larchet has emphasized Maximus' clear insistence on this point that creatures can never share the "nature" of God (*La divinisation*, 589–94), a claim that goes back at least to Clement and Origen (Russell, *The Doctrine of Deification*, 121, 136–37, 149–50).

4. *Ambig.* 7.19 (DOML 28, 100–101); *ambig.* 71.6 (DOML 29, 322–23).

5. *Ambig.* 42.26 (DOML 29, 172–75).

6. Such is the language Maximus can use to name the total difference between creaturely and divine essence: "God is apophatically [ἀποφατικῶς] separated from all existing things according to his essence [κατὰ . . . τὴν οὐσίαν]" (*qu. dub.* 173 [CCSG 10, 120]).

7. Larchet, "The Mode of Deification," 342–44.

transformation of a creature's "mode" or "way" of existence, its *tropos*, and *not* a transformation of its natural or essential existence, its *logos*. Some of these illustrations of the "tropological" reality of deification are as follows. Maximus suggests that when creatures "become God," it is not *being* the same as God; it is *"acting"* (ἐνεργῶν) the same (or having the same "activity" [ἐνέργεια]). [8] It is not like possessing; it is like "sharing" (or "participating": μετέχων, μεταλαμβάνων, and cognates).[9] It is not becoming another person; it is living with another person, indwelling their "place" (τόπος)[10] or "position" (θέσις).[11] It is not like being twins; it is like being a "copy" or "image" (εἰκών) of an "archetype."[12] It is not being perfect; it is resting on someone else's "perfections," their "beauty" and "goodness."[13] It is not what one is owed; it comes "graciously" (κατὰ χάριν).[14] Maximus offers many other such qualifying descriptions, ways

8. *Ambig.* 7.12 (DOML 28, 90–91); qu. *Thal* 59 (CCSG 22, 55); *myst.* 24 (CCSG 69, 66). See also Larchet, *La divinisation*, 545–53, 563–67.

9. E.g.: "God is apophatically [ἀποφατικῶς] separated from all existing things according to his essence . . . But according to his providential emanation he is participated [μετέχεται] by many things" (*qu. dub.* 173 [CCSG 10, 120]); "what God is by essence [κατ᾽ οὐσίαν] the creature might become by participation [κατὰ μετουσίαν]" (*carit.* 3.25 [PG 90, 1024B–C]); "One receives communion and identity with him by participation [κατὰ μέθεξιν] through likeness, by which the human is considered worthy to become God" (*myst.* 24 [CCSG 69, 58]). See also Larchet, *La divinisation*, 600–601.

10. *Cap. theol.* 1.68 (PG 90, 1108C); qu. *Thal.* 61 (CCSG 22, 105). For more on this image of "place," see Portaru, "The Vocabulary of Participation," 298–99.

11. *Myst.* 21 (CCSG 69, 48); *myst.* 24 (CCSG 69, 66); *ambig.* 20.2 (DOML 28: 408–9); *ep. sec.* prol. (CCSG 48, 37). See also Larchet, *La divinisation*, 601–3. The term θέσις can also mean "adoption."

12. *Myst.* 24 (CCSG 69, 65); qu. *Thal.* 8 (CCSG 7, 77); *ambig.* 7.12 (DOML 28, 90–91); *ambig.* 7.25 (DOML 28, 110–11); *ambig.* 21.5 (DOML 28, 444–45). Maximus offers a parallel to this image at *ambig.* 10.41 (DOML 28, 212–13): when united with God the Word, human nature does not change but becomes a "mirror" or "reflection" of the Word.

13. On "participating" in divine "perfection," see *ambig.* 10.93 (DOML 28, 296–97); in divine "beauty," see *ambig.* 10.2 (DOML 28, 152–53); and in divine "goodness," see *cap. theol.* 1.48 (PG 90, 1100D); *ambig.* 7.21 (DOML 28, 102–3); *ambig.* 7.38 (DOML 28, 132–33); *qu. thal.* 60 (CCSG 22, 78); *ambig.* 10.23 (DOML 28, 184–85); *ambig.* 63.2 (DOML 29, 272–73); *qu. dub.* 180 (CCSG 10, 123). Maximus sometimes summarizes God's perfections as "the things around God" (*cap. theol.* 1.48 [PG 90, 1100D]; *carit.* 1.100 [PG 90 981D–984A]).

14. The clearest expression of this is *ambig.* 20.2 (DOML 28, 408–11). See also *myst.* 24 (CCSG 69, 66); *ambig.* 7.22 (DOML 28, 104–5); *qu. dub.* 61 (CCSG 10, 48); *qu. dub.* 180 (CCSG 10, 123). See Larchet, *La divinisation*, 594–600. Incidentally,

of saying "deification is less like *this* and more like *that*."[15] And scholars have noticed that these descriptions often overlap or are roughly synonymous.[16] In short, Maximus resists any single theoretical definition of deification, and instead spreads out the burden of definition and explanation amongst a variety of descriptions, which point to each other and intertwine to make a single picture of deification, and the non-"essential," "tropological" transformation it involves.

### *"Likeness" and "activity"*

Included amongst Maximus' many qualifying "tropological" descriptions of deification is the term "likeness": deification does not entail being God *by nature*, but becoming God *by "likeness."* It is "by receiving communion and identity with him in participation, through likeness [ὁμοιότητος], that man is deemed worthy to become God," Maximus says.[17] The assumption that "likeness" is a category of deification is also clear in

---

Maximus employs this phrase—κατὰ χάριν—to qualify the potentially misleading claims about "becoming God" found in Scripture, namely, 2 Pet 1:4, "we become sharers in the divine nature [φύσεως]" (*ep.* 24 [PG 91. 609C]/*ep.* 43 [PG 91, 640B–C]), and Ps 81:6, LXX: "you are gods" (*ambig.* 20 [DOML 28, 408–9]). On the important role this latter verse played in the early development of the patristic doctrine of deification, see Mosser, "The Earliest Patristic Interpretations," 30–74.

15. Larchet points out that the word "mode" (τρόπος) itself, along with "state" or "habit" (ἕξις) and "quality" (ποιότης), are among the other caveats that Maximus employs to resist any notion of deification as a natural or essential change (*La divinisation*, 603–8).

16. There is an overlap in Maximus' mind between "participation," "grace," and "activity," e.g.: "the one who is able to act well and does so is truly God by grace and participation [κατὰ χάριν καὶ μέθεξιν], since he has taken on in successful imitation the activity and character of God's own good action" (*myst.* 24 [CCSG 69: 68]). The overlap between "participation" and "grace" is especially common: "the deification that will be given to the worthy, since it is beyond nature [ὑπὲρ φύσιν], perfects those who participate [μετόχους] into gods from men, by grace [κατὰ χάριν]' (*qu. dub.* 61 [CCSG 10, 48]); "God will be wholly participated [μετεχόμενος] by whole human beings . . . Man will remain wholly man in soul and body, owing to his nature [διὰ τὴν φύσιν], but will become wholly God in soul and body owing to the grace [διὰ τὴν χάριν] and splendor of the blessed glory of God" (*ambig.* 7.26 [DOML 28, 112–13, including trans.]). Scholars have highlighted that for Maximus "participation" and divine "activity" are also closely intertwined (Portaru, "Classical Philosophical Influences," 136–37), and that divine "activity" and "grace" are often synonyms (Larchet, "The Mode of Deification," 350–51; Tollefsen, *The Christocentric Cosmology*, 208, 220; Portaru, "Classical Philosophical Influences," 142).

17. *Myst.* 24 (CCSG 69, 58).

Maximus' predecessors.[18] We noted in the previous chapter that Maximus understood the "likeness" of God as a "tropological" transformation, a transformation of a rational creature's "mode" (*tropos*) of existence, whereas, the "image" of God is something fixed in the rational creature's "principle" (*logos*) of existence. It is therefore not surprising to find Maximus choosing the language of "likeness" to describe the "tropological" reality of deification: "Having completed his course [towards God], such a person becomes God, receiving from God to be God, for to his beautiful nature that is 'in the image' [of God] he freely chooses to add the exact 'likeness' [see Gen 1:26] by means of the virtues."[19]

What more can be said about "likeness" to God, beyond the fact that it describes the deification of a creature's "mode" of existence? As with Maximus' other illustrations of deification, the concept of "likeness" to God gathers its meaning in context, from its environment of linked terms. When probing this context it immediately appears that one already-mentioned "tropological" vocabulary of deification—"activity"—closely neighbors and intertwines with that of "likeness" to God. In the *Questions and Doubts*, Maximus says that "likeness" to God refers to virtues—like "detachment, meekness, long-suffering"—that "are all displays of God's activity [ἐνεργείας]."[20] Or again, in the *Mystagogia*, he says that deification occurs when "through successful imitation [εὐμιμήτως] one takes on the activity [ἐνέργειαν] and character of God's own good action."[21] Finally, in his *Questions to Thalassius*, Maximus clarifies that "likeness" to God "is the reception, among those who participate through likeness, of identity of activity [κατ' ἐνέργειαν . . . ταυτότης] with the very thing participated. And this identity . . . is the deification of those made worthy of deification."[22] All these passages suggest that, for Maximus, "likeness" is a genuine form of deification insofar as it means sharing in, or identity with, God's "activity."

---

18. Russell takes "likeness" or "imitation" as one of his fundamental categories for summarizing patristic concepts of deification (*The Doctrine of Deification*, 2–3).

19. *Ambig.* 7.21 (DOML 28, 104–5; modified trans.). For other passages in which Maximus describes deification as the attainment of the "likeness," rather than the "image," of God, see *ambig.* 7.31 (DOML 28, 118–19); *ambig.* 42.31 (DOML 29, 180–81). For secondary literature on likeness as a form of deification in Maximus, see Larchet, *La divinisation*, 156–65; Russell, *The Doctrine of Deification*, 265–66, 295.

20. *Qu. dub.* III.1 (CCSG 10, 170).

21. *Myst.* 24 (CCSG 69, 68).

22. *Qu. Thal.* 59 (CCSG 22, 53).

When exploring the theme of divine "activity" in any patristic author, there is a temptation to become involved in the long debate over this term's relation and distinction to divine "essence." But, as Louth says, for Maximus and his predecessors the distinction between "essence" and "energy" (or "activity") "is not a systematic distinction."[23] And it will suffice to underline here that although Maximus occasionally contrasts God's "essence" with God's "activity," he also contrasts God's "essence" with a range of other "tropological" concepts—like "perfections," "grace," "things around God." This fact somewhat deflates the essence-energy debate, at least when interpreting Maximus, and we can steer clear of it; there is no need to comprehend Maximus' use of "activity" in relation to "essence," as if this distinction bore great theoretical weight, because this weight spreads evenly across varying concepts.

Let us then consider ἐνέργεια on its own terms. I will be content to observe two things about divine ἐνέργεια in Maximus: it is a truthful communication of God's life, a real source of knowledge; and it is not anything less than God. To make the first point, one must recognize that in Maximus ἐνέργεια can simply mean "activity" (as was the case for Aristotle, the progenitor of this philosophical vocabulary[24]). Divine ἐνέργεια just means "what God does," God's "works." Scholars have acknowledged this fact by considering a passage on God's "works" (ἔργα, not ἐνεργεῖαι) to be crucial for establishing Maximus' teaching on the divine ἐνέργειαι.[25] And this straightforward definition of divine ἐνέργεια as "what God does" partly explains why, for Maximus, divine ἐνέργεια is inviting to human knowers: God's "activity" is God communicating himself, making God's self knowable. Or as Maximus puts it in *Difficulty* 22, "every divine activity intimates [ὑποσημαίνει] through itself the whole of God indivisibly."[26] Adam Cooper points out that this phrase "falls within a rhetorical question in which the matter is regarded as an impenetrable mystery."[27] In other words, Maximus takes for granted here that there is a communication of the simple super-existent God into the multitude of creation through his "activities," but he expressly prohibits any attempt to solve how this might work, and even forbids "reflecting and speaking

---

23. Louth, review of *La Théologie de énergies*, 748.

24. This is the claim of Kosman, *The Activity of Being*.

25. *Cap. theol.* 1.48 (PG 90, 1100C–1101A). E.g. Tollefsen, *Christocentric Cosmology*, 160–66; Portaru, "Classical Philosophical Influences," 141.

26. *Ambig.* 22.3 (DOML 28, 450–51; modified trans.).

27. Cooper, *The Body in St Maximus*, 110.

with precision [ἀκριβῶς]" on the subject.²⁸ The divine "activities" are not
the metaphysical solution, but are part of the mystery. Thus, one should
doubt any attempts to construct Maximus' metaphysical system from this
passage.²⁹ Nonetheless, Maximus is clear here that, however God does it,
God's activities certainly do "indicate" or "communicate" the fullness of
God. Maximus elucidates something of this communicative character of
divine "activity" in the following passage from his *Questions and Doubts*:

> And the fire "which proceeds before the face of the Lord" burn-
> ing "his enemies" is the activities of God. For they characterize
> the face of God, that is, his goodness, love of humankind, meek-
> ness, and things like these. These activities enlighten those who
> are akin [οἰκείως] to them and burn up those who oppose and
> have been alienated from the likeness [ὁμοιότητος].³⁰

When the soul becomes "akin" to God's "activities," sharing in God's
work, these "activities" light it up as if by fire and illuminate it with the
knowledge of what God is like.

Secondly, and leading on from this, the divine ἐνέργεια is not less
than what God is. Maximus clarifies this in his christological writings
when assembling his claim that Jesus possessed two natural "activities."
An ἐνέργεια is a "constitutive and inherent mark [συστατικὸς καὶ ἔμφυτος
χαρακτήρ] of a nature."³¹ "Without it there is only nonbeing,"³² and thus a
nature is never without its ἐνέργεια. To deny a nature its ἐνέργεια—only
ever hypothetically of course—is to deny it what makes it what it is, to
deny its "what, who, where, and how."³³ Moreover, this is true for the
uncreated divine ἐνέργεια as well as for created human ἐνέργειαι: "we
do not regard the divine and uncreated nature to be without existence
or will or activity; and nor do we consider that our human and created
essence is without existence or will or activity."³⁴ God's "activity" is part
of what makes God God. It would thus be misapprehended to suggest

28. *Ambig.* 22.3 (DOML 28, 450).

29. For example, Tollefsen takes this passage as a proof text for his theory of Maximus' theory of "participation," a term mentioned not once in *ambig.* 22 (*Christocentric
Cosmology*, 221–22).

30. *Qu. dub.* 99 (CCSG 10, 76; trans. modified from Prassas, *Questions and Doubts*,
96).

31. *Pyrr.* (PG 91, 348A).

32. *Ambig. Thom.* 5.2 (DOML 28, 32–33; modified trans.).

33. *Ambig. Thom.* 5.12 (DOML 28, 42–43, including trans.).

34. *Op.* 8 (PG 91, 96A).

that Maximus finds God's "activities" inferior to what God "really" or "ontologically" is—just as strange as it would be to suggest that for him "grace" is inferior to what God really is, or that God's "existence" and "will," to take the examples from the passage above, are inferior to what God really is.

Let us tie these findings together. For Maximus, knowledge of God unfolds as the believer imitates or achieves likeness to God. In his mind such likeness to God is not different from "deification": "likeness" is one among his many ways of naming the "tropological" reality of deification. Maximus also often identifies this deifying "likeness" to God as a sharing in God's "activity." In turn, this link makes sense of Maximus' assumption that likeness is productive of knowledge, because, we have seen, God's "activity" is "what God does"—that aspect of the divine life that is communicable and knowable. Thus we have located a likely conceptual foundation of Maximus' likeness epistemology. Knowing God by likeness works, in Maximus' mind, because it means nothing other than "knowing by tropological identity with God" (deification), and more specifically "knowing by identity with that aspect of God that makes God knowable" ("activity").

## The rule of "proportion"

Now it falls to examine another notion with which Maximus paints his "tropological" picture of deification. It runs as follows: when creatures achieve identity with God, it is not an unqualified meeting, but unfolds in a way that suits. It unfolds "in proportion" (κατὰ τὴν ἀναλογίαν), as Maximus often puts it; but he can also express the same thing with synonyms of ἀναλογία like δύναμις ("capacity"), μέτρον ("measure"), and τάξις ("rank"). And this "rule of proportion" (as I will call it, after its common terminology) is basic to his thought more generally. To summarize it with an analogy that is unsophisticated but helpful (for me at least): for Maximus, divine and creaturely interaction works a bit like a children's shape-sorting toy. The triangle hole alone can accommodate the triangle shape, the square hole can only welcome the square, and so on. Similarly, a creature receives more from God as their shape conforms more closely to God's shape. In this way, as we will see again and again, the rule of "proportion" is how Maximus makes sense of diversity in God's relation to creatures—the fact that diverse creatures do not respond to and receive from the single and simple God in a single and simple way. Maximus expresses this basic rule of "proportion" in at least three interlocked ways: one theological, one epistemological, and one biological. His theological doctrine of "proportional" deification is the most common expression: creatures are deified "in proportion" to their closeness or likeness to God. Secondly, Maximus' likeness epistemology is nothing other than this same logic of divine and human interaction, but cashed out in the terms of knowledge: a basic assumption behind Maximus' likeness epistemology is that knowers and objects of knowledge possess character or shape and are therefore not flatly available to one another; there are standards of compatibility to be met before knowing can take place, and the rule of "proportion" is Maximus' way of spelling out these epistemic standards. Thirdly, Maximus often grounds and clarifies his rule of "proportion" in a biological source of analogy: the body, which he sees as a kind of living shape-sorter. I am going to examine these first two renditions of Maximus' rule of "proportion" together—the theological and epistemological—and show how they follow on from each other. Then I will explore the third point about how Maximus roots his rule of "proportion" in the analogy of the body and its workings. To do this, we will have to expound Maximus' rule of "proportion" at greater length and go into its history, which will be worthwhile at least to make up for the lack of scholarly attention given to this guiding principle of Maximus' thought.[35]

### The rule of "proportion" in Maximus' doctrine of deification and likeness epistemology

When Maximus proposes, as we have seen him do prolifically, that the mind knows God according to its likeness to God, he is setting out one subsidiary conclusion of a wider understanding that divine and creaturely interaction with God in general occurs "in proportion," or as he tersely puts it, "deification is bestowed in proportion [ἀναλόγως]."[36] But to demonstrate this link, we must ask: in proportion to *what* does deification unfold? What is the currency or measure of "proportion"? Gregory Nazianzen and Dionysius—from whom, we will see, Maximus

35. As far as I can find, the only other scholarly work on Maximus' concept of "proportion" are the summaries offered by Larchet, *La divinisation*, 647–52, and Lévy, *Le créé et l'incréé*, 174–77, 200–201.

36. *Qu. Thal.* 22 (CCSG 7, 141).

inherited this logic—clarified, respectively, that a creature's "proportion" was a measure of its "nearness" to God[37] and its "imitation" of God.[38] Maximus follows them; for him a creature's "proportion" means its level of fittingness, or nearness, or likeness to God. This much is clear when Maximus describes deification as follows: "God wholly embraces the soul along with the body . . . and proportionately likens them to himself [ἀναλόγως αὐτὰ ἐξομοιοῖ ἑαυτῷ]."[39] "Likeness" to God is the measure, the shape in the shape-sorter; "proportion" refers to the degree to which the shape matches its object. In fact, Maximus sometimes simply substitutes his normal vocabulary of "proportion" (ἀναλογία, δύναμις, μέτρον, τάξις) for the terms "likeness" and "fittingness": "the worthy will receive the promised, ultimate beatitude of deification, and be gathered to God by fittingness 'according to likeness' [Gen 1:26] [τῇ καθ' ὁμοίωσιν ἐπιτηδειότητι]."[40] Elsewhere, Maximus specifies that the measure or currency of his rule of "proportion" is "nearness [to God] in virtue,"[41] or "the quality and quantity of each one's virtue,"[42] and we highlighted in Chapter 2 that in Maximus' eyes "virtue" equates to nothing other than likeness to God. In summary, when Maximus says that God deifies a creature "in proportion," he means that, as with a shape-sorter, God deifies a creature as far as the creature has become like God.

Importantly, aspects of Maximus' *epistemology* run along the same lines: just as the creature's proportion of likeness to God shapes its deification, so does its likeness to God condition its knowledge of God. This conceptual link between Maximus' rule of "proportion" and his likeness epistemology is clear in *Difficulty* 21. On three occasions here, Maximus invokes the rule of "proportion" to clarify how God the Word can be *known*: Christ appears as flesh or spirit "depending on the proportion of knowledge in each person" (κατὰ τὴν ἑκάστῳ τῆς γνώσεως ἀναλογίαν);[43] "the Word . . . reveals himself in proportion [ἀναλόγως] to those who

37. *Or.* 34.8 (SC 318, 212–13).

38. As Vladimir Lossky points out, in "La notion des 'Analogies,'" 289–90, 293–94. E.g., *c.h.* 3.2: "Each member of the hierarchy finds its perfection in being uplifted into imitating God according to its own proportion [τὸ κατ' οἰκείαν ἀναλογίαν ἐπὶ τὸ θεομίμητον ἀναχθῆναι]" (SC 58, 90).

39. *Ambig.* 21.10 (DOML 28, 434–35; modified trans.).

40. *Ambig.* 46.4 (DOML 29, 204–5; modified trans.).

41. *Ambig.* 31.9 (DOML 29, 50).

42. *Ambig.* 10.85 (DOML 28, 280–81, including trans.).

43. *Ambig.* 21.4 (DOML 28, 424).

receive him";[44] the Word "will be known according to the capacity [πρὸς τὴν . . . δύναμιν]" of those who know him.[45] Maximus clarifies this last formula as follows:

> For even though the Word is always himself and never changes, becoming neither greater nor lesser, yet "he becomes all things to everyone" [1 Cor 9:22, 12:6, 15:28; Eph 1:23] out of his exceeding goodness—lowly to the lowly, lofty to the lofty, and, to those who are deified through his grace, he is God in his nature, that is, surpassing every cognition of his divinity, God beyond God . . .[46]

It is clear here that when Maximus applies the rule of "proportion" to the issue of knowing God, it appears as the thesis that "like is known by like." To say that the Word reveals himself "in proportion" is the same as to say that the Word makes himself known to the degree that knowers are like him, whether "lowly," "lofty," or "deified." And as one's proportion conforms more closely to God, one achieves greater likeness to God and God appears more God's self. As we also saw in Chapter 2, the zenith of this progress is in fact an *unknowing-by-likeness*, an encounter with God "surpassing cognition" (ἐκβεβηκὼς ἔννοιαν).

## The rule of "proportion" and the workings of the body

Maximus' likeness epistemology is, then, an expression of a wider thought pattern to which he is habitually inclined, a rule of "proportion." To better understand the context and imagery behind his epistemology it is worth taking a closer look at this rule. One feature is particularly unexpected and worth staying with: Maximus' perhaps seemingly arid and abstract logic of "proportion" is inspired from a very lively, concrete reality: the *body*. The rule of "proportion" is an analogy that Maximus uses for theology but takes from biology: the understanding of how living bodies work, grow, and stay alive. This primary, biological context of the rule of "proportion" makes it a fund of metaphor that Maximus finds reliable and clarifying for talking about theological realities, namely deification. Consider the following passage, in which Maximus invokes the rule of "proportion" to navigate the difficulty of deification, describing

44. *Ambig.* 21.15 (DOML 28, 444–45; modified trans.).
45. *Ambig.* 21.16 (DOML 28, 444, 446).
46. *Ambig.* 21.16 (DOML 28, 444–47; modified trans.).

how multiple and finite humans are conformed and united to God whose nature is one and infinite:

> [T]he location of the saved will be God himself, who is unlimited, undivided, and infinite, "becoming all things to all men" [1 Cor 9:22] in proportion to their righteousness [κατὰ τὴν ἀναλογίαν τῆς δικαιοσύνης], or rather granting himself to each person according to the measure [κατὰ τὸ μέτρον] of what they have consciously undergone in this world for the sake of righteousness, just as the soul shows itself by acting in the body's parts according to the capacity [κατὰ τὴν . . . δύναμιν] underlying each part, binding the parts through itself to keep the body in existence, and keeping them under control to keep it alive.[47]

To strip this passage to its basic analogical form: "deification works in proportion like this, just as the body works in proportion like that." This is an argumentative trope that recurs in Maximus, and from it we can draw the following conclusion: when Maximus employs the language and rule of "proportion" (normally to describe divine and creaturely communion, or deification) the body and its workings are near the front of his mind as a favorite clarifying metaphor.[48] In the above passage and elsewhere, Maximus says that the rule of "proportion" fittingly describes deification by primarily describing a particular aspect of the body's constitution: its diverse animation by an indwelling soul.[49] But this is just one among a number of ways that Maximus believes bodies (human and non-human) work "proportionally." Elsewhere, Maximus uses different examples of the body's "proportional" behavior to help parse different aspects of the mystery of deification.

We will look at some of these examples, but first it is worth outlining the logic's history and origins. In doing so, importantly, it will become clear why Maximus treated the rule of "proportion" as a tool for explaining the workings of bodies: namely, because the rule of "proportion," in its Christian parlance, originated in the context of a biblical discussion of the *body*.

---

47. *Qu. Thal.* 61 (CCSG 22, 105).

48. This is a theme unfortunately absent from Cooper's monograph, *The Body in St Maximus.*

49. For the same point, see *qu. Thal.* 2 (CCSG 7, 51); *ambig.* 7.26 (DOML 28, 112–13); *ambig.* 7.31 (DOML 28, 120–21); *ambig.* 7.37 (DOML 28, 130–31); *ambig.* 7.39 (DOML 28, 134–35); *ambig.* 31.9 (DOML 29, 50–53).

The rule of "proportion" and its vocabulary wind their way to Maximus in two traditions, one originating in Paul, the other in Aristotle. More than anybody before him, Maximus adopted both traditions of thinking "according to proportion," and they merge together somewhat in his thought. They are still distinguishable, however. To summon again his favorite philosophical distinction, the Pauline tradition is concerned with *tropos*, "mode," the Aristotelian with *logos*, "nature" or "principle." In the former case, the rule of "proportion" clarifies how a rational creature's changing "mode" of existence—which might include, for example, its level of virtue, knowledge, faith, or righteousness—shapes its relation with God. In the latter case, the logic of "proportion" clarifies how a creature's fixed "nature" determines its interaction with God. The former is a tool for describing ascetic endeavor, the latter for describing metaphysics. Maximus' use of the Pauline, ascetic tradition of the rule of "proportion" will be my main concern, and this for three reasons: it is more prominent in his thought than the Aristotelian, metaphysical strand; he draws upon this tradition, and not the Aristotelian tradition, to describe deification; and, in its origins and development we find the crucial link with the body, along with links to eschatological reasoning that surely explain why Maximus associated this rule with deification in particular.

Nonetheless, it is worth briefly introducing the Aristotelian strand and showing how Maximus puts it to work. "God who is beyond fullness did not bring creatures into being out of any need of his," Maximus says, "but that they might enjoy participating proportionately [ἀναλόγως μετέχοντα] in him, and that he might delight in his works, seeing them being delighted and ever insatiably satisfied with him who is inexhaustible."[50] For Maximus, the rule of "proportion" is a metaphysical fact that accounts for the diversity of the created order.[51] Creation is diverse because it is made up of creatures with diverse natural shapes or likenesses to God, according to which they variously receive a share in existence from God's "beyond fullness" (ὑπερπλήρης—a term that points back to Dionysius, who had also used the word to describe the

50. *Carit.* 3.46 (PG 90, 1029C; trans. modified from Berthold, *Maximus Confessor,* 67).

51. More passages reflecting the Aristotelian, metaphysical rule of "proportion" include: *qu. Thal.* 51 (CCSG 7, 395); *carit.* 3.46 (PG 90, 1029C); *ambig.* 7.16 (DOML 28, 96–97); *ambig.* 20.4 (DOML 28, 414–15); *ambig.* 33.2 (DOML 29, 62–63); *ambig.* 35.2 (DOML 29, 68–71).

proportioned enjoyments of God's bounty that are the building blocks of creation).[52]

Maximus' metaphysical notion that the cosmos is distributed "in proportion" originated from a single clause in Aristotle. In a discussion in *Nicomachean Ethics* 1.6 on the topic of homonymity, Aristotle asks how diverse things can all be called "good." Perhaps, he suggests, "by way of proportion" (κατ' ἀναλογίαν). For example, he says, there is a "proportion" between the way sight is "good" in the body and the way intelligence is "good" in the soul. Aristotle's Neoplatonic commentators amplified his little phrase, κατ' ἀναλογίαν, into a metaphysical scheme, surely thanks also to Plato's praise of ἀναλογία in *Timaeus* (31C) as the "most beautiful" (κάλλιστα) structuring relationship of the cosmos. In this Neoplatonic scheme, each being takes its share of existence according to its natural "proportion," its capacity of reception.[53] Among pagan Neoplatonists this picture found its clearest expression in Proclus, and was then appropriated with equal clarity by Dionysius,[54] from whom it passed to Maximus, as Maximus acknowledges:

> He [God] brought forth beings out of nothing and endowed them with existence, and also willed to impart himself without defilement to them in a manner proportionate [ἀναλόγως] to all and to each, bestowing upon each the power to exist and remain in existence, according to the great and godlike saint, Dionysius the Areopagite, who said that ". . . He exists without diminution [ἀμειώτως] in each of the created things in a manner proportionate [ἀναλόγως] to each . . ." [see *d.n.* 2.11].[55]

Before Dionysius, Gregory Nazianzen offered an earlier Christian metaphysical rendering of the rule of "proportion." Gregory says, in orations that Maximus would have been familiar with, that the cosmos is

---

52. See *c.h.* 10.3 (SC 58, 142), where creatures enjoy God's "superabundant [ὑπερπλήρους] light" in proportion to (ἀναλόγως) their hierarchical position; and *d.n.* 2.11 (PG 3, 649C): God is "beyond fullness" and creatures are deified "according to each one's capacity" (κατὰ δύναμιν ἑκάστου).

53. For scholarship on the appropriation and transformation of this Aristotelian vocabulary of ἀναλογία, see Courtine, *Inventio analogiae*, 158–215. See also de Libera, "Les sources," 319–45.

54. On ἀναλογία in Dionysius, see Lossky, "La notion des 'Analogies,'" 279–309.

55. *Ambig.* 35.2 (DOML 29, 68–71, including trans.). See also *ambig.* 7.16 (DOML 28, 96–97).

ranked "in proportion [κατὰ τὴν ἀναλογίαν] to its nearness to God,"[56] with the angels and other creatures of closer "proportion" being the closest to God and most lavishly illuminated by God's light.[57] Interestingly, however, the Neoplatonic development of a metaphysical rule of "proportion" occurred after Gregory's time, so passages like these may be Gregory's own metaphysical riff upon the Pauline rule of "proportion" to which we now turn.

Although Maximus occasionally talks of "proportion" in this metaphysical context, describing fixed states of existence, he more often employs it within the context of ascetic progress towards deification. We can use Maximus' own words in his *Chapters on Knowledge* to summarize this rule of "proportion" in barest form: "from his fullness we receive grace proportionate [ἀναλογοῦσαν . . . χάριν] to our every progress [προκοπήν]."[58] God is an infinite[59] fullness, and dispenses himself by molding around the finite, developing "proportions" or shapes of rational creatures. These proportions vary in "spiritual quantity and quality," as Maximus puts it a few paragraphs later,[60] and they change as creatures progress towards deification, where "when he appears we shall be like [ὅμοιοι] him" (1 John 3:2).[61] This ascetic rule of "proportion" ultimately stems from Paul, and in this Pauline origin we find a reason for Maximus' close association of the rule of "proportion" with the workings of bodies, and also with eschatology.

Paul used the language of ἀναλογία (Rom 12:6), along with μέτρον (Rom 12:3; Eph 4:13, 16), to explain nothing other than how believers make up the *body* of Christ. Paul's language was transformed into a principle of Christian philosophy when Origen interpreted Romans 12:6, on the Spirit's distribution of gifts among Christ's body: "We have gifts that differ according to the grace given to us: prophecy, in proportion

---

56. *Or.* 34.8 (SC 318, 212–13).

57. *Or.* 28.4 (SC 250, 108); *or.* 28.31 (SC 250, 172).

58. *Cap. theol.* 2.76 (PG 90, 1160D).

59. Maximus can use "proportion" as a means for expressing how God's infinity and creaturely finitude interact, e.g. *qu. Thal.* intr. (CCSG 7, 23); *qu. Thal.* 61 (CCSG 22, 105).

60. *Cap. theol.* 2.89 (PG 90, 1168B). See also *cap. theol.* 2.93: "For all are given the coming grace in proportion [κατὰ τὴν ἀναλογίαν] to the quality and quantity [ποιόν τε καὶ ποσόν] of their righteousness" (PG 90, 1169B).

61. *Cap. theol.* 2.76 (PG 90, 1161A).

to faith [κατὰ τὴν ἀναλογίαν τῆς πίστεως]."[62] Origen read this verse as
a summary of his own wider, also Pauline, conception that one's level of
spiritual maturity, in faith or virtue, conditions how one receives grace
from God.[63] He therefore understood Paul to be saying that the Spirit
bestows his gifts in general—and not just the gift of prophecy—"in proportion to the faith" of each member of the body of Christ. Moreover,
Origen thought this verse paralleled and summarized 1 Corinthians 12,
with its much more elaborate account of the collaboration of Christ's
body.[64] Origen's interpretation of Romans 12:6[65]—which saw "proportion" as the governing principle of the Spirit's grace at work in the body
of Christ, and which coupled the concept with the lengthier treatment of
the body of Christ in 1 Corinthians 12—caught on among his Alexandrian successors,[66] and it eventually passed to Maximus.[67]

However, the Pauline rule of "proportion" did not always maintain
its original context of the *body*. The phrase and logic of Romans 12:6
that Origen highlighted were adopted by his successors as a generic rule
for all kinds of divine interaction with creatures.[68] In fact, even before
Origen this Pauline language and logic had departed from its Pauline
context to elaborate a different theme: eschatology. As far as I am aware,
Clement of Alexandria was the first to make this move. Paul's language
of "proportion" was, for Clement, a means of navigating questions raised
in particular by the "many mansions" of God's kingdom in John 14:2.[69]

62. Trans. NRSV.

63. Origen often grounds this conception in Paul's analogy of different kinds of
food: milk for spiritual infants, and meat or solid food for the spiritually mature (1 Cor
3:1–3 and Heb 5:12–14).

64. *Comm. in Rom.* 9.3.2–3 (SC 555, 98–101).

65. Origen employs the phrase from Rom 12:6 in the same way on numerous other
occasions. For example: *comm. in Rom.*, fr. XXV (Ramsbotham, "The Commentary of
Origen," 359); fr. *in Jo.* (GCS 10, 493); *or.* 16.2 (GCS 3, 337); *comm. in Mt.* 11.14 (GCS
40, 58).

66. E.g. Gregory Nazianzen (*or.* 27.8 [SC 250, 90]; *or.* 32.11 [SC 318, 108–11]) and
Basil of Caesarea (*comm. in Is.* 2 [PG 30, 121B]).

67. The best example is *qu. Thal.* 29 (CCSG 7, 211–13).

68. For a very generic application, see Didymus the Blind, *Gen.*: "Out of goodness
God gives himself, since the created nature is incapable of seeing him lest he give himself to be contemplated, 'in proportion to the faith' [Rom 12:6] of each" (SC 244, 232).

69. E.g. *strom.* 6.14.108 (SC 446, 276–77): ἄλλης αὐλῆς καὶ μονῆς ἀναλόγως τῆς
πίστεως κατηξιωμένα. For more on "proportion" as a tool for eschatological reasoning
in Clement, see Mortley, "Ἀναλογία chez Clément," 83–85.

Origen followed Clement,[70] and Origen's successors followed him.[71] Gregory Nazianzen is one example. In *Oration 27*, which Maximus knew and commented on in *Difficulties* 13 and 14, Gregory reasons that there are "many rooms" in God's house because "there are different patterns of life and avocations" which "lead to different places 'according to the proportion of faith' [Rom 12:6]."[72] Surely it is this Alexandrian tradition of eschatological reasoning "in proportion" that led Maximus to establish the rule of "proportion" as a rule that applied to deification in particular.

So then, as the inheritors of Clement and Origen appropriated this rule of "proportion"—for eschatological thinking or in other contexts— the original Pauline theme of the body was often lost. One exception is Gregory of Nyssa, who brought the rule of "proportion'" to numerous theological discussions whilst also improvising on Paul's original use of "proportion" to describe the body. In his *Commentary on the Song of Songs*, for example, he considers the rule of "proportion" to be illuminating for theological discussion insofar as it primarily describes bodily phenomena, like breastfeeding,[73] smell,[74] maturation of the human body and of fruit,[75] and the biological progression and events of the female body.[76]

Maximus somewhat summarized the Pauline/Alexandrian tradition of the rule of "proportion." Following many before him, he adapted the rule of "proportion" to reason about eschatology, or deification,[77] along with all the transforming interactions between God and man that

70. For links between "proportion" language and eschatological inheritance in Origen, see *princ.* 4.3.10 (GCS 22, 337–38); *hom. in Lev.* 14.3.1 (SC 287, 234–37); *hom. in Jos.* 10.1 (SC 71, 270–71); *hom. in Jos.* 23.4 (SC 71, 462–67).

71. For example, even Methodius of Olympus, who disagreed variously and vigorously with Origen, adopted the phrase from Rom 12:6 to describe the different kinds of salvation God will grant to different people (*symp.* 7.3 [SC 95, 184]).

72. *Or.* 27.8 (SC 250, 88–91; trans. Williams and Wickham, *On God and Christ*, 31). See also, *or.* 30.4 (SC 250: 232–33); *or.* 14.5 (PG 35, 864B); *or.* 19.7 (PG 35, 1049C–D); *or.* 32.33 (SC 318, 152–54).

73. *Cant.* 1 (GNO 6, 33).

74. *Cant.* 3 (GNO 6, 91).

75. *Cant.* 3 (GNO 6, 96–97); see also *instit.* (GNO 8/1, 44–45).

76. *Cant.* 15 (GNO 6, 460–61).

77. See for example: *Cap. theol.* 2.88 (PG 90, 1168A–B); *myst.* 7 (CCSG 69, 35); *qu. Thal.* 22 (CCSG 7, 141); *ambig.* 48.3 (DOML 29, 216–17). On the cognate theme of God's proportional distribution of the inheritance of the kingdom of God, see *cap. theol.* 2.93 (PG 90, 1169A–B).

deification involves.[78] But he also stays close to the original Pauline context of the body, preserved by Gregory of Nyssa: Maximus often adapts the rule of "proportion" to the context of deification by first grounding it in the body's various biological processes. Let us, then, consider three examples of how, for Maximus, the logic of "proportion" offers biological processes to interpret theological quandaries.

In one of his *Questions and Doubts*, Maximus invokes the rule of "proportion" to grapple with the ways of divine mercy and forgiveness. Here he reveals that thinking "according to proportion" is useful for him because it involves thinking back to the body, and in this case, the body's ability to receive different substances from outside itself—like air, light, and sound—without getting them confused:

> While the mercy of God is balanced, it is also fittingly circumscribed . . . [J]ust as we have an optical, auditory, and respiratory ability and these things do not receive all the air or the light or the sound . . . , but in proportion to the ability that is present in each [κατὰ τὴν ἀναλόγως προσοῦσαν δύναμιν ἑκάστῳ], each participates according to their ability, thus, also the mercy of God grants both forgiveness and grace according to the quality of the underlying disposition of each person.[79]

By saying that humans receive mercy from God "in proportion," Maximus is not attempting to tackle the question with a neat notion of reciprocity or just deserts, but rather suggests a metaphor, that is, an image from a different context that reveals the truth about the issue at hand. The metaphor here is as follows: mercy is something that humans *sense* or *breathe*, as if they were eyes or lungs. Presumably, Maximus thinks that this bodily metaphor might lead the reader towards promising and

---

78. For example, Maximus uses the logic and language of proportion to clarify: the Holy Spirit's distribution of grace (*qu. Thal.* 29 [CCSG 7, 211–13]; *qu. Thal.* 54 [CCSG 7, 255]); Christ the Word's presence to believers (*cap. theol.* 2.13 [PG 90, 1131A]; *cap. theol.* 2.27 [PG 90, 1137A–B]; *or. dom.* [CCSG 23, 59]; *qu. thal* 25 [CCSG 7, 161]; *ambig.* 21.15 [DOML 28, 444–45]; *myst.* 24 [CCSG 69, 68]; we will explore the additional examples of *ambig.* 47 and 48 later in this chapter); sharing in God through virtue (*ambig.* 10.85 [DOML 28, 280–81]; *ambig.* 21.10 [DOML 28, 434–35]); different ways of reading Scripture (*cap. theol.* 1.97 [1122C–1124A]; *myst.* 10 [CCSG 69, 39]; *qu. Thal.* 48 [CCSG 7, 331]); and epistemology (*qu. dub.* 168 [CCSG 10, 117]; *qu. Thal.* intr. [CCSG 7, 21]; *ambig.* 10.64 [DOML 28, 254–57]; *ambig.* 21.16 [DOML 28, 444–47]).

79. *Qu. dub.* 102 (CCSG 10, 77; trans. modified from Prassas, *Questions and Doubts*, 97).

hopeful conclusions about God's mercy: perhaps, just as light is good and serviceable for an eye and not for a lung, so the mercy that God gives each person is supremely fitting and good for them; or, just as ears and eyes do not fight over sense-data, so is there no competition for God's mercy; or maybe divine mercy, like sound or air, has no shortage. Whatever the specifics, it is clear in this passage that Maximus invokes the rule of "proportion" because it describes a bodily process that lends itself as a metaphor for theological reasoning.

In the remaining two examples, Maximus reveals that he finds the "proportional" behavior of bodies a particularly felicitous source of metaphor for reasoning about *deification*, or union with God and Christ, and its fundamental rule—that it is "tropological" and can never take place on the level of nature or essence. During the introduction to his *Questions to Thalassius*, Maximus suggests that the rule of "proportion" tackles the problem of how the divine Word, whose "nature" is infinite, can accommodate himself among finite creatures.

> Now the divine Word is like water: to those whom he waters, as if they were plants of all kinds, and shoots, and different living things, to those he shows himself proportionately (ἀναλόγως) through knowledge and through practice of the virtues, and then he appears like a fruit, according to the quality of each one's virtue and knowledge, and makes his home in different ways on different people. For, on account of his natural infinity, he is never tied down by one thing, or held and imprisoned within a single manifestation.[80]

Here Maximus thinks that the rule of "proportion" helpfully describes union with the Word insofar as it describes watering plants, and specifically the biological nourishment and transformation that water causes in plants. (Perhaps Maximus is developing the image from Matthew 5:45 of God sending rain on all kinds of people, good and bad.) One can begin to understand how the simple, infinite Word can accommodate himself amongst diverse and finite humanity, Maximus suggests, by considering how boundless water can find a finite home by causing a garden of different plants to bear fruit and flourish.

Our third example presents *eating* as another bodily process that the rule of "proportion" explains. In one of his *Chapters on Knowledge*, Maximus summons the metaphor of eating to address the following question

80. *Qu. Thal.* intr. (CCSG 7, 23).

about "the kingdom of God," or "deification": "Some people wonder what the state will be like of those deemed worthy of perfection in the kingdom of God: whether it will involve progress and change or a fixed sameness." In reply, Maximus suggests that deification works like a body:

> One might sensibly answer with the example that in the life of the body there is a twofold reason for food, namely, the growth and sustenance of those who are fed. For we are fed for growth until we reach the maturity of the body's stature, and then . . . the body is no longer fed for growth but for sustenance. Well, in the same way there is a twofold reason for the soul's food. For while it grows it is fed with virtues and contemplations, until it no longer passes among all the things that exist and arrives at "the measure [τό μέτρον] of the stature of the fullness of Christ" [Eph 4:13]. When it reaches this point, it stops its progress of increase and growth through mediating things and, without any mediation, is given food beyond intellection, and thereby beyond growth. This is a form of incorruptible food whose purpose is to sustain the godlike perfection granted to the soul and to manifest the food's infinite splendors. And in this way, as eternal wellbeing comes to indwell it, the soul becomes God by participating in divine grace . . .[81]

The soul's progression towards deification depends upon its "measure" [μέτρον], and here Maximus cites Ephesians 4:13, a passage in which Paul invokes the rule of "proportion" in the context of "building up Christ's body" (Eph 4:12). Maximus plays upon Paul's theme of bodily growth to suggest that the differences in statures amongst souls growing towards perfection in the kingdom of God can be understood when one thinks of deification as a progressing diet, from "virtues and contemplations" and on to "food beyond intellection," just as the body eats different appropriate foods on its journey to maturity. Interestingly, Maximus goes on to say that not only the soul but the body too will have a "proportionate participation in deification" (ἀναλογοῦσαν αὐτῷ μέθεξιν τῆς θεώσεως).[82] And by applying the rule of "proportion" to the fate of the body as well as the soul, he intriguingly suggests that, in the eschaton, human bodies might also find themselves fed by God in a way that first grows or transforms them and then sustains them in a new "measure" of life.[83]

---

81. *Cap. theol.* 2.88 (PG 90, 1165D–1168A).

82. *Cap. theol.* 2.88 (PG 90, 1168A).

83. On the deified fate of the body as recognizably still bodily but yet transformed,

### Conclusions on Maximus' rule of "proportion"

We have seen that Maximus' rule of "proportion" manifests itself in at least three intertwined discussions: he commonly deploys it to elucidate the theological topic of deification; the rule of "proportion" also (at times explicitly) underpins his likeness epistemology; and finally, this rule is a resource of metaphors of bodily functions that lend themselves to theological reasoning. To spell out these three linked points: different creatures are deified not by essence or nature, but "in proportion" to their likeness to God; in the same way, different minds know God in the degree to which they are like God; in the same way again, and most basically, the body is diversely animated, diversely processes its environment, and diversely feeds, according to the proportions of its members and of its maturity. In conclusion, Maximus has a widespread habit of thinking "in proportion," whose base logic parallels that of his likeness epistemology, and which must partly account for the ease with which he adopts and improvises on the knowing-by-likeness motif.

## Christ's incarnation in the believer

So far in this chapter we have seen two ways in which Maximus' doctrine of deification lies behind his assumption that "like is known by like." On the one hand, "likeness" to God itself is a form of deification. In this light, God is the teacher of theology in a really radical sense: he teaches his students by becoming his students; or, his students learn by living the divine life and "activity" of their teacher. On the other hand, Maximus habitually reasons about deification with a logic or rule of "proportion," rooted in metaphors of the body and its workings, a logic that echoes and underpins the logic of his likeness epistemology.

It remains now to highlight how the Confessor could apply these same two features of his thought—his conviction that "likeness" to God is a genuine form of deification or identity with God, and his proclivity for thinking "in proportion"—to the question of the believer's relationship and communion with Christ. First, Maximus thought that when individuals imitate Christ they can hope to have Christ incarnated within them, teaching them ever more deeply about himself. Secondly, this imitative

---

see *ambig.* 7.26 (DOML 28, 112–13). For the polemical context in which Maximus honed his views on this issue, see Benevich, "Maximus the Confessor's Polemics," 5–15.

and transformative "Christofication" is defined by the rule of "proportion." Indeed, Maximus is most original in his appropriation of the Pauline rule of "proportion" when he applies it to describe Christ the Word's incarnation in believers, and the consequent formation of the body of Christ. This exploration of how Maximus conceptualizes the imitation of Christ will set the scene for our final three chapters, on Maximus' later doctrinal method of discerning Christology.

### Imitating Christ and Christ's incarnate presence

In one of his *Chapters on Knowledge*, Maximus presents two ways in which God the Word can be known. First, he says, although the divine Word is unknowable in himself, he is knowable "in part" (1 Cor 13:9) by his divine activities. Maximus suggests that Paul attained this kind of knowledge. Secondly, the divine Word gave himself to be known when he became visible flesh in the incarnation. This is the kind of knowledge that John the Evangelist had, and Maximus spells out what it looks like to follow John in his epistemological achievement:

> The holy John, who, whilst being one among men, was initiated completely into the meaning [λόγον] of the Word's becoming man, said he had "seen the glory" of the Word as "flesh" [see John 1:14]. In other words, he saw the meaning, or rather the plan, according to which God became man . . . Consequently, the person who in himself keeps inviolable the complete meaning of the incarnation of God the Word for us will attain the glory "full of grace and truth" [John 1:14] of the one who for us "glorifies" and "consecrates" himself in us by his presence [παρουσίαν] [see John 17:10, 19]. For he [John] says, "when he appears we will be like him" [1 John 3:2].[84]

This is an intriguing passage because Maximus suggests a link between how someone sees the mystery of the incarnation in all its "glory," beholding its real "meaning" (λόγος), and how they appear themselves. This fullness of sight occurs "in oneself" (ἐν ἑαυτῷ), Maximus says, "in us" (καθ᾽ ἡμᾶς). Just as, we have seen, in some late-antique Greek optical theories the eye sees light because it itself is light-like, so, here, as a believer sees Christ's full "meaning" he himself attains Christ's "glory," or, in the words of 1 John 3:2, he is made "like him" (ὅμοιοι αὐτῷ). Maximus

---

84. *Cap. theol.* 2.76 (PG 90, 1160D–1161A).

actually goes further: the believer's likeness to Christ's glory is not mere appearance, but the visible sign of Christ "glorified" in him, of Christ's "presence" (παρουσία) in him. Maximus hints at a theological reality underlying his epistemology: not only does one perceive Christ as one becomes like Christ, but this likeness to Christ means having Christ present in oneself.

A handful of scholars have acknowledged Maximus' "audacious" notion of Christ's incarnation in the believer,[85] mainly focusing on the important role that "virtue"—not "imitation"—plays in this context.[86] However, as Thunberg points out, for Maximus, virtues are nothing other than imitations of Christ, who is Virtue itself: "consequently," says Thunberg, "imitation of Christ means a kind of participation in Christ's own being."[87] Thunberg's language here is somewhat unclear, and instead of using vaguely philosophical terms like "being" and "participation" it will help us to stay with the concrete terminology of "body" and "flesh," of "embodiment" and "incarnation," that, we will continue to see, Maximus hangs on to when describing this presence of Christ through the virtues/imitation. In his *Difficulties to Thomas*, for example, Maximus expressly identifies the "imitation" (μίμησις) of God's "self-emptying" (κένωσις) with the exhibition of "God embodied [σωματούμενον] in the virtues."[88] The virtues are imitations of Christ, and cultivating them makes Christ's "body" present.

As well as talking generically of "virtue" as a means of imitating Christ, Maximus thinks that even the subtle particulars of Christ's life and mission are imitable, shareable, and really bring about Christ's incarnation in the believer. One example comes in the *Commentary on the Lord's Prayer*, where Maximus comments on Galatians 3:28: when you belong to Christ, Paul says, "there is neither male nor female." With these words, Maximus suggests, Paul metaphorically instructs Christians

---

85. This is how Plested describes it. He goes on: "To speak of our becoming 'christs' through baptism and chrismation is not unusual; to speak of our becoming Christ, or what Christ is, I would suggest, is much less common" (Plested, *The Macarian Legacy*, 226).

86. Salés, "Divine Incarnation," 159–76; Thunberg, *Microcosm and Mediator*, 323–30; Larchet, *La Divinsation*, 460–62, 473–76; Cooper, *The Body in St Maximus*, 45–48; von Balthasar, *Cosmic Liturgy*, 277–83; Bathrellos, "Passions, Ascesis, and the Virtues," 291.

87. Thunberg, *Microcosm and Mediator*, 324–25.

88. *Ambig. Thom.* prol. 2 (DOML 28, 2–5; modified trans.).

to cast out "anger" (θυμός) and "lust" (ἐπιθυμία) respectively.[89] Doing so sparks off a process in the soul that ends with Christ's "incarnation" (σαρκούμενος) in the soul.[90] It is worth delineating Maximus' route to this eccentric conclusion.

He takes Elijah and his ascent to heaven (2 Kgs 2:11–12) as a figural exemplar of the casting out of male ("anger") and female ("lust") that Paul outlines. The first thing Maximus says about Elijah is that, having stopped all anger and lust, "he advances towards God bare, drawn by not a single attachment to existing things. He is simple in his desire and uncompli-cated in his will, and makes his dwelling with the one who is simple by nature."[91] (I cited this passage in Chapter 2 for its exposure of Maximus' like-by-like logic: Elijah can draw close to the "simple" God because he imitates God's simplicity.) When, like Elijah, the ascetic removes anger and lust, and in their stead discovers a desire becalmed and simplified, he achieves not only likeness to God's simple nature, but, Maximus says, his whole "life, movement, and existence" (see Acts 17:28) come to be "in Christ."[92] Maximus is supposing a definite, if not somewhat complex link between annihilating "anger" and "lust," and intimacy with Christ, a link that we need to spell out.

Maximus says here that the passions of anger and lust "expose an estrangement [ἀλλοτρίωσιν]" in the soul, a disharmony or contrari-ness, that parallels the estrangement between the opposites of "male and female." What is this estrangement that Maximus thinks is typified somehow by the opposites male and female? We get an explanation in *Difficulty* 41, written around the same time or before the *Commentary on the Lord's Prayer*.[93] Here Maximus says that the cosmos "is marked by five divisions": there is a division between uncreated and created; in the created realm there is a division between intelligible and sensible; in the sensible realm, between heaven and earth; on earth, between paradise and the world we inhabit; amongst humanity, between male and female. Humanity was made by God to unify all these differences in himself, but failed, sundering the parts, forgetting God as their beginning and

89. *Or. dom.* (CCSG 23, 47).

90. *Or. dom.* (CCSG 23, 92). For a summary of this section of *or. dom.*, interesting especially for the apparent influence of Gregory of Nyssa, see Squire, "The Idea of the Soul," 456–61.

91. *Or. dom.* (CCSG 23, 48–49).

92. *Or. dom.* (CCSG 23, 49–50).

93. Jankowiak and Booth, "A New Date-List," 28–30.

end. God became incarnate to complete his purpose and harmonize all the cosmos' divisions in a human being, Jesus Christ.[94] With his birth from a virgin, Jesus began the reconciliation process at the lowest division, subverting the cycle of procreation between male and female: "he drove out from nature the difference and division into male and female, a difference . . . which he in no way needed in order to become man . . . There is no need for this division to last 'perpetually, for in Christ Jesus,' says the divine apostle, 'there is neither male nor female' [Gal 3:28]."[95] Returning to the *Commentary on the Lord's Prayer*, it is clear, in this light, that the reason Maximus associates life "in Christ" with the simplicity of desire that comes of annihilating anger and lust/male and female is that, for him, Christ is the one who ultimately collapsed this division by his birth from a virgin. Put simply, when the soul quells anger and lust, it imitates Christ's work of reconciling the fracture between male and female in fallen humanity.

Now comes the important part for our discussion. When freed from anger and lust/male and female, an extraordinary phenomenon occurs in the soul:

> Christ is always born willingly and mystically, becoming incarnate [σαρκούμενος] through the saved. And he makes the soul that begets him into a virgin mother, who, to put it briefly, bears no relation to the marks of that nature subject to death and birth, as subject to male and female.[96]

When desire is simplified, and the male/female disjunction is reconciled, the soul imitates the ease and fullness of life shown in Christ—life without the cycle of conception and death that belongs to fallen men and women's procreation. And for Maximus, this state of imitation not only copies, but makes real Christ's incarnate life: the soul in a hidden way gives birth to Christ, and Christ becomes "enfleshed" in it.[97] Imitation brings a genuine, fleshly form of shared identity.

It is not clear in this passage what it is about imitation that results in Christ's "incarnation" in the believer. In the first part of this chapter, we specified that Maximus thinks of "likeness" to God as a sharing in

94. *Ambig.* 41.2–6 (DOML 29, 102–11).

95. *Ambig.* 41.7 (DOML 29, 110–11, including trans.).

96. *Or. dom.* (CCSG 23, 50).

97. For a list of Greek patristic expressions of the notion that the soul gives birth to Christ, see Miquel, "La naissance de Dieu," 387–89.

God's "activity," a genuine aspect of God's identity; and this provided some philosophical explanation for the connection he proposes between imitation and deification. Something similar might be going on in the context of likeness to Christ. For example, in one of his *Chapters on Knowledge*, Maximus clarifies how exactly the saints can be said to possess, in a genuine sense, "the mind of Christ" (1 Cor 2:16). Maximus says that having the mind of Christ would certainly not mean losing one's own mind, or replacing it, or having it transformed "in its essence and existence" (οὐσιωδῶς καθ' ὑπόστατιν)—Maximus' typical caveat. Rather, the mind of Christ comes to us "by illuminating the power of our mind with its own quality, and bringing to it the same activity [ἐνέργειαν]. To me at least, to have the mind [νοῦν] of Christ means thinking [νοοῦντα] like him and thinking [νοοῦντα] of him in everything."[98] When one imitates Christ, Maximus says, receiving his "mind" by "minding" like him (the cognates do not come so easily in English), one shares in Christ's "activity." It seems again that "activity" is that aspect of the divine identity that imitation gets caught up in, and in this case, it is what makes Christ present in the believer.

## *Imitating Christ "in proportion"*: Difficulties 47 and 48

In some of Maximus' writings, and indeed in Maximus scholarship, the ascetic life can sound flat and predictable—a difficult undertaking, but one that unfolds straightforwardly into inevitable, summarizable plots: practice leads to natural contemplation, which leads to *theologia* and deification; all the virtues come down to love; imitating Christ by being virtuous invites Christ's incarnation in the soul. However, Maximus underlines that, even within such overarching plots, attempts at asceticism are in reality as complex and diverse as their weary practitioners, and that God has grace enough to accommodate them all. In *Difficulties* 47 and 48, Maximus takes a set ascetic plot that we have begun to explore— imitating Christ invites Christ's incarnate presence—only to point out the countless unexpected ways that this might actually unfold. In both *Difficulties*, moreover, it is his rule of "proportion" that gives him the framework to account for this diversity and complexity in the ascetic life.

In the short *Difficulty* 47, the passage at hand is from Gregory's excursus on Exodus 12: "We need not be surprised that . . . a lamb is

98. *Cap. theol.* 2.83 (PG 90, 1164B).

required 'in each and every house.'"[99] Or, if a lamb cannot be afforded for each house, Gregory goes on, "a lamb is supplied, 'in the houses of the families' [Exod 12:3]."[100] This passage incites in Maximus the following conundrum: "if Christ . . . is one, how is it that the law, when ritually celebrating the type of Christ, commands that a multiplicity of lambs be slain 'in the houses of the families' [Exod 12:3]?" How, in other words, can one understand Scripture's figurative suggestion that Christ the one sacrificial lamb is multiplied into numerous lambs, slain amongst numerous people? To help with the dilemma, Maximus applies the ancient tactic of interpreting *Homerum ex Homero*, or Scripture from Scripture in this case: "we can surely learn the hidden intention of Holy Scripture by joining the present passage to a similar one from the holy apostle: 'I decided to know nothing in you except Jesus Christ and him crucified' [1 Cor 2:2]."[101] This passage is "similar" to Exodus 12:3 in that it too portrays Christ, the lamb, slain or crucified in multiple people, "in you" (plural, ἐν ὑμῖν). Maximus then introduces the rule of "proportion" as the key to his explanation of how this diversifying of the one Christ is possible: each person "is crucified and crucifies Christ together with himself according to his own ability and the underlying habit and quality of virtue in him"; or again, "each person brings about his crucifixion according to his corresponding mode of virtue."[102] Maximus proceeds to give *eleven* examples of such varying proportions of virtue, in ascending order, and it transpires that these are in fact varying proportions of *imitating* Christ's crucifixion, varying ways of negating, or "crucifying," realms of activity that normally busy the body and mind. Maximus begins with the example of the person who does not "actively" sin, but yet cannot muster positive virtue. Even such velleity, which only just forgoes sin, can be said to be a real imitation of Christ, a real "crucifixion." He continues with examples of increasingly closer imitations of Christ's crucifixion, so that eventually the ascetic passes from "practice" to "natural contemplation," that is, from Christ's "flesh" to his "soul," and from there to Christ's "mind" in *theologia*, and finally, in a supreme negation and "apophatic" embrace, from Christ's mind to his "divinity."[103]

99. *Or.* 45.14 (PG 36, 641C–D), cited in *ambig.* 47.1 (DOML 29, 206–7, including trans.).

100. *Or.* 45.14 (PG 36, 641D).

101. *Ambig.* 47.2 (DOML 29, 206–7, including trans.).

102. *Ambig.* 47.2 (DOML 29, 208–9; modified trans.).

103. *Ambig.* 47.2 (DOML 29, 208–11).

"Crucifixion" might seem in this passage to be little more than a metaphor for practical and spiritual abstemiousness. But when Maximus finishes and reflects on his list of examples, he points to a deeper theological reality:

> So each person, as I have said, according to his own ability and the grace of the Spirit granted to him according to his worthiness, has Christ in him proportionally [ἀναλόγως], who leads him through increasing mortification on lofty ascents. Thus it happens that, as if in a kind of "household" [Exod 12:3], "each" of us "in his own rank" [1 Cor 15:23] established to fit his virtue, sacrifices the lamb, partakes of his fleshes, and takes his fill of Jesus. For to each person Christ Jesus becomes his own lamb, to the extent that each is able to contain and eat him: he becomes Paul's own lamb . . . , and distinctively Peter's own lamb . . . , and distinctively a lamb of each of the saints, "according to the measure of faith" [Rom 12:3] in each and the grace bestowed by the Spirit: to one in this way, and to another in that, so that Christ is found to be wholly present in the whole of each, "becoming all things to everyone" [1 Cor 9:22].[104]

I wish to draw two points from this passage. First, imitating Christ results in Christ's real, bodily presence. Maximus clarifies that his talk of "crucifixion" and "mortification" was not only intended to highlight that ascetic negation imitates the pattern of Jesus' crucifixion, but was intended to describe Jesus bodily present in ascetics: "wholly and in the whole of each" (ὅλος καὶ ὅλῳ), owned, or even "eaten," by those who imitate his crucifixion in different ways. Here the language of the body—in this case, Jesus' "fleshes" (σάρκες), eaten up like a sacrificial lamb by the believer—rather than philosophical or metaphysical categories, is Maximus' preferred means for describing Christ's presence. Secondly, Maximus elucidates this picture of Christ's self-distribution with his rule of "proportion," in all its linguistic expressions: each ascetic partakes of Christ "proportionally"—according to their "ability," their "rank," their "measure." Maximus applies the rule of "proportion" in this context to justify and unfurl the mysterious fact that every ascetic truly encounters the incarnate Christ, however they might diversely succeed or fail to imitate him. A more concise passage from his *Chapters on Knowledge* confirms this picture of Christ embodied in the believer in proportion to their level of imitation. Maximus notices how Paul says that he sees Christ "crucified" amongst

104. *Ambig.* 47.2 (DOML 29, 210–11; modified trans.).

the Corinthians (1 Cor 2:2) but Christ "raised" amongst the Ephesians (Eph 2:6). What Paul indicates, he says, is that "the Word of God comes to exist [among us] according to the proportionate ability in each person [κατὰ τὴν ἀναλογοῦσαν ἑκάστῳ δύναμιν]." Consequently, the Word "is crucified among those who are still being introduced to piety in their practice," but the Word "is raised and ascends into the heavens among those who have stripped away the whole of the old self . . . and put on the new."[105]

In preparation for seeing how Maximus continues his train of thought in the next *Difficulty*, number 48, let me highlight one image summoned above at the end of *Difficulty* 47: "to each person Christ Jesus becomes his own lamb, to the extent that each is able to contain [χωρεῖν] and eat [ἐσθίειν] him." Of course, the image of a "lamb" and of eating is appropriate here simply insofar as it belongs to the passage at hand from Exodus and Gregory's commentary on it, and insofar as the lamb is a generic type of Christ; but, as we will see, in *Difficulty* 48 Maximus finds the image of eating—perhaps a deliberately eucharistic image[106]—especially accurate when it comes to theorizing the ascetic's imitative relationship with Christ.

In *Difficulty* 48, Maximus continues to move through the same oration by Gregory, this time attending to the following sentence: "Whatever is a fleshly and nourishing part of the Word, together with the intestines and hidden recesses of the intellect, will be eaten and given up to spiritual digestion."[107] The theme of "eating" often triggers Maximus' habit of thinking according to proportion,[108] but here there is especially good reason to invoke the rule of "proportion" because, as Maximus immediately notices, Gregory posits *diverse* parts of Christ's body that can be eaten. As we have seen, the rule of "proportion" is Maximus' way of making sense of diversity in God's relation to creatures. So, from Gregory's words

105. *Cap. theol.* 2.27 (PG 90, 1137A–B).

106. Although, as Blowers puts it, "the Eucharistic overtones" of language like this may seem "unmistakable" (*Maximus the Confessor*, 187), I am cautious about labelling Maximus' talk of "eating" Christ the "lamb" "eucharistic" talk. This is because of Maximus' wider reticence on the subject of the Eucharist. For one attempt to identify eucharistic references in the Confessor's thought, see Thunberg, "Symbol and Mystery," 285–308.

107. *Or.* 45.16 (PG 36, 645A), cited in *ambig.* 48.1 (DOML 29, 212–13, including trans.).

108. See, for example, passages in which Maximus considers Jesus' description of himself as "bread": *or. dom.* (CCSG 23, 59); *cap. theol.* 2.56 (PG 90, 1149A–B).

Maximus takes away the message that diverse believers eat of Christ in proportion to their likeness to Christ. He sets out to make this point about appropriate eating with the following opening warning: as believers eat Christ the lamb, his body must not be disarranged.

> [We must] maintain the Lamb's body parts distinctly and usefully in their unbroken and unmingled harmony lest we be condemned for breaking and tearing to pieces the well-arranged harmony of the divine body—either because we eat of the flesh of the Lamb and Word overconfidently, beyond our ability, or profanely, that is, averse to our ability. Rather, let each of us, in line with his ability, rank, and the grace of the Spirit given to him, partake of the divine Word in line with the meaning of each part [of his body].[109]

As in *Difficulty* 47, Maximus warns that Christ is not identically available to all; a person's proportion—their spiritual ability, rank, and openness to grace—is going to shape how and what they can eat. With Christ the Lamb, as with any food, you cannot just eat; you can only eat what you can digest.

Maximus then explains what this proportional eating of Christ's body might look like with a long list of examples that move down the different parts of Christ's body. Importantly, in this passage he reveals that a person's "proportion," or "ability," or "rank," boil down to their individual *likeness* to Christ. Here are just a few of the examples he gives:

> For example, the head shall be partaken of by whosoever has grasped, from indemonstrable first principles, a faith that has entirely set free the principles of *theologia*, from which faith the whole body of virtues and knowledges "is knit together and grows with" spiritual "growth" [Col 2:19]. The ears shall be partaken of by whosoever spiritually receives the divine words with knowledge, and because of these words "becomes" in actual deeds submissive and "obedient" to God "unto death" [see Phil 2:8]. The eyes shall be partaken of by whosoever beholds creation spiritually, and blamelessly gathers together all the principles pertaining to sensation and intellect . . . The breast shall be partaken of by whosoever has filled his heart with theological contemplations, like the great Evangelist John, and like an inexhaustible source he piously pours forth . . . the reason and mode in which the providence of the universe is comprehended . . . The stomach shall be partaken of by him whose fecundity of

109. *Ambig.* 48.4 (DOML 29, 216–17; modified trans.).

soul is ceaselessly productive, and so he abounds with spiritual
contemplations, and never quenches the burning desire of his
dispassionate appetite for intercourse with the Divine. The intestines shall be appropriately partaken of by whosoever "shall
probe into," by means of a more hidden inquiry and knowledge,
"the depths" of the mind "of God" [1 Cor 2:10], taking his fill
of ineffable mysteries. My discourse will dare to venture something even more. Of those—yes *those*—members of the Word
let him partake chastely who stands in the strength of his reason
when confronting matter, and who together with his soul keeps
his flesh perfectly undefiled, and who by means of the virtues
completely forms within his flesh the whole Word who became
flesh.[110]

Maximus' words here may have been inspired by a passage from
Gregory Nazianzen's *Oration* 40, which he had surely read.[111] At the least,
the two texts bear many parallels. Like Maximus, Gregory seeks to express
how believers may share in Christ and, like Maximus, he chooses for his
method a spiritual interpretation of parts of the body, descending from
head to foot.[112] Other similarities include their shared association of the
"head" with the language of Colossians 2:19,[113] and their shared refusal
to shy away from the body's "indecorous" or "unpresentable" (ἀσχήμων,
1 Cor 12:23) parts, as Gregory puts it, which he argues can be purified,
and the lust (ἐπιθυμία) knotted up in them unleashed toward God.[114]

However, it is the ways in which Maximus differs from Gregory that
are more interesting. Maximus is more daring than Gregory in at least
two ways. First, his account is ampler. He seems to want to stress that
every kind and variation of ascetic achievement imaginable proportionally imitates and partakes of some aspect of Christ's body—indeed, as
he says at the end of his list, "who would be able to enumerate all the
aspects of God our Savior . . . according to which he has made himself
edible and participable to all, in proportion to each [ἀναλόγως ἑκάστῳ]?
For in addition to all these, the Lord has locks of hair, a nose, lips, throat,

110. *Ambig.* 48.5–6 (DOML 29, 216–21; modified trans.).

111. *Or.* 40.39–40 (SC 358, 288–93). Passages from *or.* 40 are the subject-matter
of *ambig.* 42–44.

112. Gregory in turn was perhaps inspired by Antony the Great's short *ep.* 1, which
contains a very similar account of purifying the different parts of the body, eyes down
to feet.

113. *Or.* 40.39 (SC 358, 288–89).

114. *Or.* 40.40 (SC 358, 290–91).

shoulders, fingers, and whatever else belongs to our human frame."[115] In short, Maximus stresses that Christ is abundantly *generous*, as generous as human attempts at imitation of him are diverse. The second difference is that Maximus assigns to Christ a capacity for metaphysical generosity and outlandishness only hinted at in Gregory's account. Gregory had sought to explain how ascetics imitate and thereby share in *Christ's life* by purifying *their bodies*: when human shoulders are purified, for example, they can bear Christ's cross, and as the feet are purified, Christ himself comes to wash them.[116] Maximus turns this upside down. He claims that ascetics imitate, and thereby eat or share in, each part of *Christ's body* by purifying *their lives*. And with this reversal come more metaphysically bold claims about the nature of the sharing or eating that imitation inculcates. When Maximus "dares" to consider (but not quite spell out) "*those* parts," i.e., the genitals, of Christ's body, he does not follow Gregory and take this as the moment to discuss lust and its purification, but instead suggests that whoever spiritually eats of these most intimate parts of Christ will stare created matter in the face and remain undefiled, having "formed within his own flesh the whole Word who became flesh." You *are* what you eat, Maximus says in effect, and he draws this out in the summary:

> In this manner, according to that holy and great teacher [Gregory], the Lamb of God "is eaten, and given up to spiritual digestion," transforming into himself [μεταποιῶν πρὸς ἑαυτὸν] by the Spirit those who partake of Him, leading and transposing each of them into the place and position in the body's frame of the part that was spiritually eaten by them, so that out of his love for mankind the Word, who is in all things yet is alone beyond nature and mind, takes on substance in these deeds [τοῖς πράγμασιν οὐσίαν γίνεσθαι].[117]

As each ascetic eats of that part of the Word's body that their life and practice imitate, the Word "transforms" or "remodels" them to himself, so that he takes "substance" or "essence" (οὐσία) in their deeds. Whether Maximus means that the Word manifests his own οὐσία among humans, or takes on a human οὐσία as in the incarnation, this is a completely extravagant metaphysical claim, and runs quite contrary to Maximus'

115. *Ambig.* 48.7 (DOML 29, 220–21; modified trans.).
116. *Or.* 40.39 (SC 358, 288–89).
117. *Ambig.* 48.7 (DOML 29, 220–23; modified trans.).

consistent emphasis elsewhere that divine and human interaction *never* occurs according to "essence." Perhaps with this in mind we could soften the translation to read "he becomes real" or "he comes to exist." However one navigates this curious passage, it is clear that Maximus believed that a metaphysical and bodily intimacy with and transformation into the incarnate Christ results from imitating and eating Christ, in whatever degree the ascetic can swallow.

The last thing to point out about this passage from *Difficulty* 48 is that epistemological themes are close at hand. In the examples cited in the abridged passage above, Maximus says that when believers imitate Christ they not only invite the fleshly, edible presence of Christ; they also come across new attainments of "knowledge" or "contemplation." In the believer's relationship with Christ, knowledge derives from imitating and becoming intimate with the incarnately present Christ. And this final observation turns our gaze towards the ensuing chapters of this study, on the relation between imitating Christ and knowing Christ in Maximus' christological method.

## Conclusion

I have argued in this chapter that Maximus' doctrine of deification grounds his likeness epistemology in two ways: first, Maximus understands "likeness" to God itself to be a genuine form of deification or identity with God, and therefore a supremely revealing standpoint for knowing God, and secondly, in Maximus' doctrine of deification, there persists a rule of "proportion" that neatly parallels and informs his epistemology. In the second part of the chapter we saw that both of these features of Maximus' doctrine of deification are present in his accounts of the believer's relationship with Christ. Just as, for Maximus, likeness to God equates to deification, so the imitation of Christ equates to the incarnate presence of Christ. And he delineates both theological phenomena with the same rule of "proportion": deification unfolds "in proportion" to the believer's likeness to God, and Christ becomes bodily present "in proportion" to the caliber and kind of the believer's imitation of Christ.

In the final chapters, we will examine Maximus' likeness epistemology in practice, specifically, in his practice of Christology in his letters. We will find that Maximus encouraged Christians to find their way through the polemical, rhetorical, and political landscape of christological debate by adhering to a particular pattern of discovery that depends on imitating Christ. And once we have inspected in detail this epistemic role of imitation in his christological letters, the conclusion to our study will return to the findings of the current chapter, and suggest that the closeness in Maximus' outlook between the imitation of Christ and the indwelling of Christ discovered here perhaps offers the theological key to his imitation-centered christological method.

# 4

## *Praise and persuasion*

### *The rhetorical rationale of Maximus' letters*

> For praise of achievements induces in those who have
> accomplished them a more vehement desire for better things.[1]

Much research has been done on Maximus' Christology. In the remaining three chapters, I am going to approach his Christology from a new angle, and focus not on the content of his claims but on his method—the means by which he communicates and defends his claims and brings his listeners to understand and accept them. The central specific proposal of these remaining chapters is that Maximus' christological method was defined by a likeness epistemology. I will focus on the Confessor's introductions to his christological letters and argue that he upholds in them a model of discernment according to which the imitation of Christ is an essential condition for correctly grasping the mystery of Christ and its finer doctrinal points.

The present chapter deals with the fact that, in his letters, this epistemological model and method is an assumption, lying hidden from any straightforward or even "close" reading of the propositions on offer in the text. Instead, it is embedded amongst the tissue of assumptions made by the text itself, the rules and conventions about how to communicate and persuade that Maximus took for granted when writing:

1. Gregory of Nyssa, *Cant.* 3 (GNO 6, 72–73; trans. Norris, *Homilies*, 81).

his rhetoric.[2] Cornelia Tsakiridou has said that "Maximian theology is written in the modality of the mysteries that envelop it . . . *It is a theology that is ascetic and mystical not only in subject-matter but in form as well.*"[3] We will see in this chapter that something like this is indeed the case, that the literary "form" and rhetorical structure of Maximus' late writings genuinely reveal aspects of his thought—namely, his epistemology and christological method—that are largely absent from his "subject-matter." Andrew Louth has pointed out that Maximus' writings are, on the whole, "occasional."[4] And this occasionality most fundamentally demonstrates itself in a recurring basic literary form: the *letter*. Maximus' use of the letter form and its rhetorical tropes have been scarcely specified or examined in the scholarship. For example, "The letter" does not merit its own subsection in Van Deun's recent summary of "Maximus the Confessor's Use of Literary Genres."[5] Yet not only does Maximus' corpus contain a large collection of letters (including many of his *Opuscula theologica et polemica*, as well as his *Letters*), but many of his works normally considered "treatises" for their length also exhibit the basic literary marks of Maximus' epistolary procedure, stamped there by the raw fact of occasionality, the physical phenomenon of sending (consequently, we will see, the manuscript tradition shows some confusion over how to class Maximus' works—letters or treatises?).

So how do the literary form of "the letter" and its rhetorical tropes tell us anything about Maximus' epistemology or christological method? This chapter will argue that there is a specific connection, worth preliminarily laying out. Maximus' favorite and most consistent rhetorical epistolary convention, found mainly in the introductions of his writings, is *praise of the addressee,* presented in a form that recalls the traditional rhetorical genre of the praise speech. And he does not hide the fact that "praise" is exactly what he is up to: "What speech [λόγος] could worthily

2. By "rhetoric" I do not mean eloquent oratory. As Daley summarizes, "anyone who has tried to read Maximus' works in Greek knows he was not an accomplished rhetorician!" ("Making a Human Will Divine," 101). Rather, in referring to Maximus' "rhetoric" I am simply pointing to the fact that he employs conventional literary tactics of persuasion.

3. Tsakiridou, *Icons in Time*, 175 (my italics).

4. Louth, *Maximus the Confessor*, 15, 33.

5. Van Deun, "Maximus the Confessor's Use," 274–86. Van Deun acknowledges that Maximus wrote many letters (280–81), but the only epistolary literary form that he mentions is the somewhat unremarkable "epistolary preface"—that is, simply, the opening formula, "To [someone], from Maximus" (275, 277, 278, 282).

praise [ἐπαινέσειε] you?" Maximus puts to John, a bishop, in the prologue of his *Difficulties to John*, before attempting his own formal adulation of John's excellent episcopal qualities, Christ-likeness, and humility.[6] Although Maximus' lasting habit of praising his addressees has been briefly noted before,[7] these opening epistolary praise addresses have themselves been largely ignored in the scholarship and, equally importantly, have not been identified as a distinct and coherent rhetorical form. The task of this chapter is to argue that these epistolary addresses showcase the kind of epistemological endeavor that Maximus thinks he and his addressees are involved in. Specifically, I will demonstrate that Maximus' recurring literary form of the epistolary praise address, far from being a stylistic or decorative or even sycophantic device, bears an argumentative and epistemological function. It aims to encourage and instill virtues in his addressees that *imitate* their object of study—whatever theological topic that might be—in the hope that they might more easily comprehend it. Maximus' praise rhetoric thus manifests his likeness epistemology in practice.

The first part of this chapter will take *Letter* 2, on divine love, as a model case study. I will contextualize our analysis of this letter by pointing out some important features of Byzantine epistolary protocol, and then I will turn to *Letter* 2's opening address. I will argue that the address performs two functions. On the one hand, it is an introduction: it introduces the broad themes and particular points of the letter's content. On the other hand, this content is introduced obliquely, through a rhetorical device: praise. Maximus attempts to introduce his hearers to his letter's teachings on divine love by praising them for manifesting that teaching in their own lives. I will explore how the details and structure of Maximus' praise rhetoric in *Letter* 2 resemble conventional features of late-antique praise rhetoric. However, I will ultimately suggest that Maximus' rhetorical strategy—of introducing his letter's content not by straightforwardly outlining it, but by encouraging his readers, through praise, to mirror that content themselves—is his own invention. *Letter* 2 will thus provide a first example of how Maximus' rhetorical praise address translates his likeness epistemology into a literary form, working on the assumption that imitation brings understanding, that "like is known by like."

6. *Ambig.* prol. 3(–6) (DOML 28, 62–63[–67], including trans.).
7. E.g., Blowers, *Maximus the Confessor*, 281.

In the second part of the chapter, I will identify this same signature strategy of praise rhetoric and its like-by-like methodology in another letter, the *Second Letter to Thomas*. Unlike *Letter* 2, this is not a letter of spiritual teaching but of detailed dogmatic Christology. By attending to its praise rhetoric, we will begin to see what ascetic dispositions of imitation Maximus thinks fit a person for *christological* reflection in particular. This will give a good introductory example of how, fascinatingly, we largely find Maximus' signature praise address, with its subtle but consistent epistemological force, in his christological writings, which we will approach in the final two chapters.

The chapter will end by contextualizing Maximus' methodology, pointing out how, although it is unique to him, it shares some essential assumptions with Gregory Nazianzen's epistolary rhetoric and theological method.

First, however, it is worth giving our coming discussion a bit more context. In the remaining chapters we will consistently find that Maximus' letter addresses take for their object of praise and manipulation the *character* of his audience. This fact tells us that these addresses have an epistemological or pedagogical purpose, since the Confessor is elsewhere very clear that it is precisely a listener's character and attitude that determines how and what they can hope to know. In *Difficulty* 13, Maximus says that certain "dispositions" (διαθέσεις)—inward attitudes of will that accrue over time and shape the soul's movement and behavior[8]—make men deaf to the truth. Maximus considers Gregory's image of people with "itching ears and tongues,"[9] which Maximus identifies as a description of a "disposition" of encompassing resentment: an inability to stand by and let another succeed, "so that, even before the object of their cynicism and envy has had a chance to complete a sentence . . . , their 'ears' and their 'tongues' are poised to seize upon a particular word . . . , not of course in order to relish it, but to revile it."[10] Maximus goes on to paint this "disposition" as a "bitter and thick secretion that has accumulated deep within the body," which pricks when irritated by the sound of "whatever is well spoken."[11] At the beginning of the *Centuries on Love*, he similarly warns

8. This is my own rough definition, assembled from tracing Maximus' numerous uses of the word. To add an extra detail: "disposition" means something very like "habit" (ἕξις), and Maximus often pairs the two.

9. *Or.* 43.58 (SC 250, 70).

10. *Ambig.* 13.4 (DOML 28, 352–33, including trans.).

11. *Ambig.* 13.5 (DOML 28, 354–55, including trans.)

that if somebody "takes up this or any other work whatsoever, not for the sake of spiritual profit but of ferreting out phrases serving to revile the author . . . there will never come any profit of any sort."[12] One gets the feeling that Maximus was himself familiar with this kind of unworkable audience.

On a couple of occasions during his bewailing of bad listeners and learners of theology, Maximus specifies, unsurprisingly by now, that the soul's best dispositions for attaining knowledge would be those that *imitate* the object of knowledge. In a *Difficulty* on a passage from Gregory's *Oration* 27, where, we saw in Chapter 2, Gregory spells out the fitting spiritual conditions for theological reflection, Maximus says that those who are "insolent and disorderly [ἀτάκτους], who know no order [τάξιν] in general," are at a loss "especially when it comes to speaking about God." And this is because God himself works and creates in an "orderly" (εὐτάκτως) way. Only those who speak and work with order themselves, picking the "appropriate situation" (τὸ εὔκαιρον), may hope to speak appropriately about the God who authors order.[13] Another example comes in *Difficulty* 19, where Maximus examines a passage by Gregory that he says "enumerates for us the different forms of prophecy." First, Maximus says, Gregory himself could speak about prophecy with understanding only because his own ascetic achievements led him to "experience the same things as the holy prophets." In turn, the reader will only grasp Gregory's words by sharing in this same prophetic experience of ascetic purgation: "these words . . . are far beyond the grasp of anyone who is not himself like [οἷος] the teacher [Gregory]."[14] Imitation is the key condition for understanding, for Gregory and for his reader.

Maximus was very aware, then, of the potentially disastrous or, conversely, profitable link between disposition and reception of truth, so much, indeed, that he can call wrong doctrinal "confession" a kind of "disposition."[15] In short, Maximus is clear on a number of occasions that the teachings or doctrines in a text become available to the listener who has the right kind of disposition. As rhetorical devices that mean to shape the habits and dispositions of his readers, Maximus' epistolary praise

---

12. *Carit.* prol. (PG 90, 960C–961A; trans. ACW 21, 137).

13. *Ambig.* 14.2 (DOML 28, 356–59, including trans.).

14. *Ambig.* 19.2 (DOML 28, 402–3, including trans.).

15. *Qu. Thal.* 28 (CCSG 7, 205).

addresses will, therefore, offer us clear windows into his epistemological method.

## Letter 2: a case study in Maximus' epistolary praise rhetoric

### Sending and receiving letters

Letter 2 ("about love," περὶ ἀγάπης) is quite an early work[16] and bears a rhetorical rationale. To identify this rationale we first need to highlight that the text is indeed a letter, with its own particular style and conventions, and not a bulk of content lacking any genre. Because it is a letter, it is written for a particular audience, in this case, John the Cubicularius, a chamber-master to the emperor Heraclius, whose connection to Maximus is unclear.[17] Maximus' use of the second person plural indicates that the letter addresses a group,[18] maybe of other court officials, maybe whom Maximus also knew.[19] Here at the very heart of Byzantine officialdom, the polished ceremonial of epistolary correspondence no doubt proceeded as typically as the centuries of evidence suggest.[20] The modern reader of Byzantine letters should remember that a letter's text itself functioned as but one part of a multimedia event, or "feast" as Gregory Nazianzen calls it:[21] a physical and always oral and audible interplay between the re-

16. "[P]robably before or around 633" (Jankowiak and Booth, "A New Date-List," 37).

17. For a brief prosopography of John, see Jankowiak and Booth, "A New Date-List," 24.

18. Louth, *Maximus the Confessor*, 81.

19. Most scholars now downplay Maximus' Constantinopolitan roots. It is not clear when or for how long Maximus spent time in Constantinople. But even a scholar who most forcefully aims to scrap the once-prevalent picture of Maximus the Constantinopolitan suggests that he was indeed there long enough to form relations such as this one with John (Boudignon, "Maxime le Confesseur," 36). Recently, Booth has compounded scholars' doubts over Maximus' roots in Constantinople, but he too suggests the Confessor may well have visited the city (*Crisis of Empire*, 150–51).

20. In presenting the following picture of Byzantine letter reception, I draw heavily from the exceptional work of Margaret Mullett, especially: *Theophylacht of Ochrid*, 31–43; "The Language of Diplomacy," 203–16. For a good summary of twentieth-century scholarship on Byzantine epistolography, see Hatlie, "Redeeming Byzantine Epistolography," 213–48.

21. *Ep.* 115 (Gallay, *Lettres*, vol. 2, 9–10).

cipients, the text, the epistle-bearer,[22] and often accompanying gifts[23]—or rather, *other* gifts, since letters were recognized as gifts themselves.[24]

For the modern reader, the most unfamiliar player in this set piece is probably the bearer. Maximus would have chosen for his bearer an appropriately worthy man, perhaps another monk,[25] whose task was not only to deliver the written message but also, and sometimes principally, to recite an oral and perhaps confidential message.[26] This is why Basil calls the bearer the "living epistle" (ἐπιστολή ἔμψυχος),[27] who brings to life, adds to, and interprets the written epistle. Basil describes bearers as informed improvisers, who "can by their own words easily supply what is lacking in the letter."[28] In turn, the written epistle was intended and expected to spell out the content or theme of the "living epistle" and, vitally, to provide its rhetorical wrapper. *Letter* 14 to Peter the Illustris offers a glimpse of how Maximus could wield the "living epistle."[29] In this letter, written around 633,[30] Maximus includes for Peter a formal introduction to and recommendation of the letter's bearer, Cosmas, a deacon apparently recently converted from monophysitism.[31] Maximus then offers a short summary of the dyophysite confession. After this he once again commends Cosmas to Peter, and says that he has written Cosmas a "summary response" to some of the convert's questions about the "principal dogmas" of the faith—and Maximus is probably referring to the dyophysite christological summary he has just provided.[32] Then he implores Peter, "help Cosmas with your fine explanation of the issue at hand, and

22. Normally called a "cursor" (κούρσωρ) (Allen, "Prolegomena to a Study," 491).

23. See Mullett, "The Language of Diplomacy," 213–14; Allen, "Prolegomena," 489. Maximus' *ep.* 3 (PG 91, 408C–4012C) evidences such gift giving.

24. Karlsson, *Idéologie et cérémonial*, 113; Mullett, "The Classical Tradition," 77.

25. Letter bearers were normally, or ideally, men of high repute or rank—this included monks. See Allen, "Prolegomena," 484–86.

26. Allen, "Prolegomena," 487–88.

27. *Ep.* 205 (LCL 243, 174–75). A generation later, Synesius of Cyrene also calls the bearer by this term (*ep.* 85, cited in Gustav Karlsson, *Idéologie et ceremonial*, 17).

28. *Ep.* 205 (LCL 243, 174–75, including trans.).

29. On the uncertain identity of this "Peter," see Jankowiak and Booth, "A New Date-List," 24–25.

30. Jankowiak and Booth, "A New Date-List," 44.

31. Maximus says that Cosmas has "gladly welcomed" the confession of Christ's two natures (PG 91, 537C). For more details on *Letter* 14, see Jankowiak and Booth, "A New Date-List," 44–45.

32. Larchet thinks that he does ("Introduction," in Ponsoye, *Lettres*, 52).

supply his mind with what was left out of the summary."[33] We can see from this interaction that Maximus' written letter aims to provide the necessary rhetorical framework—generous personal introductions and a summary of key talking points—for the living conversation between Peter the recipient and Cosmas the bearer.

With most of Maximus' letters, however, including *Letter* 2, there is no mention of the bearer,[34] and it is impossible to reconstruct the living reception or accompanying oral message. But I nonetheless draw attention to the living epistle to contrast it with the written epistle. Whereas the living epistle is to an extent improvised and unpredictable, especially if there is an ebullient recipient or talkative bearer,[35] the written epistle is written because, as with *Letter* 14's dyophysite summary above, its content or literary flourish is too difficult, precise, or important to commit to memory or to be heard only once.[36] Often, indeed, the written letter was but an artistic cover-letter for a message.[37] The Byzantine written letter is thereby a thoroughly honed piece of rhetoric, a shiftless fundament and frame of reference within which a message will be received and understood. It is as indispensable and highly conventional as, for example, the introduction to a dissertation or the trailer for a film, exactly preparing and persuading its hearers to digest and respond to a particular content in a particular way. In this light, while *Letter* 2 straightforwardly shows what Maximus thinks "'about love," it more fundamentally shows how Maximus thought such love could be effectively broadcast and encouraged amongst a spiritually promising group of Constantinopolitan elites.[38]

33. *Ep.* 14 (PG 91, 537C).

34. Exceptions are *ep. D*, whose bearer is called Zacharias (see Jankowiak and Booth, "A New Date-List," 36–37; this letter is preserved in *Cantanbrig. Colleg. S. Trinit.* O.3.48, s. XII, f. 64ᵛ-65ᵛ); *ep.* 44, whose bearer is called Theocharistus (PG 91, 644D–645A), and *ep.* 45, whose bearer is mentioned, but not by name (PG 91, 649C). In all cases, the bearer is highly commended and praised by Maximus.

35. John Mauropous in the eleventh century expresses his frustration with overly lively bearers: "Letters are as useless as a lantern at midday . . . when you have a talkative and many-voiced bearer" (*ep.* 2; cited by Mullett, *Theophylacht of Ochrid*, 36).

36. On the performance and re-performance of letters, see Mullett, *Theophylacht of Ochrid*, 39–40.

37. Littlewood, "An Ikon of the Soul," 219–20.

38. At the most elementary level, Greek rhetorical artistry demanded that one fit one's speech to one's hearers and object of discourse. Consequently, different genres of rhetoric are classified not according to style but according to context, falling most

## The tactic of introduction

Let us look in full at the opening address of *Letter* 2 to begin to identify its rhetorical rationale:

> You, the God-protected ones, cleave through grace to holy love towards God and your neighbor and care about appropriate ways of practicing it. Already when I was present with you I had learnt, and now I am absent it is no less true, that you suffer those things that are, and are said, to belong to divine love, in order to possess this divine thing, which in its power is beyond circumscription or definition. For you not only do good to those who are present, but you long to do good to those who are absent, however great the distance in space, and thus on each occasion I learn of the greatness of the largess of your love both from what has come to pass amongst you, and also from your honored words, in which I can see the form of the divine grace that has been imprinted in you, as in a mirror, so that I am gladdened and rejoice. And I give thanks for you to God, the giver of good things, and I do not cease to cry out with the Apostle, "Blessed is the God and Father of our Lord Jesus Christ, who has blessed us with every spiritual blessing in the heavenly places" (Eph 1:3). For I know quite certainly that your holy soul is indissolubly bound to my wretchedness in the spirit through love, having the law of grace as a bond of friendship, in accordance with which you invisibly embrace me, making my sinful shamefulness vanish in comparison with your own excellence.[39]

We can note two obvious but fundamental points here. First, this passage (which is in fact one long sentence in the Greek) works as an introduction, not simply because it comes first, but because it makes known the subject of the letter, "love," along with some subtopics that Maximus will focus on. Secondly, this long introductory sentence is a piece of praise, a fact we will deal with in the next section.

Firstly, then, Maximus' introduction functions like a good introduction should, showing forth the letter's general theme, divine love, as

---

generally into the three γενή of deliberative, forensic, and epideictic rhetoric (Stowers, *Letter-Writing*, 53–55). See also, Pernot, *La rhétorique de l'éloge*, 664–67. In the letter-writing handbook, *Epistolary Types*, Pseudo-Demetrius shows that the letter was not exempt from this maxim: they "can be composed in a great number of styles, but are written in those which always fit the particular circumstance" (Malherbe, *Ancient Epistolary Theorists*, 30–31, including trans.).

39. *Ep.* 2 (PG 91, 392D–393B; trans. Louth, *Maximus the Confessor*, 82).

well as the specific claims that the author will make about it. The first specific claim anticipated in the introduction is that divine love collapses distances. Maximus exemplifies all three facets of the common epistolary trope of *distance*:[40] twice he deploys the couplet of *presence-absence*,[41] and then summons the notion of distance itself (the conceptual poles being *near-far*), and then towards the end of the introduction the conception shifts to *separation-unity*, as Maximus claims that despite his absence "your holy soul is indissolubly [ἀλύτως] bound to my wretchedness." These are conventional tools for introducing letters in late-antiquity, and Maximus employs them in other letters from his first period of exile (c. 626–33).[42] Here, however, this rhetorical trope plays a theological role. It introduces the patterns by which divine love expresses itself, as Maximus will describe it in the body of the letter. Love collapses distances, making present what is absent:

> Love grant[s] enjoyment of those things believed in and hoped for, by itself making present the things to come . . . [L]ove gives faith the reality of what it believes and hope the presence of what it hopes for . . .[43]

Or again, love gathers all things into inseparable unity with each other and with God:

> [T]he power of love . . . gathers together what has been separated . . . It levels off and makes equal any inequality or difference in inclination in anything, or rather binds it to that praiseworthy inequality, by which each is so drawn to his neighbor in preference to himself and so honors him before himself, that he is eager to spurn any obstacle in his desire to excel. And for this reason each one . . . is gathered to the one singleness and sameness, in accordance with which nothing is in anyway separated from what is common to all, so that each is in each, and all in all, or rather in God and in others, and they are radiantly established as one . . .[44]

---

40. Mullett, *Theophylacht of Ochrid*, 13–15.

41. Presence-absence (παρουσία-ἀπουσία) is the most common form of this trope, identified and traced by Karlsson, "Formelhaftes in Paulusbriefen," 138–41, who suggests that Paul (Col 2:5) is the archetype for this epistolary convention amongst Christian writers. See also Karlsson, *Idéologie et ceremonial*, 40–45.

42. See *eps.* 4, 5, 8, 13, 23, 24, and 27, noted by Jankowiak and Booth, "A New Date-List," 34.

43. *Ep.* 2 (PG 91, 393D, 396C; trans. Louth, *Maximus the Confessor*, 83).

44. *Ep.* 2 (PG 91, 400A–B; trans. Louth, *Maximus the Confessor*, 85).

Another of the letter's specific claims is introduced in the address when Maximus speaks, in a way redolent of Philippians 2:6–7, of the "form" (μορφή) of divine grace conspicuous in his addressees. This theme will appear later in the letter: "God is thus manifest . . . , taking shape [μορφούμενος] according to the specific character of the virtue of each [κατὰ τὴν ἰδιότητα τῆς ἀρετῆς ἐχάστου⁴⁵] through love for humankind."⁴⁶

A third specific claim is introduced at the end of the address when Maximus uses another familiar rhetorical trope, this time of *comparison*. Maximus says, addressing John, "you make my sinful shamefulness vanish in comparison with your own excellence." The word for "comparison" is normally σύγκρισις in the textbook accounts of praise oratory (known as "encomion" or "epideictic"),⁴⁷ but Maximus chooses the alternative term παράθεσις, which is also sometimes used.⁴⁸ The comparison was one of the longstanding exercises that would have been practiced as part of the *progymnasmata*, or preparatory exercises, of late-antique Greek education. In the comparison, the student or orator compares their object of praise with a familiar figure of the past (and sometimes present), to demonstrate the superiority, equality, or, in the case of blame oratory, inferiority of the object at hand.⁴⁹ In epistolary literature, however, which always

45. We can note in passing yet another characteristic expression of the rule of "proportion."

46. *Ep.* 2 (PG 91 401A–B; trans. Louth, *Maximus the Confessor*, 86).

47. At least three influential textbooks include "comparison" as a crucial ingredient of praise oratory: Hermogenes' *Progymnasmata* 8 (Rabe, *Hermogenis Opera*, 19); Aphthonius' *Progymnasmata* 8 (Rabe, *Aphthonii Progymnasmata*, 22); and Menander's *On Epideictic* 376–77 (Russell and Wilson, *Menander Rhetor*, 92–93). On the "comparison," see Webb, "Praise and Persuasion," 130. For brief discussions of how the rhetorical trope of "comparison" was appropriated in Byzantine letters, see Karlsson, *Idéologie et cérémonial*, 79–81, and Kennedy, *Greek Rhetoric*, 31. For case studies on Christian appropriation of the "comparison" trope, see Young, *Biblical Exegesis*, 109–12, 115–16.

48. E.g., Aphthonius, *Progmymnasmata* 8 (Rabe, *Apthonii Progymnasmata*, 22). Gregory of Nyssa, a seasoned rhetorician, also uses this term for the laudatory comparison. He interprets Song 7:1–5 as an epideictic speech (ἐγκώμιον), orated by the divine Bridegroom in praise of the bride, a speech that, he says, proceeds through παράθεσις, "setting [two things] alongside [each other]," and ὁμοίωσις, "likening" them to each other (*cant.* 7 [GNO 6, 232]). Later he says that the beauty of the Bride is praised "by way of some appropriate comparison and juxtaposition" (διὰ τινος καταλλήλου συγκρισεώς τε καὶ παραθέσεως, *cant.* 15 [GNO 6, 450]), using σύγκρισις and παράθεσις synonymously. Gregory also uses this term, as Maximus does here in *Ep.* 2, to describe the tactic of comparing good with bad to make the good seem better (*cant.* 8 [GNO 6, 250–51]).

49. Kennedy, *Greek Rhetoric*, 25, 63–64; Pernot, *La rhétorique de l'éloge*, book 2, 692–97. On the teaching of praise rhetoric in late-antique Greek education, specifically

borrowed and appropriated the tropes of formal and theorized rhetoric, the comparison is normally set up (usually in the introduction) between the recipient and the author himself, in order to praise the recipient and establish the author's humility.[50] In these cases, the praise normally took for its subject-matter the correspondent's and the author's own literary artistry.[51] By contrast, in Maximus' writings, we will see again and again, the comparison is between levels of virtue and spiritual achievement. As Blowers summarizes, Maximus "abases himself as author, confessing his own poverty of linguistic or intellectual ability and moral virtue while esteeming that of his addressee." Blowers characterizes this rhetorical move as a "pattern of authorial κένωσις . . . paralleling the kenosis of the Logos in his incarnation." Blowers suggests that this proves how, for Maximus, theological writing is itself a "participation in the grand *oikonomia* of divine revelation" and the self-emptying of the Word.[52] There is surely some truth in this: as we will continue to see, Maximus' tactic of comparison does indeed typically praise acts of writing and theological questioning for being imitations of the Word's kenotic condescension. However, these are always *other people's* writings, never Maximus' own. My smaller suggestion is that the introductory comparison is a rhetorical tactic that Maximus generally uses to prepare his reader to understand the topic of the self-emptying of the Word. In the case of *Letter* 2's opening address, Maximus paints a salvific "comparison" or "placing together," "making my sinful shamefulness vanish in comparison [παραθέσει] with your own excellence." This introductory comparison anticipates the salvific comparison of God and man, divine love and sickly human love, in Jesus, that Maximus will elucidate in the body of the letter with the language of Philippians 2.[53] By the time his hearers reach this account, Maximus has already prepared them for it with his rhetorical comparison in the introduction, which spelled out this same pattern in their own lives.

It is perhaps unremarkable to point out that Maximus' introduction introduces the themes of his letter, or reveals what he thinks the letter is about. Nonetheless, this is a tactic that I suggest lasts his writing career

---

in the *progymnasmata* form, see Pernot, *La rhétorique de l'éloge*, book 1, 57–59.

50. On epistolary humility see Mullett, "The Classical Tradition," 76.

51. Littlewood, "An Ikon of the Soul," 203. See, for example, the long epistolary correspondence between Basil and the rhetor Libanius (Basil, *ep.* 335–59 [LCL 270: 285–329]), in which the two take turns to praise one another's eloquence.

52. Blowers, *Maximus the Confessor*, 71–73.

53. *Ep.* 2 (PG 91, 397B–400A).

and offers indispensable but overlooked insight into his christological letters. What are we to conclude, for example, when Maximus introduces a
dry and polemical account of Christ's wills with praise of his addressee's
infinite and divine desire? This and other such questions will occupy us
in the next chapter.

## The tactic of praise

What is remarkable about Maximus' introduction in *Letter* 2 is that,
unlike any introduction a modern reader will be familiar with, it not
only introduces the letter's claims—that divine love collapses distances,
imprints the form of God in people, and brings salvation through Jesus—but it declares that the addressees breathtakingly model all of these
claims in themselves. Blowers is surely correct when he says of *Letter*
2's opening address that here "[l]ove must be approached . . . from the
standpoint of what John . . . has experienced, the gracious activity, and
indeed *affect*, of divine love that has formed or taken possession of him
over time, rather than from the standpoint of an antecedent love-logic."[54]
Maximus tells his readers, in effect: you are only going to be able to discuss and understand divine love once you see how divine love has already
taken shape in you. Put simply, one knows divine love by likeness. But
something more precise is going on here, that we have noted in passing
when discussing the "comparison" tactic above: *Letter* 2's introduction is
a rhetorical device, namely, an exemplary piece of *praise*. Maximus' aim
is thus rhetorical: he wishes not to explain but to *argue* and *persuade*; he
wishes not to outline how divine love might be known or understood,
but rather actually to set this epistemology going, to stimulate John into
an affective stance whereby he might be persuaded of what Maximus has
to teach him. Here in *Letter* 2, then, and elsewhere as we will continue to
see, Maximus aims to identify and instill the content of his teaching in
the practice of his hearers by suggestively pointing his praise, attempting
to persuade his readers of his claims by praising them for having already
practically adopted them.[55]

---

54. Blowers, *Maximus the Confessor*, 255.

55. For another example, in a brief letter to the same John on the topic of "godly
sorrow" (2 Cor 7:10), Maximus opens by praising John as an exemplar of nothing
other than "praiseworthy [ἐπαινετήν] sorrow" (*ep.* 4 [PG 91, 413A]).

A caveat is in order before examining Maximus' praise rhetoric any further. The term "praise rhetoric" is in danger of translating "flattery" or "sycophancy" in a modern reader's mind. This is by no means what Maximus thinks he is up to. As Krastu Banev has emphasized in his study of the rhetoric of Theophilus of Alexandria, in Greek oratorical culture rhetorical conventions and their aim of persuasion were considered a genuine "argumentative strategy." Modern readers miss a huge amount if they assume that rhetoric simply meant a "stylistic" strategy. Rhetoric was not imagined to decorate argumentative content but to *contribute* to it.[56] Maximus, too, takes for granted that praise, as a rhetorical form, is a valid argumentative device. Specifically, in *Letter* 2 and in the letters that will concern us for the rest of this study, Maximus adopts praise rhetoric as a tool in the service of pedagogy and epistemology: his aim is to make readers understand and assent to the teaching on offer in the letter. In *Opusculum* 9, Maximus wonderfully exposes the strategy lying behind his use of praise. During his stay in Sicily, on the way to Rome in 646, the Confessor was stung by criticism levelled against him for adulating Pyrrhus, now a key monthelite spokesman, in a letter during the nascent years of the monoenergist controversy.[57] In the face of this criticism, Maximus aims to retrospectively justify his praise:

> [T]he divine Word exhorts us to love and bless those who are different from us or write against us. At the same time, instead of exasperating him [Pyrrhus], rather I was eager to make the man agreeable with praises [ἐγχωμίοις] of him, so that he would assent to the dogmas that I had piously declared in line with the teaching of the holy fathers. Whence, in this way, in the letter I sent to him, I confessed to have understood the things he wrote to me, inciting him, as I said, and inviting him to agree with the pious account [λόγου] that would procure for him the greatest salvation, if he acquiesced and confessed with us what we had written: that is, two natural energies of the one and same Christ, God.[58]

Phil Booth somewhat simplifies Maximus' defense here: "the words of praise that he had so lavished on his correspondent," Booth summarizes,

---

56. Banev, *Theophilus of Alexandria*, 69–71.

57. The letter in question is *ep.* 19, dated by Jankowiak and Booth to 633 or early 634 ("A New Date-List," 42). For more on the context of *op.* 9, see Jankowiak and Booth, "A New Date-List," 64–65.

58. *Op.* 9 (PG 91, 132A–B).

are "excused [by Maximus] as a mere expression of humble Christian
love for one's opponents."[59] Maximus does indeed say that praise follows
the divine order of love, but Booth misses the crucial point that, as Maximus specifies, praise is an argumentative weapon of orthodoxy: it "makes
someone agreeable"—literally, it "flattens" or "smoothes" out (ὁμαλίζειν)
a person—so that they might be in a mind to accept the truth handed
them. Maximus himself is clear, then, that praise is an argumentative
method that he uses in letters to persuade his recipients of his teaching. To summarize something of Maximus' defense with an analogy: if
an eight-year-old were to come to her art teacher with a grotesque and
undecipherable self-portrait and the teacher were to congratulate her,
"well done, your painting has beautiful colors," or, "I can recognize you
in that, keep going," no wise observer would accuse the teacher of flattery.
Similarly, Maximus says that he dishes out praise not as a manipulative
or deceitful tactic. Rather, he understands it as a normal, sensible, and
honest method of teaching, argument, and persuasion.

With this caveat in mind, we can examine the praise rhetoric of
*Letter* 2 in more detail. There are a number of signals in the praise passages of *Letter* 2 that firmly place Maximus as an inheritor of late-antique
Greek rhetorical traditions, which showed their appreciation for the indispensable argumentative function of rhetoric by churning out numerous rhetorical textbooks. The first thing to notice from these textbooks
is that, by the time Maximus was writing, oratory that dealt in praise or
blame—known as "encomion" or "epideictic"—had long been assigned
a specific order. This order is most clearly summarized in the late fourth
century *Progymnasmata* of Aphthonius—a text that had probably found
influence amongst Christian circles by Maximus' time (judging by the
fact that it attracted an introduction by a Christian writer):[60]

> This then is the division of the encomion. You should elaborate
> it with the following headings. You will construct a preamble
> [προοιμιάσῃ] appropriate to the subject; then you will state the
> person's origin [γένος], which you will divide into nation, home-
> land, ancestors, and parents; then upbringing [ἀνατροφήν],
> which you will divide into habits and acquired skill and prin-
> ciples of conduct; then you will compose the greatest heading of
> the encomion, deeds [πράξεις], which you will divide into those
> of mind and body and fortune: mind, as courage or prudence;

59. Booth, *Crisis of Empire*, 216.
60. Kennedy, *Progymnasmata*, 90–91.

body, as beauty or swiftness or strength; and fortune, as power and wealth and friends; after these a comparison [σύγκρισιν], attributing superiority to what is being celebrated by contrast [ἐκ παραθέσεως]; then an epilogue [ἐπίλογον], rather fitting prayer [εὐχῇ].[61]

Aphthonius recommends the following order of topics for praise oratory (or alternatively "blame" oratory [ψόγος][62]): "preamble," "origin," "upbringing," "deeds" ("the greatest heading"—τὸ μέγιστον κεφάλαιον), "comparison," and finally "epilogue," which is appropriately written as a "prayer." Aphthonius is not inventing something new, but summarizing existing practices. A few decades earlier, for example, in the late third century, a text on epideictic (praise) oratory attributed to Menander bears ample witness to the same order of praise.[63] When the scheme that Aphthonius outlines was appropriated in Christian discourse, it was stripped of its worldly ingredients—"origin," "upbringing," and deeds of "body" or "fortune"—to be left with a simplified order whose goal was praise of moral or spiritual character: "preamble," "deeds" of virtue (or vice), "comparison," "epilogue." Around the turn of the fourth century, this scheme appears in the blame discourses of the letters of Theophilus, archbishop of Alexandria, as Banev has recently pointed out.[64]

Maximus' sophistication and technical knowledge in matters of rhetoric was clearly far inferior to that of a writer like Theophilus. Nonetheless, in the introduction to *Letter* 2 he distinctly echoes this encomiastic menu. We have already noted the "comparison," but let us look at the opening passage again to identify this order fully:[65]

61. *Progymnasmata* 8 (Rabe, *Aphthonii*, 21–22; trans. Kennedy, *Progymnasmata*, 108).

62. *Progymnasmata* 9 (Rabe, *Aphthonii*, 27–28; trans. Kennedy, *Progymnasmata*, 111).

63. The author of *On Epideictic* takes this order for granted repeatedly in different contexts, whether instructing how to praise an emperor (368–77 [Russell and Wilson, *Menander*, 76–95]), an arriving guest (378–81 [Russell and Wilson, *Menander*, 94–101]), someone celebrating their birthday (412–13 [Russell and Wilson, *Menander*, 158–61]), a governor (414–18 [Russell and Wilson, *Menander*, 164–71]), or a festival or city (424–28 [Russell and Wilson, *Menander*, 182–91]).

64. Banev, *Theophilus of Alexandria*, 114–17.

65. The following analysis and categorization of Maximus' praise rhetoric owes a lot to Banev's parallel analysis of an invective passage from one of Theophilus of Alexandria's letters (*Theophilus of Alexandria*, 114–17).

[**PREAMBLE:**] You, the God-protected ones, cleave through grace to holy love towards God and your neighbor and care about appropriate ways of practicing it. Already when I was present with you I had learnt, and now I am absent it is no less true, that you suffer those things that are, and are said, to belong to divine love, in order to possess this divine thing, which in its power is beyond circumscription or definition. [**DEEDS:**] For you not only do good to those who are present, but you long to do good to those who are absent, however great the distance in space, and thus on each occasion I learn of the greatness of the largess of your love, both from what has come to pass amongst you and also from your honored words, in which I can see the form of the divine grace that has been imprinted in you, as in a mirror, so that I am gladdened and rejoice. [**PRAYER:**] And I give thanks for you to God, the giver of good things, and I do not cease to cry out with the Apostle, "Blessed is the God and Father of our Lord Jesus Christ, who has blessed us with every spiritual blessing in the heavenly places" (Eph 1:3). [**COMPARISON:**] For I know quite certainly that your holy soul is indissolubly bound to my wretchedness in the spirit through love, having the law of grace as a bond of friendship, in accordance with which you invisibly embrace me, making my sinful shamefulness vanish in comparison with your own excellence.[66]

Maximus sets the theme of sharing in divine love in a *preamble*; he ignores the unnecessary topics of lineage and upbringing; instead, he moves straight on to praise the recipients' *deeds*—of virtue, or "mind" in Aphthonius' terms, and not of "body" or "fortune"; then he ends with a prayer of thanksgiving and a *comparison* (which Aphthonius too called παράθεσις). There is no epilogue, unless we consider the prayer and comparison as together making up an epilogue.

Clearly Maximus does not neatly follow the typical procedure of praise rhetoric laid out by Aphthonius. He nonetheless takes some of Aphthonius' ingredients and maintains their order. We will continue to see that Maximus' personalized order of praise rhetoric, exemplified in *Letter* 2, occurs with consistency in a number of his other letters and sent treatises. It is worth laying out this order and its clear link with the traditional order of praise rhetoric summarized in textbooks like Aphthonius':

---

66. *Ep.* 2 (PG 91, 392D–393B; trans. Louth, *Maximus the Confessor*, 82).

| Apthonius' order of praise rhetoric | Maximus' order of praise rhetoric |
|---|---|
| 1. Preamble | 1. Preamble (topic) |
| 2. Origin | 2. Deeds ("you enact/display this topic in yourselves like this . . .") |
| 3. Upbringing | |
| 4. Deeds | 3. Comparison ("I am worthless compared to you") |
| 5. Comparison | |
| 6. Epilogue/prayer | |

This threefold order of praise is Maximus' epistolary signature, and, like Theophilus' version, it represents a Christian or monastic makeover of the traditional order: Maximus strips the worldly ingredients (lineage, upbringing, deeds of "body" and "fortune"), focuses on success in deeds of virtue, and crowns the set piece with a "comparison" between the lofty recipients and his own lowly self. The comparison, and not the deeds, perhaps forms "the greatest heading" for Maximus; its rhetorical role has been amplified by the supreme monastic ideal of humility and by the theological topic of God's own lowliness in the incarnation.

The closest semblance to Maximus' encomiastic structure that I have come across from his own period is a letter from Sergius of Constantinople to Cyrus of Alexandria, two monoenergist patriarchs. The letter is taken up with praise of Cyrus' *Announcement* or *Pact of Union*, with its nine articles of faith.[67] Analyzed in Aphthonius' terms, Sergius begins with a preamble, followed by a section recounting Cyrus' deeds, which makes up the body of the letter, and then finishes with a prayerful epilogue.[68] The comparison is missing however, and is a distinctive feature of Maximus' praise rhetoric.

Just as the address of *Letter* 2 echoes a long-established textbook procedure of praise oratory, the letter's conclusion shows Maximus' similarly distant yet engrained familiarity with other technicalities of the genre. Towards the end of the letter, Maximus introduces divine "love" itself as the speaker, who lauds John at length "through" the words of Jeremiah (Bar 4:1–4; 3:14; Jer 38:3–4; 6:16).[69] Maximus then finds his

67. For the background to the *Announcement*, and the text itself with English translation, see Allen, *Sophronius of Jerusalem*, 28, 168–73.

68. *Sergii Constantinopolitani epistula secunda ad Cyrum Alexandrinum*, in Allen, *Sophronius*, 176–83.

69. *Ep.* 2 (PG 91, 405A–D).

own voice again to praise his recipients with some more passages from the prophets. Then finally he concludes as follows:

> I have no more words to manifest the secret disposition of your soul. For I have nothing worth mentioning alongside your goods that I can offer to God and to you, except to wonder [θαυμάζειν] mightily at you, approve your right actions, rejoice that your good deeds [ἔργων] draw down the mercy of God, and through you praise [ἐπαινεῖν] virtue, and through virtue hymn [ἀνυμνεῖν] God, for virtue has united you to God.[70]

Maximus demonstrates his fluency in the basics of praise oratory by distinguishing between the different kinds of praise he offers: the virtue of his hearers receives "praise" (ἔπαινος), Maximus "wonders at" or "admires" (θαυμάζειν) the hearers themselves (and again, it is "deeds" that are the object of praise), and then "hymns" (ἀνυμνεῖν) God. These are all pieces of codified vocabulary in Greek praise rhetoric: ἔπαινος is praise in its most generic sense,[71] "wonder" is its common and emphatic substitute,[72] and "hymns" (ὕμνοι) and "hymning" (ὑμνεῖν) are reserved for the divine, or at least denote a "pious" kind of praise.[73]

In the praising introduction and conclusion of *Letter* 2, then, it is clear that Maximus has imbibed the structure and language of conventional praise rhetoric. However, Maximus' praise rhetoric cannot be straightforwardly identified as a piece of encomiastic oratory, at least for the simple fact that it is a letter and not a public speech, and takes up the praising mode only in the introduction and conclusion. Rather, Maximus adopts certain aspects of formal praise oratory in an epistolary context, and in doing so he stands in an established literary tradition. Although Greek letter-composition never crystallized into a systematic or technical

70. *Ep.* 2 (PG 91, 408A; trans. modified from Louth, *Maximus the Confessor*, 89).

71. In his *Panegyric of Saints Cyril and John*, Sophronius of Jerusalem (or "the Sophist"), Maximus' master and teacher, also distinguishes ἔπαινος as generic praise, which includes in itself other specific techniques of praise, namely, the ἐγκώμιον (Bringel, "Introduction," in PO 51, 7–8).

72. Pernot, *La rhétorique de l'éloge*, book 1, 282–84.

73. Pernot, *La rhétorique de l'éloge*, book 1, 82–84, 216–18. For examples of accounts of epideictic types that specify ὕμνοι as a subdivision of ἔπαινος, see the work probably dating from the late third century ascribed to Menander, *On Epideictic* 331 (Russell and Wilson, *Menander*, 2–3), and Nicolaus the Sophist's fifth-century synthesis of some previous progymnasmata traditions (Felten, *Nicolai Progymnasmata*, 47; trans. Kennedy, *Greek Rhetoric*, 154). Young summarizes Christian appropriation of the rhetorical genre of panegyric to the gods, in *Biblical Exegesis*, 111–12.

rhetorical form of its own, letters always harvested from the systems and rules of other kinds of familiar rhetorical speech, including praise speeches.[74] At least since the epistolary handbook falsely attributed to Demetrius of Phalerum, dating as early as the second century BC, Greek letters had been categorized into widely recognized "types," employed in different contexts or situations.[75] Pseudo-Demetrius lists twenty-one and the handbook of pseudo-Libanius in the fourth century CE has forty-two. Importantly, included in both lists is the "praising" (ἐπαινετικός) type. For pseudo-Demetrius, the praising letter "encourages" or "exhorts" (παρακαλέω) the habits of virtue and conduct of its recipient(s).[76] Pseudo-Libanius has more to say about this type than the others on his list, but his concern is to distinguish it from the formal encomium rather than to elucidate what praise consists of, beyond pointing out that *virtue*—rather than the person's origin, lineage, deeds, etc.—is its object: "The praising [ἐπαινετική] style is that in which we praise [ἐπαινοῦμεν] someone eminent in virtue. We should recognize that praise differs from an encomium. For praise is laudatory speech praising one thing [virtue], but an encomium is encomiastic speech embracing many things in itself."[77]

One can see how Maximus' rhetorical style roughly conforms to such generic late-antique categorizations. The introduction of *Letter* 2 could well be classed as the "praising" epistolary type in pseudo-Demetrius' description—that is, laudatory encouragement of the recipient. The address also neatly fits into pseudo-Libanius' category, praising the virtue enacted by Maximus' addressees, rather than cataloguing their lineage and biography like an encomium.

Textbook accounts of epistolary rhetoric like the ones mentioned are rare,[78] and Maximus probably had not read them. Rather, he echoes them in so far as they represent the conventional practice of late-antique Greek letter-writing. Epistolary rhetoric was largely learnt not through textbooks but, at the most, through imitating model letters and, at the

---

74. Stowers, *Letter-Writing*, 34.

75. For a useful analysis of the sources of evidence for ancient Greek and Latin epistolary theory, see Poster, "A Conversation Halved," 21–51.

76. *Epistolary Types* (Malherbe, *Ancient Epistolary Theorists*, 36).

77. Pseudo-Libanius, *Epistolary Styles* 30 (Malherbe, *Ancient Epistolary Theorists*, 70–71). On the distinctions in the wider epideictic tradition between ἔπαινος and ἐγκώμιον, see Pernot, *La rhétorique de l'éloge*, book 1, 118–27.

78. Kennedy, *Greek Rhetoric*, 72.

least, through sheer quotidian familiarity with the genre.[79] Maximus must have learnt to write letters in just this way, by imitation and familiarity. For example, if we look to the practice of letter-writing among Maximus' contemporaries and Christian forebears, we immediately find two features that Maximus has naturally adopted. First, praise of the addressee is a common and lasting epistolary convention, and, secondly, this praise is often placed at the outset of the letter. We find numerous letters begun in praise of their addressee amongst the epistolary corpora of the great Greek Christian writers—Cyril of Alexandria[80] and Gregory of Nyssa,[81] for example. It is clear that this was common practice in Maximus' day too. In documents that survive from the christological debates that defined Maximus' political and theological climate, we find his contemporaries opening their letters with sentences praising their addressees. For example, each of the four letters sent between Cyrus the Patriarch of Alexandria and Sergius the Patriarch of Constantinople—a correspondence that takes us from the whisperings of the monoenergist position in the year 626 right into the heart of the controversy in 633[82]—is begun in praise of the addressee with numerous lofty titles: "Honoured-by-God" (θεοτίμητος); "God-strengthened" (θεοστήρικτος); "God-taught" (θεοδίδακτος); "Most-dear-to-God" (θεοφιλέστατος); "Thrice-blessed" (τρισμακάριστος); "Your Love-of-God" (ἡ θεοφιλία ὑμῶν).[83] In Maximus' *Letter* 2, and in numerous other letters that we will examine, he adopts this basic epistolary convention: he reserves praise rhetoric for the introduction, and sometimes conclusion (with the result that the paraenetic or didactic style in the body of the letter can feel abruptly contrasting).

From this brief tour through the late-antique categorizations and epistolary applications of praise rhetoric, it becomes clear that Maximus framed *Letter* 2 with a brand of praise rhetoric that was a confection of conventional ingredients. Maximus is quite original, however, in the

79. Poster, "A Conversation Halved," 21–51.

80. E.g. *ep.* 55.1 (ACO 1.1.4, 49); *ep.* 56.1 (*Codex Vaticanus gr. 1431*, 17; trans. FC 77, 37).

81. E.g. *ep.* 10.1 (GNO 8/2, 39–40); *ep.* 12.1–2 (GNO 8/2, 42–43); *ep.* 18.1–3 (GNO 8/2, 58–59).

82. Allen, *Sophronius*, 19, 30.

83. These texts are presented with English translation in Allen, *Sophronius*, 160–67, 174–83. For two more letters that begin with praise of the addressee, see the correspondence between Sergius and Pope Honorius, presented in Allen, *Sophronius*, 182–209.

function he makes his praise rhetoric play. In the letters between Cyrus and Sergius, the praise is generic, a matter of protocol and courtesy. The praise form floats freely from the content. By contrast, in Maximus' *Letter* 2, praise is lengthy, specific, and a matter of theological epistemology. His goal is to communicate his teaching on the nature of divine love, but he seems to feel that he should struggle to fulfil that goal by simply, or even lucidly, explaining what that love is. Instead, he chooses praise rhetoric to communicate it: not to flatter his friends into accepting his teaching (which is the feeling one gets in the letters of Sergius especially), but to identify the content of his teaching in his friends, to spell it out not only onto a page but into their habits of mind and life. We have seen that he does this almost systematically in his introduction, anticipating the important themes of his letter by first ideally locating them in the lives of his correspondents. I know that divine love is a mystery diffi-cult to understand, Maximus tells them, but you might begin to grasp it when you see how your own life has become a likeness of divine love. In short, Maximus' tactic is based on a likeness epistemology, set to his own unique form of epistolary praise rhetoric.

It is worth recapping here the signature rhetorical-epistemological strategy that *Letter* 2 demonstrates, and which we will continue to see is absolutely typical of Maximus' epistolary procedure. Maximus opens his pedagogical letters with an address that introduces the letter's content with praise, and that has a structure similar to the traditional order of encomiastic oratory (preamble, deeds, comparison); the address praises the reader for manifesting and living out the letter's content; the goal of this tactic is to persuade the readers of the truth of these themes by point-ing out, or coaxing out, their own likeness to them.

## The *Second Letter to Thomas*:
### epistolary rhetoric and christological method

Maximus probably wrote his *Second Letter to Thomas* at least a couple of years later than *Letter* 2,[84] and it shows very clearly that the rhetoric of praise was still his favorite medium for viscerally communicating his teaching.

84. Janssens suggests that Maximus wrote this letter in 634 or a short while after (CCSG 48, xxii–xxiii). Jankowiak and Booth suggest 635 or 636 ("A New Date-List," 46).

As the title suggests, this text is indeed the second of two of Maximus' letters from a single correspondence. The first letter is now known as *Ambigua ad Thomam* (*Difficulties to Thomas*), as it was entitled by Migne in *Patrologia Graeca* 91 (1860).[85] This title is somewhat misleading because, although the text does comprise a short list of attempts at resolving difficult patristic passages, it is in fact a letter. One thousand years before Migne, in the ninth century, Photius of Constantinople, who evidently had both texts grouped together in one manuscript,[86] thought it very obvious that both texts were "letters" from a single correspondence,[87] and even noted Maximus' solid epistolary style.[88] However, René Henry, Photius' twentieth-century translator, failed to recognize the *Difficulties to Thomas* from Photius' description of it (as a letter) because, thanks to Migne's infelicitous title, Henry was not looking for a letter and so was led to the false conclusion that "there exists in Migne no letter to a recipient of this name [Thomas]."[89] In 1681, Thomas Gale's title for the text acknowledged that it was indeed not only a letter, but a "first letter," which included various difficulties: Ἐπιστολὴ πρώτη τοῦ αυτοῦ περὶ διαφόρων ἀπόρων.[90] The *Difficulties to Thomas* and the *Second Letter to Thomas* should thus be read together since they make up a single correspondence.[91]

Thomas the recipient is addressed ἡγιασμένος, "sanctified one." This term suggests that Thomas was a monk,[92] which becomes more likely

---

85. The term *ambigua* was first employed by Eriugena in his Latin translation of *ambig.* in the ninth century, but not as the text's title, only in his introduction to the text. The term was preserved in the introduction and notes of Thomas Gale's edition (1681), but again not in the title (Janssens, CCSG 48, xv–xvi).

86. Canart, "La deuxième Lettre," 416, n. 2.

87. Photius, *Bibliotheca*, cod. 194 (Henry, *Bibliothèque, Tome III [Codices 186–222]*, 87–88).

88. "His lack of clarity does not entail disorder, since he rightly maintains and honors the laws of the letter" (*Bibliotheca*, cod. 192 [Henry, *Bibliothèque, Tome III*, 83).

89. Henry, *Bibliothèque, Tome III*, 87, n. 2.

90. Janssens, CCSG 48, xvi; Canart, "La deuxième Lettre," 417.

91. Recently, van Deun has also made the point that *ambig. Thom.* and *ep. sec.* belong together in light of their mutual genre and addressee. He nonetheless presents the opposite conclusion to me, classifying *ep. sec.*, along with *ambig. Thom.* and *ambig.* as a third selection of "*ambigua*," rather than classifying *ambig. Thom.* as a first letter (van Deun, "Literary Genres," 277).

92. On ἡγιασμένος as a term of address for monks, see Janssens, CCSG 48, xxiii.

when Maximus calls him his "spiritual father and teacher."[93] From an improved edition of the short *Letter* 40 to Stephen, who was apparently an abbot (the title calls him πρεσβύτερος καὶ ἡγούμενος), it seems that Stephen wanted a piece of work done, very possibly a retort to monoenergist opinions, and had asked Maximus if he would carry it out. Maximus says he would gladly undertake the task, but recommends that the "abba Thomas" could also do the job well. It seems that Stephen assigned the task to Thomas, but that Thomas in turn passed it back to Maximus, or at least wrote to Maximus asking for help and clarification. Whatever Thomas' request, Maximus produced his first letter to Thomas (known as *Difficulties to Thomas*) in response, in which he analyzed four contentious or difficult passages by Gregory Nazianzen and one by Dionysius.[94] Thomas wrote back unsatisfied or confused, and Maximus responded with an attempt at further clarification, his *Second Letter to Thomas*.[95]

It might appear, however, that Maximus does little more in this second letter than closely and expressly reiterate much of the first,[96] to the extent that the letter has been largely overlooked in the history of scholarship. Maximus' seventeenth-century editor, Thomas Gale, possessed a manuscript containing both the *Difficulties to Thomas* and a fragmentary *Second Letter to Thomas* but thought it unnecessary to publish the latter because it repeated the former. Franz Öhler followed this decision in his edition of 1857. Consequently, the *Second Letter* was absent both from Migne's reprint of Öhler's edition in 1860 in PG 91,[97] and then from Sherwood's *An Annotated Date-List of the Works of Maximus the Confessor* in 1952, a touchstone resource for scholarship ever since.[98] Even Joshua Lollar, after laboring to produce the text's most recent English translation, avoids analyzing the second letter *at all* in his introduction, "since," he

93. *Ambig. Thom.* prol. (DOML 28, 2–3); *ep. sec.* prol. (CCSG 48, 37).

94. I have drawn all of this from Janssens, CCSG 48, xxiv–xxv, who includes in Greek and summarizes the key passage from *ep.* 40, with the help of a new manuscript being edited by Basile Markesinis. The poor edition available in PG 91, 633C–636A, names "Thalassius" as the recipient. Larchet also suggests that *ambig. Thom.* is the end product of the request mentioned in *ep.* 40, but inevitably gets the wrong end of the stick over the text's back-story due to the incomplete manuscript represented in PG 91 (Larchet, "Introduction," in Ponsoye, *Lettres*, 46–47).

95. Janssens, CCSG 48, xxii.

96. Janssens demarcates which texts from Gregory and Dionysius and which questions from the first letter (*ambig. Thom.*) *ep. sec.* revisits (CCSG 48, xxii).

97. Janssens, CCSG 48, cxxxiii–cxxxvi.

98. Sherwood, *An Annotated Date-List*.

explains in a footnote, "it is fragmentary and consists to a large degree of restatements and direct quotations from the *Ambigua ad Thomam*."[99] In the 2015 date-list compiled by Jankowiak and Booth, this text is included and merits a paragraph.[100] This historic lack of attention is unfortunate because, with a closer glance, the *Second Letter* in fact begins to manifest differences—mainly rhetorical—which are intriguing for my purpose.

For a first difference, in the *Difficulties to Thomas* we can observe that Maximus conducted the letter's conventionally laudatory conclusion in the second person *plural*, no longer addressing Thomas the "sanctified *one*" (ἡγιασμένος) as in the letter's introduction, but the "sanctified *ones*" (ἡγιασμένοι), that is, the monks.[101] The letter was intended, in other words, to be heard by the community of monks surrounding Thomas, which perhaps indicates that this was indeed *the* piece of work that Stephen the abbot originally requested, presumably for the benefit of his monks. As Constas notes, there is a grammatical flexibility between the second person singular and plural in a number of Maximus' letters, which demonstrates that the Confessor expects "that his work will be read by others in addition to the primary addressee." Constas cites the introduction to *Questions to Thalassius* as an example: "I therefore beseech you, most holy ones, as well as all those who, as is likely, will read this work."[102] In the *Second Letter*, however, the second person addresses are *all* in the singular, which suggests Maximus may have expected this letter to be read by the primary addressee alone. Why this shift in Maximus' assumed audience? Perhaps it is explained by the fact that the *Second Letter* is an addendum to the first, concerning a second round of questions and qualms from Thomas. Its subject-matter is to an extent closed to anyone other than Thomas, private simply in virtue of being a second stage in a now self-referencing dialogue, twice removed from Stephen's original request. So, while Thomas may have found the *Second Letter* a useful aid for expounding the ambiguities of the first letter to his fellow monks, Maximus seems to have written it to Thomas alone.

For a second difference, although the *Second Letter* seems to be a private or personal letter in this regard, Maximus heightens his polemical rhetoric and praise rhetoric. As Margaret Mullett has argued, it was

99. Lollar, "Introduction," in CCT 2, 23, n. 41.

100. Jankowiak and Booth, "A New Date-List," 46.

101. *Ambig. Thom.* 5 (DOML 28, 58–59).

102. DOML 28, 59, n. 23; citing *qu. Thal.* intr. (CCSG 7, 21).

not unusual for epistolary rhetoric and convention to be employed across public *and* private letters.[103] Indeed, perhaps Maximus leans more heavily on rhetorical devices in the *Second Letter* precisely because the correspondence is now at its second stage, one-on-one, and Maximus must somehow persuade his recipient of what he has already explained to him very clearly once and finds himself forced to repeat verbatim. Maximus is running low on things to say, I mean; he has no more to add. So instead of saying more he repeats himself more persuasively, with amplified rhetoric. For this or some other reason, a stronger rhetoric undoubtedly distinguishes the *Second Letter* from the *Difficulties to Thomas*. For example, Maximus makes a point of bringing up the monophysite heretic Severus,[104] and he associates those who deny the "essential movement" (οὐσιώδης κίνησις) that belonged to the incarnate Word's human nature with a host of heretics including Severus.[105] By contrast, Maximus felt no need to bolster his previous longer discussion in *Difficulties to Thomas* 5[106] with such a *reductio ad monophysitismum*.[107]

As well as amplifying his polemical rhetoric in this way, Maximus adorns his *Second Letter* with a great deal more *praise* rhetoric than the first. Along with a praise address, a second piece of praise introduces section three on the passage from Dionysius, and then the letter concludes with a third praise passage.

Let us look first to the letter's praise address:

> [PREAMBLE:] They say that virtue is the instantiation of wisdom, and wisdom is the essence of virtue. Accordingly, [1a] the *tropos* of life belonging to contemplatives unwaveringly manifests wisdom, and [2a] the *logos* of contemplation of those engaged in the practical life establishes the firm foundation of virtue. [3a] And the most truthful mark of both is an unswerving, devoted gazing upon that which really is, a gaze

103. Mullett, "The Language of Diplomacy," 212–15. In the same vein, Stowers argues that private and public, or "natural" and "conventional," is not a useful or representative distinction "for either Greco-Roman society in general or for letter-writing" (*Letter-Writing*, 19–20).

104. *Ep. sec.* 2 (CCSG 48, 43).

105. *Ep. sec.* 3 (CCSG 48, 47).

106. Maximus had argued that, with his human nature, Christ possessed a natural human power of κίνησις (*ambig. Thom* 5 [DOML 28, 38–39]). Here in *ep. sec.* 3, Maximus responds to Thomas' further query about this κίνησις.

107. This is the label given by Louth for Maximus' characteristic rhetorical portrayal of his enemies as monophysites ("Dogma and Spirituality," 202).

made up of fear and longing. Longing leads it on by beauty, and fear astounds it with the greatness of the Creator. [4a] Out of this comes the pure [literally "unmixed"] mixture [ἀκραιφνής . . . σύγκρασις] of the worthy with God in union, which makes them undergo by adoption what the Maker is called by nature.

[DEEDS:] Therefore, sanctified one, since more than any other person you have preferred all of these things over created things, [1b] you displayed the appearance of unwavering wisdom in your *tropos* of acting and [2b] you established firmly founded virtue in your *logos* of thought. [3b] And as the marks of both, you have made the convergence with that which truly is, a convergence mixed with longing for and fear of the Creator, [4b] according to which the whole of you has been mixed with the whole of God in spiritual relationship. Truthfully, "you walk in faith" [2 Cor 5:7] towards participation in the form of good things, and this manifests in deification . . . Hence, laboring only for that insatiable desire for deifying knowledge, you possess an ever-moving desire, whose satisfaction in you fathers more longing, paradoxically increasing your appetite for participation.

[COMPARISON:] On account of this [desire for knowledge], you the pearl enquire once again of the mud. "The one who tends himself with grain enquires of the one who covers himself in dung" [Lam 4:5]. The one who is pure and illuminated, I mean, who bears not a hint of matter, enquires of the one who is fleshly and unpersuaded that anything exceeds this slack life. The one who delights in bright and enflamed thoughts enquires of the one who has made the stench of the passions his only sign of life. And you force me, with the unbearable weight of the extremity of your God-imitating emptying, to attach myself to your spiritual words, I who have not yet received "the baptism of John" through practice, nor "heard if there is a Holy Spirit" [Acts 19:2–3] through spiritual contemplation.[108]

First comes the *preamble*, specifying the topic of praise, which in this case is quite a complex piece of theorizing about the ascetic life. In the text above I have labelled four distinct points covered in the preamble (1a–4a). In the *deeds* section that follows, Maximus praises Thomas for enacting each and every one of these points (1b–4b), effectively repeating the preamble but in the second person. Thirdly comes the *comparison* section. Maximus conjures a series of images that contrast Thomas' sparkling spiritual achievements with his own baseness. In short, we have

---

108. *Ep. sec.* prol. (CCSG 48, 37–38; trans. based at points on CCT 2, 77–78).

here a brazen reappearance of Maximus' epistolary "signature," as I called it before: the same threefold rhetorical structure—preamble, deeds, comparison—that we identified in *Letter* 2's introduction. But did he have the same rhetorical goal in mind? In *Letter* 2, he praised his recipients for enacting divine love in order to teach them the content of the letter, namely, divine love. Is Maximus opting for a similar epistemological tactic in the *Second Letter to Thomas*? There is no single theme introduced and carried through in the *Second Letter* as there is in *Letter* 2. Nonetheless, the introduction anticipates at least one crucial theme from the body of the letter and, through its rhetoric of praise, aims to make room for it in Thomas' heart and mind. This is the theme of "mixture."

In the praise address to the first letter of this correspondence, *Difficulties to Thomas*—which, we will point out in the next chapter, also bears the encomiastic order of preamble, deeds, comparison[109]—Maximus had praised Thomas for imitating the "mixture [μίξις] of opposites" that Christ displayed, being at once exalted and lowly.[110] In the introduction to the *Second Letter* above, Maximus improvises more daringly on this theme of "mixture," saying that Thomas has become mixed with God: he praises Thomas for having "made the convergence with that which truly is, a convergence mixed with longing for and fear [πόθῳ καὶ φόβῳ συγκρατουμένην] of the Creator, according to which the whole of you has been mixed [συγκραθείς] with the whole of God in spiritual relationship."[111] Maximus deploys the vocabulary of "mixing" (σύγκρασις and cognates, rather than μίξις) on but a few occasions, three of which shed light on his language here in the address to the *Second Letter*. First, in the opening of his *Commentary on the Our Father*, Maximus uses precisely the same language. He describes "making mixed [σύγκρατον]" "fear" (φόβος) and "desire" (πόθος). These make a difficult and precarious confection whose potential dangers he spends some time exploring. However, when balanced just so, this mixture produces a love (ἀγάπη) oriented "towards God and each other."[112] Similarly, here in the address of the *Second Letter*, Maximus goes on to say that this mixture, so expertly decocted by Thomas, releases a throng of hurtling desires toward God—mentioning three different terms for "desire" in one short

109. *Ambig. Thom.* prol. 1–2 (DOML 28, 2–5).
110. *Ambig. Thom.* prol. 2 (DOML 28, 2–3).
111. *Ep. sec.* prol. (CCSG 48, 38; trans. modified from CCT 2, 78).
112. *Or. dom.* (CCSG 23, 27–28).

sentence, ἔφεσις, πόθος, and ὄρεξις—desires that are "ever-moving," awarded with a satisfaction that "paradoxically" always increases desire. This love is paradoxical and unending because the reality that "mixture" language describes is "deification."[113] So too, and secondly, in *Questions to Thalassius* 54 Maximus maps out the deifying power of love by saying that love "enlaces around God himself, in an erotic mixture [ἐρωτικήν τινα σύγκρασιν], as far as it is possible for human nature, and it forms an immaculate symbiosis with God."[114] Thirdly, in *Difficulty* 10, Maximus describes man's "becoming God" and God's reciprocal "becoming human" as a "mixing [ἐγκεραννύναι] through the Spirit."[115] In summary: in all three of these cases, and in the *Second Letter*'s address, Maximus chooses the language of "mixture" to paint the tension that desire introduces into the reality of deification, a reality authentic but mysterious, thronged about with but ever beckoning and eluding longing.[116] In the address of the *Second Letter*, however, Maximus does not simply describe this deifying mixture, but rhetorically envisions and admires it unfolding in Thomas, his addressee. Why? What is it about this particular letter that requires Thomas to recognize this extraordinary mixing with God, in which, Maximus assures him, he has become involved?

The answer comes in the letter's second section where Maximus has a second go at clarifying a passage in which Gregory makes a strange claim about nothing other than "mixture": "in that he became man," Gregory says, "he was God below, since it [his flesh] was mixed with God and he has become one. In this, the better part achieved the victory."[117] Gregory uses a rare verb here, συνανακεραννύναι, "to be mixed together," which in the praise address Maximus mirrors in his double use of the root verb κεραννύναι (rather than μίξις or cognates, as in the first letter's address). Since the council of Chalcedon, christological languages of "mixture" were highly suspect, and it is thus not surprising that Thomas wrote worriedly asking Maximus for further clarification. But Maximus insists on interpreting Gregory's language exactly as he had done in his

113. *Ep. sec.* prol. (CCSG 48, 39).

114. *Qu. Thal.* 54 (CCSG 22, 202).

115. *Ambig.* 10.9 (DOML 28, 164).

116. For other passages where Maximus uses "mixture" (κρᾶσις and cognates) to describe deification, see *ambig.* 10.35 (DOML 28, 204–5) and *ambig.* 10.41 (DOML 28, 212–13).

117. *Ep. sec.* 2 (CCSG 48, 42; trans. CCT 2, 81), citing Gregory Nazianzen, *or.* 29.19.

first response, in *Difficulties to Thomas* 3: with the notion of mixture, Maximus says, Gregory meant to convey how "the Word actually assumed flesh, deifying it by identifying it with His own hypostasis."[118] Maximus clarifies these words of his for Thomas, saying that he intended them to emphasize "how great an extent to which the victory has become manifest . . . since that which was 'actually' assumed hypostatically was assumed to the point of deification."[119] "How could I make it any clearer?"[120] Maximus asks: "mixing" means deification—in this case as it came about in the man Jesus. Maximus stresses that he has said all he can already, but he also knows that Gregory's words are genuinely difficult and that Thomas may be just as unsatisfied as before. So, instead of solving the difficulty as such, Maximus heightens his rhetoric. On the one hand, he polemically clarifies what Gregory's mingling language does *not* mean, namely, a sort of "vanquishing" (ἐκνικᾶν) of one nature by the stronger, an opinion he polemically attributes to Severus.[121] And with this caveat he also steers clear of any connotations of the mixture of predominance model propounded by Aristotle and some Stoics.[122] On the other hand, and more interestingly, Maximus has prepared Thomas for this second attempt at understanding Gregory's "mixing" language by praising Thomas for his own deifying "mixing" with God in the letter's address above. He has already rhetorically placed Thomas precisely within the difficult, paradoxical knot of desires where this mixture takes place in human lives, on the assumption that this spiritual location or condition will give Thomas a good chance of grasping the paradoxical and deifying mixture of God and man in the incarnation.

The remainder of the *Second Letter* bears this same rhetorical tactic, whereby Maximus encourages in Thomas, through praise, ascetic conditions that imitate the specific aspects of the mystery of the incarnation

118. *Ambig. Thom.* 3.3 (DOML 28, 18–19; modified trans.); Maximus recalls and repeats this phrase at *ep. sec.* 2 (CCSG 48, 42).

119. *Ep. sec.* 2 (CCSG 48, 42–43; trans. CCT 2, 81).

120. *Ep. sec.* 2 (CCSG 48, 42).

121. *Ep. sec.* 2 (CCSG 48, 43).

122. The *locus classicus* is *genn. corr.* 328A, where Aristotle uses the example of a drop disappearing into a greater body of liquid. For an example of a Stoic appropriation of Aristotle's image, see Plutarch, *comm. not.* 37. Gregory of Nyssa infamously employed this model of mixture—a drop absorbed in an ocean—three times (*antirrh.* [GNO 3/1, 201]; *Theoph.* [GNO 3/1, 126–7]; *Eun.* 3 [GNO 2, 132–3]), not, however, to describe the disappearance of Jesus' humanity, but because Gregory thought that the image of an "ocean" aptly expressed the divine properties by which Jesus' humanity was transformed (Steven, "Mixture," 508–16).

that he will go on to discuss. A second example comes, again, in the opening address, this time in the comparison section:

> The one who delights in bright and enflamed thoughts enquires of the one who has made the stench of the passions his only sign of life. And you force me, with the unbearable weight of the extremity of your God-imitating emptying, to attach myself to your spiritual words, I who have not yet received "the baptism of John" through practice, nor "heard if there is a Holy Spirit" [Acts 19:2–3] through spiritual contemplation.[123]

As in the address of *Letter 2*, Maximus clearly deploys the conventional encomiastic trope of *comparison* to paint the pattern of the incarnation in the life of his hearer. He praises Thomas for his "self-emptying" (κένωσις) into what is "fleshly" (σαρκικός), into the "stench of the passions [παθῶν]," and in doing so aims to prepare Thomas to grapple for a second time with the words from his first letter that Maximus will go on to repeat at length:

> Therefore the Word himself has really been emptied out [κενωθείς], without change, into the passibility [παθητόν] of our nature, truly becoming subject to what is naturally perceptible by being made flesh [σαρκώσεως], God made visible; and he was called "God below," making manifest the super-infinite power through naturally passible flesh [σαρκὸς φύσει παθητῆς] . . . [124]

Again, instead of honing a new analysis or explanation of the difficulty, Maximus cites what he has already said, but this time primes it within an intensified rhetorical context of praise, having attempted in the address to bring to life the terms and reality of this difficulty in his hearer.

In the third and final section of the *Second Letter*, Maximus approaches again what he said in the final section of the *Difficulties to Thomas* about movement and activity in Christ in relation to an excerpt from Dionysius' *Letter 4*. Some of the text is missing, but what remains is nearly all rhetorical material: a praising introduction for the section, a denouncement of some heretics, and the letter's praising conclusion. First, then, let us look at the section's praising introduction. After reciting his words from *Difficulties to Thomas* over which Thomas has expressed

---

123. *Ep. sec.* 2 (CCSG 48, 38).

124. *Ep. sec.* 2 (CCSG 48, 42), citing *ambig. Thom.* 3 (DOML 28, 18).

concern, Maximus opens his second attempt at analysis by praising Thomas for imitating the incarnation:

> I wonder at your wisdom, truly beloved, and I will never cease being astounded by its firmness. For you teach by asking questions, you impart wisdom by wishing to become a disciple, you raise up by coming low, and you rectify opposites through opposites, exactly imitating the Lord's saving and philanthropic self-emptying in all and for all.[125]

Next, he cites Thomas' question, praises him at length for asking it, and then affirms briefly that Christ's human nature had its own integral "essential movement." Then comes another *reductio ad monophysitismum*, as Maximus lists some traditional heretics and briefly details the absurdity of their position. Perhaps it is not surprising that, in a tenth-century manuscript, the first part of the third section is preserved by itself,[126] since it would have made a reasonably self-sufficient epistolary unit: the quotation from Dionysius, the long introduction where Maximus praises his recipient and cites and praises his question, and then the affirmation that Christ assumed human flesh not empty of its natural "movement," which merges into a denouncement of heretics who think differently.[127] What is important to note for our purposes is that amidst Maximus' volley of rhetorical devices comes the familiar like-by-like pedagogical move. Maximus aims to teach Thomas the intricacies of the mystery of the incarnation by first praising him for "imitating" it, rhetorically positioning this imitation as the condition for understanding.

Lastly, some manuscripts preserve most of the letter's concluding paragraphs, where Maximus simplifies his christological argument in terse summary: "Thus, if we believe that Christ is actually true God in essence and nature, and that he is actually true man in essence and nature, then nothing is more necessary than to think and to say that he is both."[128] Then follow some final intriguing statements that aptly recap and press forward the argument I have been making so far. Referring to his terse summary, Maximus says that one can either affirm this christological axiom (πίστωσις) by "demonstrating the numerical . . .

---

125. *Ep. sec.* 3 (CCSG 48, 46; trans. modified from CCT 2, 84).

126. Lines 1–58 in CCSG 48, 46–48.

127. *Vaticanus graecus 1809*, folios 195ᵛ–96, detailed by Janssens in CCSG 48, lxxx–lxxxii.

128. *Ep. sec.* 3 (CCSG 48, 49; trans. CCT 2, 87),

distinction" between the two natures, or, "better yet" (μάλιστα), it is sometimes necessary,

> ... to exhibit [this axiom] in the truth [τῇ ἀληθείᾳ συνίστασθαι] and to make visible [ἐμφανῆ ποιεῖσθαι] [see 2 Cor 4:2] the disposition surrounding it, by outlining the right principle of reason [λόγου] and fittingness [καιροῦ], so that we may not only be justified by piously "believing in the heart," but that we may also be saved, by "confessing with the mouth" [Rom 10.10] absolutely everything correctly ... [129]

Maximus thinks that believers manage their christological data best (μάλιστα) with a certain "reason" and "fittingness." What does he mean? Well, Maximus seems here to be making a distinction between a subtle and recondite kind of confirmation (for example, "demonstrating the numerical quantity involved in the distinction—according to essence alone—of those [natures] from which, in which, and which he always is"[130]), and a confirmation certified by an outward and manifest coherence—a "reason" and "fittingness." He expresses this distinction with two pieces of Scripture. First, in the citation above, he adopts the language of 2 Corinthians 4:2 ("we refuse to practice cunning or to falsify God's word; but by the open statement of the truth [τῇ φανερώσει τῆς ἀληθείας συνιστάνοντες] we commend ourselves to the conscience of everyone in the sight of God"),[131] and then summarizes his point with Romans 10:10: we are not only to believe "in the heart," Paul says, but to confess "with the mouth." By the words "reason" and "fittingness" Maximus seems to intend to express the appropriateness of the latter option portrayed in these verses: a doctrine is best communicated and affirmed through its obvious and "visible" coherence or integrity, embodied in the manifest "disposition" of the claimant. In other words, a particular kind of visible habit or temperament must accompany Christology if it is to be grasped by the christologian and their audience. And, as I have been suggesting throughout this analysis, for Maximus such a temperament is nothing other than content embodied, in this case, the pattern of the incarnation imitated and embodied. He immediately makes this clear in the concluding rhetorical comparison:

129. *Ep. sec.* 3 (CCSG 48, 49).
130. *Ep. sec.* 3 (CCSG 48, 49).
131. Trans. NRSV.

> I pray you, my dear Leader, become to me now even more than
> before a most philanthropic judge of what I have written—in-
> asmuch as I have been brought lower by the slackening of my
> virtue and have transfixed the intellectual power of my soul
> with the corruption of the passions—so that by encompassing
> the mass of my evil, that so easily besets me, with the greatness
> of your virtue, you might encourage me . . . and make me new
> by putting off the old [Eph 4:21–24], able to contain only the
> more mystical teaching about Christ, by which the seething of
> the Spirit has been secretly united to you, arousing and warming
> the soul to the love of the Creator alone.[132]

Maximus is explicit here: he pleads that Thomas might understand his
meagre elucidation of the mystery of Christ by himself becoming the
location of that mystery, might view Maximus' sorry words through
Christ's own eyes. Indeed, taken out of context Maximus could very
well be praying to Christ himself in this passage. He assigns to Thomas a
miscellany of christological traits: he hopes that Thomas will receive his
words in *philanthropia*, the term that Maximus always uses for the divine
initiative in the incarnation; then he suggests that Thomas might enable
Maximus to put off his old self and become new, Christ's command in
Ephesians 4, and might lead him to grasp "the more mystical teaching
about Christ," a teaching bound up somehow with the "seething of the
Spirit" that inspires intense love of God.[133]

Maximus asks all this of Thomas "even more than before" (νῦν
μᾶλλον ἢ πρότερον), surely referring to the praise conclusion of the first
letter, *Difficulties to Thomas*, which summoned this same perplexing
bunch of themes:

> As you possess this [confession of Christ's two natures], sancti-
> fied ones, which takes shape in your speech and life, imitate his

132. *Ep. sec.* 3 (CCSG 48, 49; trans. modified from CCT 2, 87).

133. Maximus attributes this same "seething of the Spirit" (ἡ ζέσις τοῦ Πνεύματος)
to Marinus in the praise introduction of another letter (*op.* 7 [PG 91, 69C]). He perhaps
inherited this language from the Cappadocians. Gregory Nazianzen used it to describe
the uncontrollable commotion of the soul brought about through sense perception
(*or.* 17 [PG 35, 965B]). Gregory of Nyssa uses it in his *Homilies on the Song of Songs*:
"when every bodily disposition has been quelled, our mind within us may boil with
love, but only in the Spirit" (*cant.* 1 [GNO 6, 27; trans. Norris, *Homilies*, 28); or again,
like the heat spreading out from the heart throughout the body, the bride accustoms
every aspect of her life "to seethe with the Spirit that spreads from her heart [ζέειν . . .
τῷ ἐκ τῆς καρδίας διήκοντι πνεύματι], and no lawlessness chills the love of God in any
member of her body" (*cant.* 3 [GNO 6, 94–95; trans. Norris, *Homilies*, 242]; see also
*cant.* 9 (GNO 6, 283).

"patience" [see 1 Tim 1:16]; and when you receive this writing, show yourselves to me to be philanthropic judges of what it contains . . . And become to me mediators of reconciliation with him, working "peace which surpasses all understanding" [Phil 4:7], of which the savior himself is the "prince" [Isa 9:6]—who sets free "those who fear him" [Ps 24:14, LXX] from the disorder of the passions—and "Father of the age to come" [Isa 9:6], who begets in the Spirit through love and knowledge "those who will fill the world above" [Gregory Nazianzen, *or.* 38.2].[134]

Again, christological confession is a disposition, something that "takes shape in speech and life," and Maximus' recipients exemplify this disposition by receiving his words in *philanthropia*. He portrays them as possessing a christlikeness that somehow "mediates" Christ's redemption, just as, in the *Second Letter*, Thomas is said to enable Maximus to put off his old self and put on the new; and, again, this reality is shot through with the activity of the Spirit in love.

These parallel conclusions to Maximus' first and second letters to Thomas show clearly enough a single methodological assumption: that the mystery of the incarnation is only ever going to be pondered fruitfully and expressed reliably when one is assimilated to it, when that mystery is allowed to take shape amongst those trying to grasp it.

## Maximus' method in the context of Gregory Nazianzen

The rhetorical-epistemological strategy that this chapter has identified, as far as I can find, is Maximus' own impressively unique invention. He made it up himself. He did not, however, make it out of nothing. We have already seen how Maximus' strategy shows signs of many conventional features of praise rhetoric. It is also worth briefly comparing Maximus' method with the communicative strategies of his most influential predecessor, Gregory Nazianzen, to understand the inheritance upon which Maximus was improvising. My suggestion is not that Maximus consciously drew from Gregory in developing his epistolary strategy. Rather, I simply wish to point out that Maximus was an avid reader of Gregory, that Gregory greatly influenced his theological culture and environment, and that in Gregory's works we find at least three assumptions about literary and epistemological protocol that would have shaped Maximus' intellectual landscape and that come together in Maximus' epistolary praise rhetoric. These assumptions are: that it is often proper to begin a letter

134. *Ambig. Thom.* 5 (DOML 28, 58; trans. modified from CCT 2, 73–74).

with praise of the addressee; that the order of a text or speech has an epis-temological significance; and that certain ethical and ascetic dispositions enable certain epistemic options and, more specifically, christological convictions. Let me take these in turn.

I have already mentioned the fact that by beginning his letters with praise of the addressee Maximus was following a convention practiced by Christian writers for centuries. Gregory commonly exemplifies this same epistolary protocol,[135] and it is one of the basic features that his otherwise more restrained and artistic praise rhetoric shares with Maximus'.

Secondly, for Gregory the opening of a discourse is especially im-portant because it can bear a crucial epistemological value. Christopher Beeley has laid emphasis on the importance and priority that Gregory gives to "purification" as a condition for knowledge.[136] Intriguingly, Beeley furthermore notices that this "priority of purification is also rep-resented in the literary structure of several of Gregory's works." Since purification is the condition for knowledge and understanding in mat-ters of theology, Gregory's exhortations to purification often come *first* in his discourses. And Gregory trusts that this rhetorical placement brings an epistemological advantage. For example, Beeley points out that on a number of occasions in the *Orations* Gregory makes the transition from his introductory discourse on holiness to the oration's doctrinal substance with the following phrase: "Now that we have purified [the listener] with our discourse" (Ἐπεὶ δὲ ἀνεκαθήραμεν τῷ λόγῳ).[137] Beeley does not observe, however, that Gregory in fact takes this maxim straight from Jesus' mouth: "You have already been purified by the word that I have spoken to you" (John 15:3: ἤδη ὑμεῖς καθαροί ἐστε διὰ τὸν λόγον ὃν λελάληκα ὑμῖν).[138] Following the rules of Christ's own discourse (λόγος), then, Gregory assigns an epistemic value to the order of *his* discourse: a well-ordered—and specifically, a well introduced—discourse can genu-inely carry out in the audience the purification necessary to occasion their understanding. Maximus makes just the same move. He develops

135. E.g. *ep.* 8.1 (Gallay, *Lettres* vol. 1, 11); *ep.* 37.1 (Gallay, *Lettres* vol. 2, 46); *ep.* 44.1–3 (Gallay, *Lettres* vol. 1, 576–77); *ep.* 83 (Gallay, *Lettres* vol. 1, 105); *ep.* 140.1–3 (Gallay, *Lettres* vol. 2, 28–29); *ep.* 198.1–2 (Gallay, *Lettres* vol. 2, 90); *ep.* 223.1–2 (Gal-lay, *Lettres* vol. 2, 114–15).

136. Beeley, *Gregory of Nazianzus*, 64–90.

137. Beeley, *Gregory of Nazianzus*, 88. Beeley refers to the following examples: *or.* 28.1; *or.* 20.5; *or.* 39.11. The same phrase also appears at *or.* 4.12 (SC 309, 102–3).

138. Trans. modified from NRSV.

a standard introduction of praise that encourages the appropriate epistemic conditions in his audience.

Thirdly, although "purity" is, for Gregory, a central and generic condition for knowledge because it imitates the objects of theology, he often presents Christ-likeness as the apt condition for knowledge in the context of Christology. He appropriates his likeness epistemology—normally centered around the theme of "purity"—to the task of christological discernment, and Maximus follows him in this. As Andrew Hofer has shown in his recent book, Gregory's favorite and enduring christological method consists in rhetorically identifying the mystery of the incarnation and the events of Christ's life with the events of his own life and the lives of his hearers. Hofer demonstrates this, for example, in an examination of some of Gregory's festal orations (*or.* 38–40),[139] as well as some letters. He gives the example of *Letter* 101, the first of the polemical christological letters to Cledonius,[140] sent in response to news that some followers of Apollinarius were gaining a foothold in the church in Nazianzus.[141] As Hofer summarizes, in this letter Gregory suggests that "[j]ust as the reward of orthodox belief in Christ proposed by Gregory makes right believers to be like Christ himself . . . , so the punishment for the disbelievers makes them resemble, in Gregory's rhetoric, their grotesque account of Christ."[142] To take some examples from the anathema of *Letter* 101, "Whoever does not accept Holy Mary as the Mother of God has no relation with the Godhead,"[143] "Whoever imports two 'sons' . . . and not one and the same Son, loses the adoption promised to those who believe aright,"[144] and, "Whoever does not worship the Crucified is . . . ranked with the God-slaughterers."[145] Gregory summarizes his argument in *Letter* 102 to Cledonius, "Our objection, then, and counter-argument to their mindless opinion on the mind [of Christ], in brief is as follows: they are almost alone in actually suffering the same fate as the object of

---

139. Hofer, *Christ in the Life*, 161–75.

140. Hofer, *Christ in the Life*, 123–51.

141. Williams and Wickham, *On God and Christ*, 149.

142. Hofer, *Christ in the Life*, 131.

143. *Ep.* 101.16 (SC 208, 42–43; trans. Williams and Wickham, *On God and Christ*, 156).

144. *Ep.* 101.18 (SC 208, 44–45; trans. Williams and Wickham, *On God and Christ*, 157).

145. *Ep.* 101.22 (SC 208, 46–47; trans. Williams and Wickham, *On God and Christ*, 157).

their dogmatizing, when they mindlessly amputate the mind."[146] Those who doubt Jesus had a human mind (νόος), Gregory says, are themselves mindless (ἀνόητος). Right or wrong doctrinal confession mirrors one's conduct of life. We find the same assumption at work, also in the context of Christology, in Maximus' *Second Letter to Thomas* and, we will see shortly, in many more of his christological letters.

In summary, Gregory was perhaps Maximus' single greatest patristic influence, and after devotedly reading and interpreting a great number of Gregory's works, Maximus may well have picked up something of Gregory's rhetorical and epistemological methods and applied them with his own, admittedly less sophisticated, rhetorical capacities. At the least, Maximus' unique strategy of epistolary praise rhetoric is redolent of Gregory in its motivating assumptions.

## Conclusion

With the help of two case studies, Maximus' *Letter 2* and the *Second Letter to Thomas*, this chapter has identified a recurring rhetorical tactic: Maximus opens his letter with a passage that introduces the letter's key themes, but obliquely, praising the addressee for reflecting the letter's themes in their own Christian life and practice. By analyzing this typical introductory praise passage in the terms of late-antique rhetorical handbooks, and noticing in particular that its structure (preamble, deeds, comparison) echoes the conventional order of an encomion (preamble, origin, upbringing, deeds, comparison, epilogue), we identified it as a coherent rhetorical form whose aim is to persuade and to improve the communication of the letter's teaching. Crucially, in this rhetorical method, which orders the reader's route to understanding with the patterns and proportions of the reality they are straining towards, we spotted a like-by-like epistemological assumption: Maximus considers theology or doctrinal discernment to be a task requiring dispositions which imitate the divine reality in question. So, the one who manifests divine love in his or her life will understand what divine love is like; the one who imitates the incarnation will be capable of grappling with and expressing its mystery. It is now time to explore how this like-by-like rhetorical and epistemological strategy unfolds in Maximus' other christological letters.

146. *Ep.* 102.5 (SC 208, 72–73; trans. Williams and Wickham, *On God and Christ*, 167–68).

# 5

# *Descending, ascending, and doing Christology by likeness*

Maximus: "Seeing that God has stirred you to accept the expressions of the holy Fathers . . . you—I mean the Emperor and the patriarch and his synod—must make a written dispatch on this matter to the see of Rome . . ."

Bishop Theodosius: ". . . But advise us by the Lord whether this can be done."

Maximus: ". . . Let the Emperor and the patriarch admit to imitate God's condescension [μιμήσασθαι τοῦ θεοῦ τὴν συγκατάβασιν] and let the former make a supplicatory rescript and the latter an entreaty by synodical letter to the pope of Rome . . ."

Bishop Theodosius: "Of course this will be done."[1]

This excerpt comes from Maximus' dispute with Bishop Theodosius of Caesarea Bithynia in the summer of 656, towards the end of his life. Maximus was being held at the fort of Bizya on modern Turkey's north-east coast, in an exile to which he was condemned at his trial for treason in Constantinople.[2] In the course of the dispute, Maximus begins to wrestle Theodosius round to admit Christ's two wills. Upon gaining this ground

1. *Bizy.* 4 (Allen and Neil, *Maximus the Confessor and his Companions*, 98–99, including trans.).

2. For the story of Maximus' arrest, trial, and exile, see Allen and Neil, *Maximus the Confessor and his Companions*, 22–25; Blowers, *Maximus the Confessor*, 54–62.

he demands, in the above extract, that Theodosius compel the emperor, Constans II, and the patriarch of Constantinople to dispatch to Rome their official written acceptance of the dyothelite conclusions of the 649 Lateran Council. Unfortunately for Maximus, his demand was never fulfilled. His demand is nonetheless interesting, however, in that he seemingly envisioned this potential bureaucratic act to partake of the saving mystery of the incarnation. It genuinely "imitates" God's "condescension." Here, through his public habits of speech and negotiation, Maximus apparently suggests that the right government of Christian doctrine, even and perhaps especially in the hands of politicians and emperors,[3] comes about only with a mimetic share in the Christian mysteries themselves.

Up to this point we have been uncovering a deep epistemological assumption of Maximus' thought: that imitation is the key to knowledge of divine things. I have lengthily endeavored to demonstrate and clarify this assumption in this study, and now I wish to show that this assumption characterizes how Maximus approaches *doctrine* in his late christological output. The contention of this chapter and the next is that, as we glimpse in Maximus' remarks above, the principle of knowing-by-likeness animates his doctrinal method, by which I mean those conditions and sequences of discovery that Maximus recommends for discerning orthodox dogmas, about Christ in particular.

To set the scene, this chapter will begin by asking what kind of object doctrine is in Maximus' mind. We will first examine how Maximus uses the word "doctrine" (δόγμα), and then we will read some pieces of advice Maximus gave to those seeking to understand doctrines. Through this exploration we will discover that doctrine is, for him, a matter of ascetic enterprise, a product of practice and contemplation, a product of imitation, and something taught by God. Then, in preparation for reading Maximus' christological letters themselves, we will look to the equally important doctrinal vocabulary of "initiation" (μύησις) and "mystery" (μυστήριον) that frames these letters. By observing how Maximus uses this language elsewhere, I will argue that for him "mystery" signals both a reality to be known *and* to have one's life shaped by, a reality that involves knowledge *and* imitation. In this way, "mystery" vocabulary is something of a shorthand label for a likeness epistemology. Thus, by placing

3. On the Byzantine ideal of the emperor as an imitator of Christ, see Lévy, "Liberté et 'structure profonde,'" 183–88. For an example, Cyrus, the patriarch of Alexandria in Maximus' day, refers to Emperor Heraclius as "His God-imitating condescension," in his *First Letter to Sergius* (Allen, *Sophronius*, 160–61).

the language of "mystery" and "initiation" on guard at the openings of his christological letters, Maximus warns of the epistemic and ascetic transformation he expects matters of dogmatic Christology will always demand.

With this general ascetic or imitative characterization of doctrine in mind, the remainder of the chapter will examine a number of Maximus' christological letters, in order to uncover the specific methods of imitation that, he thinks, christological discernment entails. We will focus closely on the opening praise addresses of these letters, a literary form identified in the last chapter, marked especially by a standard order (preamble, deeds, comparison). Although these letters have been discussed at length in the scholarship, this has almost solely been part of a search for the details of the Confessor's developing christological stance, information found most easily in the didactic body of each letter. Consequently—and perhaps also thanks to a modern tendency, touched on in the previous chapter, to consider "praise" and other non-didactic rhetorical modes as merely stylistic and thus uninformative—almost no attention has been given to the distinct literary unit that is *the praise address*, despite its recurrence and consistency through Maximus' corpus.[4] In the last chapter, we reached two basic conclusions about Maximus' tactic of praise: his praise addresses *introduce* what he thought his letter was about, or its content, and, on the other hand, they prepare his listeners for this content by mapping the content's expression in their lives, *likening* them to it. In this way, Maximus' praise addresses reveal an epistemological pattern, exemplified in an argumentative mode in the excerpt from the *Dispute* above, whereby "like is known by like": imitation is the proper condition and method for attaining clarity and truth in any given theological topic. This rhetorical-epistemological tactic will continue to appear in the praise addresses we examine from the christological letters. In these texts, I will argue, Maximus rhetorically envisions those who comprehend *christological* doctrine to be those whose lives imitate the *incarnation* of God in Christ. Imitation is the epistemic condition of doctrinal discernment, and I will show that Maximus recommends at least two distinct shapes of imitation to his readers, each of which models a different aspect of the incarnation. First, there are virtues that mirror

4. There are more praise addresses in Maximus' corpus than can be examined in this chapter, e.g. *ep.* 1 (PG 91, 364A–364B). Three introductions that are notable for their threefold encomiastic structure (preamble, deeds, comparison) are *ambig.* prol. 1–4 (DOML 28, 62–65), *op.* 7 (PG 91, 69B–72B), and *qu. Thal.* intr. (CCSG 7, 17–19).

the Word's descent. Secondly, there are ascetic achievements of ascent, which mirror the Word's transfiguration, ascension, and hidden eternal existence with the Father.

## Maximus on the character of doctrine

### *"Dogma," ascetic practice, imitation, and God the teacher of theology*

It is worth briefly portraying the character of doctrine in Maximus' writings. The first place to go is the Greek word for doctrine, "dogma" (δόγμα). In a general sense the word "dogma" means "settled opinion" or "ordinance." For Maximus, however, it is chiefly a piece of *ascetic* vocabulary, especially allied with the natural "contemplation" (θεωρία) that follows the practice of "virtue." In this context, "dogma" names those convictions about God, the cosmos, and its creatures that present themselves to the mind through long ascetic disciplining of the body and soul.[5] Of course, in Christian parlance another key meaning of "dogma" was "doctrine," the conviction and confession of the church—and for Maximus the orthodoxy of doctrines depends absolutely on the authority of the church and the fathers.[6] But such doctrinal "dogma" is still one specific sort of ascetic "dogma," learnt not simply by rote and attention to the fathers, but by ascetic endeavor. And even when Maximus stresses that "doctrines" find their validity in the confession of the church, rather than in the integrity of ascetic practice, the regulating ascetic presence of the virtues is never far off: "the orthodox faith," Maximus says, "is the true solid seat and constitution of pious doctrines, *and* the nature and everlasting fruitfulness of the virtues."[7]

In his later christological and polemical letters, when Maximus talks of "dogmas" in the ecclesial sense of "doctrines," their source in the ascetic life is clear to see. An excellent example comes at the beginning of *Opusculum* 1, in Maximus' praise address: "by your right enactment

---

5. Maximus closely associates "dogma" with "virtue" (see *ambig.* 10.27 [DOML 28, 188–89]; *ambig.* 10.53 [DOML 28, 234–35]), and with "contemplation" (see *ambig.* 10.34 [DOML 28, 200–203]; *qu. Thal.* 16 [CCSG 7, 107]; *qu. Thal.* 48 [CCSG 7, 335]; *qu. Thal.* 63 [CCSG 22, 153]), or both (see *ambig.* 10.53 [DOML, 234–35]; *qu. Thal.* 3 [CCSG 7, 57]).

6. *Op.* 11 (PG 91, 137C–140B) provides a good condensed example of this conviction.

7. *Op.* 8 (PG 91, 92A).

[κατορθώσει]"—or perhaps one could even translate this "orthopraxis"—
"of the virtues, the grasp of divine doctrines [δογμάτων] comes together
. . . Accordingly, you discerned and rejected what has been proposed
inaccurately regarding 'wills' by some people."[8] Or again in *Opusculum*
7, to keep to "the royal road of the divine dogmas of the fathers," Maximus says, a believer's "prayer" must be open to the gracious guidance of
the Holy Spirit, who leads them into "knowledge of and initiation into
Christ."[9] Right praying leads to right doctrine, Maximus suggests.

In *Letter* 14 to Peter, he intriguingly modifies this picture: *Christ-
like* praying leads to right *christological* doctrine. We mentioned this
letter briefly in the previous chapter for the interesting relationship it
shows between letter-bearer and letter-recipient. To outline the first part
of the letter: Maximus introduces to Peter a deacon named Cosmas, the
bearer,[10] then offers a summary of the right confession of Christ's two-
natures,[11] and then implores Peter to help Cosmas grasp this confession
"with your fine explanation of the issue at hand, and supply his mind with
what was left out of the summary."[12] But then, intriguingly, Maximus
immediately offers another piece of advice to Peter and Cosmas, as they
embark on this task of understanding the mystery of Christ's two natures:

> I remind you, men guarded by God, to "watch and pray" as the
> Lord commanded [Mark 14:38; Matt 26:41], so that we may not
> be caught in the traps of temptations that surround us from ev-
> ery side. For if we watch and stay aware, I know that we guard
> against the tricks of the demons. And if we pray, we bring divine
> grace to our aid as our ally, declaring us conquerors over the
> power that opposes us and drawing us back from all error and
> ignorance.[13]

In the excerpt from *Opusculum* 7 above, Maximus implied that orthodoxy is reached through Spirit-led prayer. Here in *Letter* 14, he makes
a parallel point: to understand the mystery of Christ one must remain
alert in prayer. However, Maximus has no bland or generic practice of
prayer in mind. He is careful in his choice of language: "watch and pray,"

---

8. *Op.* 1 (PG 91, 12A).

9. *Op.* 7 (PG 91, 72C–73A).

10. *Ep.* 14 (PG 91, 533C–536A).

11. *Ep.* 14 (PG 91, 536A–537B).

12. *Ep.* 14 (PG 91, 537C).

13. *Ep.* 14 (PG 91, 537C–340A).

he says. This is a biblical citation that signals a very specific episode and context of prayer: the garden of Gethsemane (Mark 14:38; Matt 26:41). To "watch" and "pray" is what Jesus himself does and asks his disciples to do "with me" in the garden (Matt 26:36–38). Maximus encourages Peter and Cosmas to tackle the mystery of Jesus' two natures by joining in with Jesus' activity in Gethsemane. He posits a link between understanding and praying, between understanding the dyophysite mystery and praying in a way that shares with Jesus in Gethsemane. In his dyophysite summary, in the letter's previous paragraph, Maximus had said that "the same Word willingly accepted the trial of human sufferings" and consequently "the same was crucified, buried, and raised on the third day, according to the Scripture."[14] Now he invites Peter and Cosmas to go to Gethsemane, to the place where that suffering of the Word began and the place where, as Maximus would later affirm, the truth of the doctrine of Jesus' two natures appeared so visibly in the apparent conflict of his two wills.[15]

Maximus unpacks this line of thought a little later in the letter. After bewailing the woes befalling Christians of his day—the invading Muslims and, in Maximus' opinion, the Jews who support their conquest[16]— Maximus attributes all this misfortune to the fact that "we all sinned . . . , we all strayed from the way of the commandments who said 'I am the way' [John 14:6], and we acted as wild beasts to one another, ignorant of the grace of *philanthropia* and the mystery of the sufferings of God who was made flesh for us."[17] Maximus blames the sufferings of his day on ignorance of the mystery of the incarnation, inattentiveness to Jesus and his "sufferings." Immediately, he exhorts Peter and Cosmas to take the same remedy as before: "Let us 'watch and pray'":

> For if we "watch and pray," we hold fast to a surer faith in our Lord and God Jesus Christ, contemplating and grasping by experience [πείρᾳ] the accomplishment of those things he foretold. And we are not baffled at all and do not submit to fitfulness of soul . . . but rather we hold fast to the faith that is surer, seeing the prophecy fulfilled through the acts of our Lord.[18]

14. *Ep.* 14 (PG 91, 537A).

15. *Op.* 7 (PG 91, 80C–81C).

16. For a brief discussion that puts *ep.* 14's invective against the invading Muslims and conniving Jews in historical and social context, see Blowers, *Maximus the Confessor*, 19–21.

17. *Ep.* 14 (PG 91, 541B–C).

18. *Ep.* 14 (PG 91, 541D).

If you want to understand the mystery of the incarnation and the Word's suffering, Maximus says, then go, join Jesus suffering in Gethsemane and grasp it "by experience," that is, by Jesus' own experience. Then, in those things Jesus "foretold" in his prayers to the Father in Gethsemane and "fulfilled" thereafter on the cross, you will see the two natures in one person: "the same Word," as Maximus summarized, "willingly accepting the trial of human sufferings; the same crucified, buried, and raised on the third day, according to the Scripture."

Only later in his career, during the monothelite conflict, would Maximus identify these prayers of Jesus in Gethsemane as evidence for his two wills and their harmony. Nonetheless, as Blowers says, this theme was not "purely a reaction to controversy."[19] Before the debate over Christ's two wills emerged, here in *Letter* 14 we see Maximus laying the foundation for his later interpretive moves, by twice invoking the episode of Jesus in Gethsemane in order to help his readers understand the mystery of Jesus' two natures. Maximus considered waiting with Jesus in Gethsemane, "watching and praying," to be an activity that aids the mind in understanding the dyophysite reality lying behind the words and deeds of Jesus in his passion. One learns doctrine through assimilation to doctrine's object. Something of the like-knows-like thesis is certainly fundamental here in Maximus' early picture of christological discernment.

We could phrase the logic of this passage differently: the real teacher of doctrine is doctrine's object. Jesus in Gethsemane is the one who teaches the mystery of the incarnation to the believer. Maximus gives examples of this pattern of doctrinal discernment elsewhere. When approaching the mystery of the Trinity, for example, he makes it clear that "the Holy Divinity itself moves us into an acknowledgement of itself and provides pious starting points [in order for us] to have the courage to examine closely the mode of its extraordinary existence."[20] Most generally, Maximus says elsewhere, the activity of God the Trinity alive in the believer is the source of all right doctrines:

> Who illumined you with the faith of the holy, consubstantial, worshipful Trinity? Or who made known to you the incarnate dispensation of one of the Holy Trinity? And who taught you about the natures of incorporeal beings and the reasons of the beginnings and consummation of the visible world? Or about the resurrection from the dead and eternal life? Or about the

19. Blowers, *Maximus the Confessor*, 157.

20. *Qu. dub.* 105 (CCSG 10, 79; trans. Prassas, *Questions and Doubts*, 99).

glory of the kingdom of the heavens and the dread judgement?
Was it not the grace of Christ dwelling in you, the pledge of the
Holy Spirit?[21]

From this brief look at the character of doctrine in Maximus' earlier
works, it is clear that for him doctrine is a matter of ascetic practice,
prayer, imitation, and being taught by God.

### "Deep cries out to deep": entering the "mystery"

Maximus signals this active, ascetic character of doctrinal discernment
with the vocabulary of "mystery," a vocabulary that permeates and often
introduces his christological letters. It is worth briefly exploring this vocabulary before examining his letter introductions in fuller detail for the
rest of the chapter.

Glancing among Maximus' christological letters, a reader might
quickly notice that "mystery" and its cognate terms (μύσται, "initiates";
μύησις/μυσταγωγία, "initiation") are a common feature. Whatever "mystery" signals, it is the environment into which Maximus rhetorically
places his reader when introducing his christological letters—and therefore, according to the conclusions about Maximus' rhetorical "tactic of
introduction" established in the previous chapter, it is the deep content
of the christological discourses themselves. Amid the openings of these
letters, the Confessor praises his recipients as "initiates," technicians of
christological dogma, skilled in the techniques of "initiation":

> I am not so much struck by the modesty of your ample rever-
> ence as I am amazed by the courage of your most great zeal,
> all-holy servant of God, all-wise initiate and initiator [μύστα καὶ
> μυσταγωγέ] of his mysteries [μυστηρίων].[22]

> So then, in an appropriate way, you come to an understanding of
> the new mystery [μυστηρίου] of the divine modeling as man of
> God the Logos . . . by willing to ask questions—not in order to
> learn the basics, for you have a grasp of all fine things, but rather
> to press on to a more perfect initiation [μύησιν], free from what
> is inferior.[23]

21. *Carit.* 4.77 (PG 90, 1068A; trans. ACW 21, 204).
22. *Op.* 7 (PG 91, 69B).
23. *Op.* 4 (PG 91, 57C).

In what does this practice of "initiation" into "mystery" consist? As Louth summarizes, "mystery" for most of the Greek fathers referred equally to the object of mystery—whether Scripture, or sacraments, or the incarnation—and to the believer's transforming encounter with that object.[24] We can recall that when we came across the vocabulary of "mystery" in Chapter 1, in the context of Alexandrian allegorical reading, the probing of "mystery" or "enigma" innately involved a sorting of the reader's character after the likeness of what they are trying to probe. Just the same leap takes place in Maximus' Alexandrian consciousness: "mystery" is an object that reveals little to spectators and considerers, but instead always demands followers or, Maximus clarifies, "imitators." In his words from the opening lines of the praise address of one christological letter, "initiation" involves "imitation":

> For those whom the Word causes to blossom with virtues, their mind is lit up with knowledgeable graces, which drive it away from all forgetfulness, just as they do from deceit. And they lead the mind towards initiation [μύησιν] into what is hidden [κρυφίου], as much as they lead it back up into imitation [μίμησιν] of him who was revealed for us. You exemplify this in the Holy Spirit, God-honored Father, striving with them in a harmony of holy ways [τρόπων] and holier practices [πράξεων].[25]

"Initiation" issues in "imitation," in "ways" and "practices" of living that follow the revealed Christ, so that the imitation of Christ is the visible sign of initiation into hidden knowledge of the mystery of Christ. The point I wish to highlight is that when Maximus characterizes his christological letters from the outset with the language of "initiation," "mystery," and "hiddenness," he invites his readers to engage in a practice of christological discernment that will involve not only abandoning deceit and getting their knowledge in order, but putting their lives in proportion with the incarnation through imitation.

One example from Maximus' earlier works will suffice to substantiate this point. In his final *Difficulty*, number 71, Maximus interprets the following line from one of Gregory Nazianzen's poems: "The sublime Word plays in all kinds of forms, judging His world as He wishes, on

24. Louth, "Mysticism," 272–73.
25. *Op.* 20 (PG 91, 228B).

this side and on that."[26] For Maximus, the strangest and most interesting thing here is Gregory's image of the divine Word "playing." In his first interpretation, Maximus lays out a syllogism which yields the conclusion that this "playing" could "signify the mystery of the divine Incarnation."[27] Before embarking on the path to this conclusion, however, he begins the *Difficulty* "by way of digression, prefacing the difficulty at hand with an example."[28] Intriguingly, however, Maximus selects for his "example" a verse from the Psalms that seems to have nothing to do with his conclusion whatsoever: "Deep cries out to deep at the sound of Your cataracts" (Ps 41:8, LXX). It turns out that Maximus considers his verse not as an "example" of the ensuing claim of this first section—that words and images of privation can signify excessive divine realities like the incarnation; nor is it a descriptive "example" of the incarnation itself; nor, as Blowers suggests, does Maximus simply offer it as an invitation into "deeper" contemplation of the passage from Gregory.[29] Rather, as Maximus explains, the psalmist's words are an "example" of the correct *method of discernment* of the Christian "mysteries." The psalm specifies the correct order and conditions by which the mind in contemplation journeys towards a "glimpse" or "impression" (ἔμφασις) of "divine providence" and the "mystery" of the incarnation that providence sets in play; the psalm sets out the condition that lets the mind look upon "the land of Jordan and Hermon" (Ps 41:7, LXX) where the incarnation took place. And this condition for discernment that the psalm recommends is nothing other than likeness. Like grasps like, "deep cries out to deep": that is, the "deep" of a purified mind grasps the "Deep" of divine Wisdom. Let me cite the appropriate passages at length:

26. Gregory, *carm.* 2 (PG 37, 624A–625A), cited by Maximus at *ambig.* 71.1 (DOML 29, 312–13, including trans.). For the context of Gregory's quotation, and an analysis of Maximus' interpretations of it in *ambig.* 71, see Steel, "Le jeu du Verbe," 281–93.

27. *Ambig.* 71.3 (DOML 29, 316–17, including trans.). Maximus reaches this conclusion through a syllogism of three premises and a conclusion, whose first and major premise is an apophatic maxim: (1) a negation or privation in our terms indicates a surpassingly excessive affirmation and possession in divine terms; (2) in our terms, childish play is a privation, of prudence specifically; (3) the incarnation is the most surpassingly excessive act of God; therefore, the Word's "play" might likely signify the incarnation (DOML 29, 314–7).

28. *Ambig.* 71.4 (DOML 29, 318–19; modified trans.). These words are Maximus' own description of his argumentative moves at *Ambig.* 71.2 (DOML 29, 313–14).

29. Blowers, "On the 'Play' of Divine Providence," 202.

When the great David, by faith alone, spiritually thrust his mind through the latches [see Song 5:4–5], as it were, of visible realities, he received from the divine Wisdom a certain impression [ἔμφασιν] of the mysteries that are accessible to human beings; and accordingly, it seems to me, he said: "Deep cries out to deep at the sound of Your cataracts" [Ps 41:8, LXX]. With these words he may perhaps be indicating that every mind in a state of contemplation, on account of its invisible nature and depth and multitude of its thoughts, is like a "deep," for after it has passed through the whole orderly arrangement of visible things and finds itself in the region of intelligible realities . . . it is then that, fittingly [δεόντως], it "cries out to" the divine Wisdom—which to our knowledge is really and truly an unfathomable "deep"—and asks that it might be given, not of course the divine "cataracts" themselves, but their "sound," which means that it asks to receive a certain cognitive impression [ἔμφασιν] of faith concerning the modes and principles of divine providence governing the universe. Through this impression, the mind will be able to "remember" God "from the land of Jordan and Hermon" [Ps 41:7, LXX], where the great and awesome mystery of the divine condescension of God the Word was accomplished through the flesh, a mystery in which the truth of right faith in God was given to human beings . . .[30]

[To summarize,] we understood the phrase "deep cries out to deep at the sound of the" divine "cataracts," as signifying the cognitive mind calling to Wisdom, and alluding to a certain small impression [ἔμφασιν] of the mysteries of the divine and ineffable descent of God. For the name "deep" is also given to the place of the deep, and the purified mind is the "place" of divine Wisdom. Thus, owing to its receptive capacity, the mind is called "deep" by convention, and Wisdom also receives the same name by nature.[31]

The phrase "deep cries out to deep" bears a latent like-by-like logic, which Maximus spots and coaxes out,[32] and which he thinks outlines the conditions for the mind's glimpse of divine "mysteries," and especially the "mystery" of the incarnation. When the mind in contemplation is purified of all visible and material concerns or distractions, then it becomes

30. *Ambig.* 71.2 (DOML 29, 312–15; modified trans.).

31. *Ambig.* 71.4 (DOML 29, 318–19; modified trans.).

32. As far as I can find, this verse had not attracted much interpretative attention amongst Greek Christian writers before Maximus.

"deep," and because God's Wisdom is also and supremely "deep," the mind can thereby call out to it and get an impression of God's providence, by which it glimpses the divine dispensation of mysteries as God sees them, in the light of divine Wisdom. Maximus puts this a different way in his summary above: as the mind begins to resemble divine Wisdom, the two begin to share the same "place," a place where the mind can receive a "small impression of the mysteries of the divine and ineffable descent of God," that is, the incarnation. One can see very clearly here that, in line with the origins of the Christian likeness epistemology discussed in Chapter 1, Maximus believes that "mystery" innately involves and demands the believer's assimilation to mystery's object.

If this is the case, then when Maximus introduces and encases his christological letters with the vocabulary of "mystery," he hints at the kind of enterprise in play: his language of "mystery" locates his christological letters, and his readers' task, within deep's call to deep, within the Christ-like mind's cry to that which it can glimpse, to Christ. To summarize this point, "mystery" sets the stage for the task of knowing Christ by likeness.

## Tackling doctrine in letters: imitating Christ and doing Christology

Andrew Louth says that Maximus' "later christological treatises are dry, technical, and polemical, and do not raise *directly* what we could call spiritual issues, except in passing."[33] This is an appropriate description of the body of Maximus' letters in large part. But it would be strange if this were the whole story, since Maximus makes clear, we have just seen, that good doctrinal reflection is always resourced by ascetic endeavor and a spiritual alertness to doctrine's object, and moreover he signposts these christological treatises with a vocabulary of "mystery" that calls the reader to make their mind the "place" or stage of a doctrine by ascetically mirroring it. It is my suggestion that, far from being fundamentally dry, "a last sophistic hurrah or scholastic pedantry at the culmination of a debate on mere christological technicalities," in Blower's deliberate caricature,[34] Maximus' later christological writing proceeds from a

33. Louth, "Dogma and Spirituality," 200.

34. Blowers, *Maximus the Confessor*, 137. Blowers promises, in a chapter from his recent book, to collapse the seeming disparity between Maximus' earlier spiritual and ascetic mode of christological reflection and his later dogmatic christological works. What follows in his chapter, however, is an examination of different christological

spiritual spring, made visible to the attentive reader by the order and rhetorical rationale by which the texts unfold. In the previous chapter, we clarified in some detail the kind of common rhetorical pattern with which Maximus presents many of his letters: at the outset of a letter, we saw, the address uses a rhetoric of praise to muster the ascetic practices that match and manifest whatever will be the letter's doctrinal content. (Presumably these praise introductions are the discourses on "spiritual" topics that Louth dismisses, above, as "passing"). For example, we saw how, in his *Second Letter to Thomas*, Maximus aimed to teach Thomas the meaning of Christ's flesh "mixing" with God, by first praising Thomas for becoming "mixed" with God himself through cultivating a "mixture" of desire for and fear of God. Through this rhetorical tactic, Maximus shows his belief not only that a grasp of doctrine grows out of ascetic endeavor, but that to grasp a particular doctrine, or even a doctrine's small detail or vocabulary, a believer's asceticism should precisely imitate it. In many of his christological letters, Maximus regularly summons this rhetorical and epistemological strategy, so that his likeness epistemology animates his christological method. As we examine these letters it will become clear that, for him, discerning doctrine is not a dry and technical occupation; rather, the technicians of doctrine are those who work to become rapt and formed by the shapes of divine life to which the doctrine attests.[35]

To discover the specific imitative shapes of life that Maximus thinks make Christology possible, let us look now at some of the praise address- es of Maximus' christological letters, where the Confessor heartens his hearers to model and manifest the fundamental patterns of the mystery of Christ. If my conclusions from the last chapter were correct, then we may read each praise address as a valid argumentative step of Maximus' christological method, introducing the christological content of each

---

themes from Maximus' early and later writings that, for all its detail and helpfulness, does not quite display how these themes come together or support one another, and one is left feeling that Blower's opening caricature may have some truth to it (135–65).

35. As far as I have found, Blowers is the commentator who has come nearest to spotting at work, in one of Maximus' letter addresses, a christological and epistemo- logical method. Blowers suggests that Maximus' later dogmatic works seem to have their "foundation" in his earlier ascetic theory, and he takes the praise address of *op. 7* for his example: "When . . . in *Opusculum 7* (*c.*642) he addresses Marinus . . . about the emerging error of monoenergism and monothelitism, . . . he first dwells at length on how Marinus's exceptional virtue and acquired wisdom have already qualified him to grasp the mysteries of the constitution of Christ" (Blowers, *Maximus the Confessor*, 77).

letter and its mystical reality and encouraging the reader, through imitation, to be initiated into it in order to understand it.

## Descending

In a number of the christological letters, Maximus opens by wondering at the patterns of "emptying" (κένωσις) and "condescension" (συγκατάβασις) occurring in the lives of his addressees, and keenly points out that these are just the sorts of shapes of divine life that defined the incarnation. There is an inclination towards self-toppling, a trajectory of "descent," or simply a virtue of "humility," that Maximus seems to consider crucial for grasping the ins and outs of christological dogma, and which he thus obliquely kindles in his recipients with praise. Maximus gives a terse and exemplary instance of this in the prologue to his first letter of *Difficulties to Thomas*:

> [**PREAMBLE:**] From your concerted zeal in the pursuit of divine things, you have acquired, dearly beloved of God, a habit of undeviating contemplation, and have "become" a most chaste "lover," not simply of "wisdom, but of her beauty" [see Wis 7:30, 8:2]. Now the beauty of wisdom is knowledge embodied in practice, or practice informed by wisdom; and the common characteristic of both of these . . . is the principle of divine providence and judgement. [**DEEDS:**] In accordance with this principle, you combined intellect and sensation through the spirit, showed truly how God is of a nature to "fashion man after his own image" [see Gen 1:27; 5:1], and made intelligible the riches of his goodness, lavishly showing forth in yourself—by means of the marvelous mixture of opposites—God incarnated [σωματούμενον] by means of the virtues. [**COMPARISON:**] You have attained his height and the imitation [μιμήσει] of his self-emptying [κένωσιν], and have not disdained to descend [κατελθεῖν] even to me, seeking things the knowledge of which you already possess by having undergone them [πεπονθώς].[36]

Before approaching the five difficulties in this letter, four of which are on the topic of the incarnation, Maximus uses the "comparison" section of his address—in a way that is by now familiar—to praise Thomas for having like proportions to God incarnate, literally, for "being the same height" (συμμετρήσας τῷ ὕψει). Specifically, Thomas imitates

---

36. *Ambig. Thom.* prol. 2 (DOML 28, 2–5; modified trans.).

God's "emptying" through his "descent" to Maximus. Maximus implies that these christological virtues allow Thomas a kind of insider's perspective on the incarnation, a knowledge from real experience of the mystery itself—"having undergone these things, you have knowledge" (ὧν πεπονθὼς ἔχεις τὴν εἴδησιν). Importantly, in this phrase Maximus hints at the theological presumption whose foundations we unearthed in Chapter 3: namely, that imitating Christ is an activity that invites the "incarnated" or, here, "embodied" (σωματούμενος) presence of Christ, that involves "undergoing" the incarnate Christ, and therefore understanding him. In the passage that follows, Maximus suggests that something like this happened supremely to the saints Gregory Nazianzen and Dionysius (whose writings the letter examines). As part of their mastery of christological reflection, Maximus says, they themselves "took hold of the living, unique Christ, who . . . became the soul of their souls, manifest to all through their deeds, words, and thoughts, by which one is persuaded that the passages cited hereinafter were authored, not by them, but by Christ, who by grace has exchanged places with them."[37] This, the ideal epistemic state of the christologian, is the reality that Maximus coaxes Thomas towards through praise, and we will continue to see him do so in other letters.

In the address of a christological letter to the priest Theodore in Sicily, Maximus again witnesses to this methodological and theological assumption that imitative intimacy with Christ is the crucial condition for fruitfully grappling with the finer doctrinal points of the mystery of the incarnation. Here, in a praise address that is a "comparison" in its entirety, we find Maximus encouraging in Theodore the same Christ-like virtues for which he praised Thomas—condescension, abasement, and so on:

> I do not think that you, most holy ones of all, have need of the
> knowledge of any other person, you who already through simple virtue have managed to summon by your wise intellect the
> one Holy Spirit itself, the source from which you gush forth the
> divine pouring of wisdom to others in boundless gift. You make
> an outpouring of the wisdom of intelligible things through your
> speech, to fully extend out of love of humanity [φιλανθρώπως]
> divine knowledge and teaching even unto those as lowly as me

---

37. *Ambig. Thom.* prol. 3 (DOML 28, 4–5, including trans.). On the Macarian background of this theme of Christ as the second soul of the believer, see Plested, *The Macarian Legacy*, 225–26.

who share no part at all in reason. If, as I know, you consult me with questions in condescension [συγκαταβάσει] in order to push forward and, moreover, to raise to your own summit of knowledge through your most severe abasement [ὑφέσεως] those like us who lie below, weighed down with ignorance, then, purifying my sluggishness by your descent [ὑποβάσει] and the ignorance of my thinking by your inspiration, you would guide me to a gnostic habit, and a vigorous and practical eagerness, out of which salvation comes by grace to those who are saved, through those like you who are made worthy to save the worthy.[38]

In the body of the letter, Maximus distinguishes "quality," "property," and "difference" and then highlights the confusion and abuse of these concepts in monophysite talk about Christ. To prepare Theodore for this technical and polemical christological discussion, Maximus uses a rhetoric of comparison to outline the astonishing ways in which the mystery of Christ is taking shape in Theodore's life, in a way so real that he not only manifests Christ's "love of humanity" and "condescension" but wields an ability "to save" those around him. From his praise rhetoric we can see in action Maximus' conviction that "deep cries out to deep," that one grasps the intricacies of christological doctrine by likeness, especially to the divine "emptying" and "abasement."

Let us look at one more passage that yields the same conclusion, the opening lines of *Opusculum* 8, Maximus' letter to the bishop Nikandros. The tenor this time is more consciously dogmatic and polemical:

[DEEDS:] You, God-honoured and all-blessed father, courageously gain the most holy victory, as your name suggests, over all enemies who war visibly or invisibly against the holy, catholic, and apostolic church of God. From him you already receive in hope the garland he makes evergreen with graces and unfading with the activities of the Spirit. And you have grasped with your hands that which is desirable by nature, through your perfect agreement with it in blessed enjoyment. [COMPARISON:] Clearly as a result of this you delight in the Lord more than any other, and grant what this is like, even in plain speech. You avoid introducing it with worthy and blessed discourse to one who is incapable and miserable, who until now has in no way been taught to move the practical powers of his mind or the thoughts of his soul like fingers of hands in the army of God [see Ps 143:1,

38. *Op.* 21 (PG 91, 245D–248B).

LXX] and the holy war that is his and on his behalf, nor to rout
those who mount up against the Lord almighty with words and
dogmas, nor to drive them off the "good ground" [Luke 8:8]—
that is, our Lord and God himself, and the orthodox faith in
him, the truly solid ground and constitution of faithful dogmas
and the everlasting fruitfulness and nature of the virtues. You
have done this in the imitation of Christ [χριστομιμήτως], in
order that, by displaying his goodness-loving self-emptying
[κένωσιν] to me—the one who has willfully become separated
from him and who determinedly indwells a habit of evil like a
"distant land" away from him, and who actively rears disgraceful
passions like "pigs" [Luke 15:13, 15]—and by showing through
the greatness of your condescension [συγκαταβάσεως] the power in you of divine right actions [κατορθωμάτων], you might
awaken in me a desire for this and harden me towards a holy
and blessed zeal that casts away, as far as possible, the burden
of both my sluggishness that weighs me down before everyone,
and my indifference.[39]

In the body of the letter, Maximus will challenge monoenergist and
monothelite claims, and he paints a military scene from the first lines
of the introduction. In the long comparison section we see the lofty Nikandros training and energizing the lowly and lazy prodigal Maximus
for this battle against heretics, and with a single resource: "imitating
Christ." This imitation consists, again, in the "right actions" or "orthopraxis" (κατορθώματα) of some core christological virtues: "emptying"
and "condescension." Imitation of the divine Word's descent is the crucial
weapon of orthodoxy that Maximus, through praise, encourages Nikandros to take up and that, he says, supports his own dogmatic efforts in
this lengthy letter.

## Ascending

In a few other christological letter addresses, Maximus repeats this tactic
of encouraging, through praise, Christ-like humbling and abasement
in his reader, but pursues the trajectory of the incarnation from self-
emptying descent to glorious ascension. The introduction to *Opusculum*
15 is exemplary in this regard. It is a late letter full of anti-monothelite
resources from Scripture, the fathers, and heretics for Bishop Stephen,

39. *Op.* 8 (PG 91, 89C–92B).

whose job it was to depose eastern bishops with monophysite leanings for Pope Theodore.[40] Maximus prefaces these christological florilegia with praise for Stephen's Christ-likeness in the now familiar rhetorical mode of "comparison":

> Most excellent lamps of God, having known formerly by experience and today from what you hear that you are master over me, our slave, you have chosen a way, in the things you have written, to be led to the abasement of the beggar and poor man, you who have been so far raised and uplifted from the earth by God's grace as to raise up your life by the Word and your mind by the Lord of things here and beyond, assimilating and uniting the image to the archetype. Or to speak more truly, you wished to demonstrate your height by a free abasement from your highest beauty, so that you would lead us also in excess to the measure of God the Word who is beyond infinity, and who displayed the height of his own uncircumscribable glory by emptying himself for us, because he desired so much more to transform us that he conformed himself in flesh to what is more lowly. He is the pre-eminent lover of humanity, becoming man by nature without change or confusion.[41]

Stephen both imitates the Word's incarnate self-abasement and, consequently, attains to the "measure" of the Word's beyond-infinite divine life.

This theme reappears in a number of other letter introductions. *Opusculum* 4 is a short letter in which Maximus aims to clarify for the priest George, his addressee, that Christ's human nature and ours are one and the same. This all makes for "an exceedingly dense christological exposé," as Larchet puts it. However, Maximus prefaces the discussion in a more accessible style. He offers "an exposition on the ascetic life," in Jancowiak and Booth's words.[42] But in fact, this long opening section (that takes up about a third of the letter) is not a passage of exposition but of praise, by which Maximus aims to encouraging George to "press on to a more perfect initiation"[43] into the christological mystery at hand through imitation:

> [**PREAMBLE:**] Having given wings to your intellect with divine longing, father honoured by God, and having eagerly lifted

40. Jankowiak and Booth, "A New Date-List," 65–66.
41. *Op.* 15 (PG 91, 156B–C).
42. Jancowiak and Booth, "A New Date-List," 59.
43. *Op.* 4 (PG 91, 57C).

up your reason and risen beyond matter and what relates to it, you hold insatiable converse with the words of holy Scripture, and you possess, like no one else, an inexhaustible capacity for thinking over them with careful attention. For what is beyond sense-perception knows no satiety; and what is beyond intellection knows no restraint. The one stands beyond nature's every ebb and flow; the other lifts beyond every form and shape. The one, as is proper, manifests what is hidden [κρυφίου]; the other grants the possibility to comprehend what is boundless, as much as it nears a grasp of sufficient thought and a handle on the Holy Spirit. To this end there came about the manifest philanthropic condescension [ἡ φιλάνθρωπος . . . συγκατάβασις] of him who is beyond humanity, which makes gods by grace those who willingly ascend with him and those who, by the Word's self-emptying [κενώσει], receive his fullness in the completion of the work of the commandments. **[DEEDS:]** In accordance with this, having yourself been led up to a perfection of prudence and courage, you wisely compress what is visible [τὸ . . . φαινόμενον] and justly expand what is hidden [τὸ κρυπτόμενον], so that in the former case you exhibit the mortification of Jesus, which utterly destroys all sin, and in the latter case you show forth his life, which, in a way that surpasses this world, brings forward all virtue. From all this, by rightly enacting [κατορθώσας] holy practice and contemplation, you finally reaped holy salvation. **[COMPARISON:]** To share this salvation with others and, in the imitation of God, to make it known to me—the one who is unworthy, lowly, and ignorant—you chose to use words, first to give wisdom and understanding by reason, and second to bestow holiness through the grace that is in you and that is spread to everyone everywhere, since this grace has for its cause the uncaused and uncircumscribable Word.[44]

Maximus does indeed introduce the broad content of his letter, namely, the mystery of the incarnation, "the philanthropic condescension that took place through the manifestation of him who is beyond humanity"; but he introduces this indirectly, praising the manifestation of this content in George the abbot, whose "right-acting" or "orthopraxis" (verb: κατορθόω) is stamped with the shape of the incarnation—with the lowliness of Christ the Word's emptying and death, but also with the lofty fullness of his divine life. George is "ascending with him," bearing the features of Christ's risen and deified life, like unparalleled virtue and

44. *Op.* 4 (PG 91, 56D–57C).

familiarity with what is hidden. This last detail is especially important. Through the passage Maximus plays with the words "manifest" and "hidden" in a way that alludes to a distinction between the Word's visible and hidden existence that he dwelt upon at length in earlier works, especially when discussing the transfiguration.[45] Maximus had argued that "hiddenness" is "characteristic of the Word's being," and that his true hidden reality was shown forth momentarily at the transfiguration, in Jesus' face filled with dazzling light.[46] As for Jesus' shining garments, which are themselves visible, they conceal the Word's true hiddenness, while his body hidden beneath them manifests his hiddenness. Put simply, the Word is "concealed through manifestation" and "manifested through concealment."[47] Maximus had made the following injunction, that he drew from this reflection on the Word's hidden nature, concealed in the visible "garments" of Christ's human flesh, of nature's appearances, and of Scripture's words:

> Let us, then, make manifest what is hidden by means of an apophatic negation—leaving aside every capacity to picture truth by means of figures and signs, being lifted up in silence by the power of the Spirit from written words and visible things to the Word Himself . . .[48]

In the praise address above, Maximus reproduces this christological injunction, encouraging George towards "the manifestation of what is hidden," not only imitating Christ's manifest life, but encountering the boundless hidden life of the Word beyond "form and shape." This is how imitating Christ fulfils its course, as Maximus clearly summarizes elsewhere: "in his incarnation Jesus passes through all things on our account, so that by following him we also may pass through all things with him and may come beside him, that is, if we know him not in the limitedness of his incarnate condescension, but in the majestic splendor of his natural

---

45. This aspect of Maximus' thought has been identified as an "apophatic" Christology, because of the way he appropriates Dionysius' apophatic scheme to reflect on the incarnation and the Word's presence in creation and Scripture. See de Andia, "Transfiguration," 293–328; Louth, "Recent Research on St Maximus," 79–80; McFarland, "Developing an Apophatic Christocentrism," 208–11. Both de Andia and McFarland highlight the way in which Maximus reverses Dionysius' scheme, so that apophatic encounter comes first, as the condition that makes possible kataphatic theology.

46. *Qu. dub.* 191 (CCSG 10, 134). See also *ambig.* 10.28–29 (DOML 28, 190–91).

47. *Ambig.* 10.31 (DOML 28, 196–97; modified trans.).

48. *Ambig.* 10.31 (DOML 28, 196–97, including trans.).

infinitude."[49] George moves from the visible garments to the hidden flesh of Christ, as it were, finding through imitation an apophatic intimacy with the Word that Maximus recommends as the proper context for digesting the complex christological points he will turn to in the remainder of the letter.

A comparable passage comes at the beginning of *Opusculum* 20, an anti-monothelite letter to the priest Marinus. Maximus' signature procedure of praise is again easy to spot:

> [**PREAMBLE:**] For those whom the Word causes to blossom with virtues, their mind is lit up with knowledgeable graces, which drive it away from all forgetfulness, just as they do from deceit. And they lead the mind towards initiation into what is hidden, as much as they lead it back up into imitation of him who was revealed for us. [**DEEDS:**] Exemplifying this in the Holy Spirit, and striving with them in a harmony of holy ways and holier practices, God-honored Father, you exceed praise as much as you are able to muster your strength, making extension the end of your course and making the ever-moving ascent to the Word the end of your reason, so that you might surpass even nature, and break through all figures, and consort in purity with him who is most pure, by his detachment from all things and towards all things—a perfect state of crossover. This crossover steers a boundless happy course by grace, a course which traces out all that has bounds and then passes beyond it, and fast prepares the advance into the "Holy of holies" [see Heb 9:3]—where "Jesus," who is above us, "entered on our behalf" what was our own, "as a forerunner" [Heb 6:20; see Heb 9:1–3, 11–12]—for that person who, practically and through virtue, goes up with Jesus "from glory to glory" [2 Cor 3:18], and who, through understanding, passes through the heavens from knowledge to knowledge, to the "mysteriously hidden" [κρυφιομύστῳ] and polyphonic "silence" [see Dionysius, *myst.* 1], where all intellectual activity gets abandoned, and where he unknowingly meets with the "Father of spirits" [Heb 12:9]. [**COMPARISON:**] You, who have been extraordinarily led up to the Father by grace and by blessed eagerness for holy works, you lead up those like me who lie below, extending a hand in sympathy through your letter, and extending your reason through the hidden [κρυπτομένης] meaning within it, and persuading us by your eagerness to depart from those who have departed from

49. *Cap. theol.* 2.18 (PG 90, 1133B; trans. modified from Berthold, *Maximus Confessor*, 151).

God and to honor unreservedly his love that alone unites one
to him with the whole heart. By this love, which is simple and
formless, you command us to get rid of every compound veil of
shape and of thought itself and of what is visible, and to rightly
enact [κατορθοῦν] that virtue which brings true happiness and
is an exhibit of kinds of happiness. If only, being kept in your
most holy prayers, I might achieve this virtue and cut off sin's
easy onset.[50]

Maximus depicts Marinus on an unending upward journey with Jesus.
Marinus "imitates" and shares in the Word's stretching down in condescension to lowly creatures—like Maximus. But Marinus voices his call
of "deep to deep" unflinchingly, holding to Jesus' course with such eagerness that he is led up into the Word's secret divine life, hiddenly convers-
ing with the Father in a state beyond human knowledge and all it deals
in—finite things, visible things, thought. Maximus portrays this with the
language of Hebrews here, but he seems to be encouraging Marinus up
just the same path from the visible to the hidden existence of the Word
that he dwelt upon in his earlier works. Marinus, like George, models the
whole breadth of the Word's economic and immanent life—the perfect
preparation for comprehending the mystery of his incarnation.

    We have seen so far that, with a rhetoric of praise, Maximus repeat-
edly recommends a select array of promising conditions for christological reflection, all of which consist in imitating and finding intimacy with
different aspects of the Word's incarnate dispensation. I have presented
these conditions in two groups: virtues of descent—like humility, emptying, condescension, abasement—and consequent attainments of ascent—like surpassing visible reality, encountering infinity, and above
all entering into God's hiddenness. These two groups reflect the Word's
incarnation, death, and fleshly manifestation on the one hand, and the
Word's transfiguration, ascension, deification of humankind, and hidden
life with the Father on the other. Altogether, these conditions summarize
a human life saturated in the mystery of the incarnation, and thereby,
Maximus thinks, matchlessly prepare a believer for right dogmatic reflection upon that mystery.

50. *Op.* 20 (PG 91, 228B–229B).

## Conclusion

In this chapter we first set out to get a feel for the kind of endeavor Maximus embarks upon in his christological letters. We considered the ascetic nature of doctrine in his early works, and then we explored the like-by-like, or "deep-by-deep," epistemology implied in the vocabulary of "mystery" and "initiation" that attends his dogmatic Christology. Then we sought to identify these themes in some of his christological letters. We read through a number of letters that exhibited a consistent rhetorical pattern: the dogmatic christological content is preceded by a praise address that prepares the reader by encouraging them to imitate Christ. We saw that Maximus both praises virtues that imitate the Word's descent into humanity, and praises spiritual achievements that ascend to imitate the Word's hidden divinity. Maximus' consistent rhetorical endorsement of these acts of imitation shows that, for him, they make up the basic epistemic conditions for approaching the mystery of the incarnation. In the next and final chapter, I will specify my enquiry, and ask whether a parallel model of knowing-by-likeness is at work in Maximus' communication of his dyothelite doctrine—his teaching of Christ's two natural wills—in particular.

# 6

## Imitation, desire,
## and discerning dyothelite Christology

While they were embracing each other the consul Theodosius
said: "Look, everything has turned out well. Is the Emperor then
still expected to make a supplicatory rescript?"

And Father Maximus said: "Of course he will do so, if
he wills [θέλῃ] to be an imitator [μιμητής] of God and to be
humbled and emptied together with him [συνταπεινωθῆναι καὶ
συγκενωθῆναι] for the sake of the common salvation of us all,
considering that if the God who saves by nature did not save until he willed [θέλων] to be humbled, how can the human being,
who by nature needs to be saved, either be saved or save when
he has not been humbled?"

And Theodosius the consul said: "I hope that, if God
prompts my memory, I will say the same to him and he will be
persuaded."[1]

We join Maximus again, towards the end of his life, in exile in Bizya. The
consul Theodosius brings Maximus and Bishop Theodosius' dispute to a
conclusion, and raises again the issue of the "supplicatory rescript." We
saw at the beginning of the last chapter that this was the document that
Maximus wished the emperor to dispatch to Rome, pledging his support
of the dyothelite confession. And as before, Maximus peculiarly suggests
that, by carrying out this task of doctrinal administration, the emperor

1. *Bizy.* 8 (Allen and Neil, *Maximus the Confessor and his Companions*, 104–7;
modified trans.).

would find himself deeply involved in the mystery of the incarnation, an "imitator of God," "humbled and emptied together with him." Imitation of the incarnation, Maximus implies, is the mark of healthy discernment and negotiation of orthodoxy. More intriguingly still, Maximus suggests that if the emperor should "will" (θέλειν) this official acceptance of the doctrine of Christ's two "wills" (θελήσεις), then he would be aligning himself with God's own "willing" (θέλων) to become incarnate. Maximus hints that there is something about human "willing" that, when done right, sets the stage for right thinking and acting in the practice of Christology, and for fruitfully approaching the mystery of Christ's own willing in particular.

This final chapter will follow this hint. My method will be the same as before. Focusing still on Maximus' literary set-piece that I have called the "epistolary praise address," I will explore how Maximus' rhetorical and epistemological tactic of praise bears upon the central issue at stake in his later christological letters: Christ's two wills. I will argue that the rhetorical approach of a number of Maximus' dyothelite letters suggests that he saw a link between the state of believers' volition and desire and their capacity to hold right convictions about Christ's volition and desire, that is, his human and divine wills. We will see this link in the way Maximus often prefaced his dyothelite teachings by encouraging in his hearers a *will* or *desire* that imitates Christ's human willing, unified and harmonized with the divine will. Again, "deep cries out to deep": Maximus posits imitation or likeness as the key to knowledge and discernment of the Christian mysteries. But this time he matches his epistemological maxim to the dyothelite cause, recommending to his listeners a divine trajectory of willing and desiring in order that they may hold firmly to the doctrine of Christ's two wills.

I will begin by pointing out that the virtue of "humility," that we have seen Maximus exhort his readers to adopt in his christological works, is for him a virtue of *will* and a virtue that imitates Christ's human will in the incarnation. Thus, when Maximus introduces his dyothelite teaching with laudatory exhortations to humility, he rhetorically introduces the imitation of Christ's will as the condition for grasping that teaching.

In the remainder of the chapter, I will explore the role of another crucial volitional category—desire—in Maximus' vision of christological discernment. I will take *Opusculum* 1 as a case study. The body of the letter is devoted to the theme of the "will" and gives a good introduction to Maximus' later teaching on the will and desire: in fallen humans, in

Christ, and in the saints or the deified. Moreover, crucially (and by now expectedly), in this letter's introductory address the Confessor praises his reader for their *imitation*: for reaching the heights of deified desire that, he will argue, belong to Christ and the saints. Maximus coaxes his hearers to understand his teaching on the will by drawing them into the dyothelite mystery, rhetorically identifying the same kind of willing and desiring in them as belonged to Christ.

Next, I will spend some time summarizing the freedom and synonymy with which Maximus can use multiple "desire" terms, both to describe human desiring and the divine and human desire animating God the Word's incarnation. This will prepare us to pursue further the conclusions drawn from *Opusculum* 1 as we turn to some final christological letter addresses, and aim to identify in them divinely oriented "desire" as a crucial epistemic condition for discerning dyothelite doctrine.

## Humility and imitating Christ's willing

In *Letter* 13 to Peter the Illustris, written before Maximus became embroiled in the monoenergist controversy in 633, the Confessor refutes the anti-Chalcedonian Severus, but not before a praising introduction:[2]

> Truly sweet is your presence, my praised master, and your absence is no less lovely than your full presence, thanks to the Holy Spirit's shining grace of poverty in you. Through this grace every person becomes a holy temple, a dwelling place of God in spirit—every person, that is, who is genuinely remade by this virtue into God, who humbled himself [ταπεινώσαντος ἑαυτόν] down to the form of a slave [see Phil 2:7–8], and by deed and speech displayed this form to men in himself. You yourself, my praised master, by imitating him have attained gentleness [πραότητα] and humility [ταπείνωσιν] in your disposition [see Matt 11:29]. One attains gentleness in order to become well-pleasing to God and to men, by quenching the passions of anger and the movements of lust. For gentleness is nothing other than the complete abatement of all anger and lust for what is against nature, by which, to those who possess gentleness, the divine will [τὸ θεῖον ... θέλημα] becomes visible. For so says the great psalmist David, "He guides the gentle in his judgement, the gentle he will teach his ways" [Ps 24:9, LXX]. One attains humility, on the

2. Jankowiak and Booth estimate 629–33 ("A New Date-List," 33–34).

other hand, to become thankful to God and thankful to all men,
by cutting out the calluses of arrogance.[3]

This passage displays Maximus' christological praise rhetoric in full swing at a very early date, presenting the imitation of God's humble abasement as the proper accompaniment to christological reflection. Maximus praises Peter for imitating Jesus in "gentleness" and "humility," christological virtues identified by Jesus himself in Matthew 11:29: "Take my yoke upon you, and learn from me; for I am gentle [πραΰς] and humble [ταπεινός] in heart."[4] Most intriguingly, as Maximus continues he suggests that these Christ-imitating virtues let one perceive "the divine will." In the body of the letter, Maximus does not, of course, deal with Christ's wills, since it would be a number of years before the outbreak of the monothelite conflict. Nonetheless, we can conclude that, in this passage, Maximus suggests that a believer might clear away their self-centered vices and know God's "will" when they imitate Christ's gentleness and humility. We have here the seed or expression of Maximus' conviction that humility is a volitional category. In his later anti-monothelite works he will clarify this conviction, arguing that aligning one's will to God's will is made possible precisely by sharing in Christ's humility, by which he submitted *his* human will to the divine will.[5] Amid a discussion of Christ's wills (θελήματα) in a letter to Marinus in 641,[6] Maximus makes this clear: "He [Christ] harmonized his natural human will with the divine will of the Father, without any difference from it out of opposition, giving himself to us as an example [ὑποτύπωσιν], submitting his own will voluntarily; and he united it to the Father's will, so that we indeed would exactly imitate [ἐκμιμούμενοι] him, rejecting our own will so that we might fulfil the divine will with all eagerness."[7] Maximus repeats this point in his dispute with Pyrrhus over Christ's wills in 645,

3. *Ep.* 13 (PG 91, 509C–512A).

4. Trans. NRSV.

5. In Blower's summary, Maximus in his later works "attended to Jesus' *human* will in its own right as a theatre of the drama of salvation and of believers' participation in the *tropos* of Christ's new humanity" (*Maximus the Confessor*, 235). Blowers shows very clearly that, even before the monothelite conflict, Maximus understood Christ's mode of human passion and volition as thoroughly salvific, opening the way for the transformation and deification of human passion and volition (234–40).

6. Jankowiak and Booth, "A New Date-List," 48–49. For a detailed summary of this letter's content see Larchet, "Introduction," in Ponsoye, *Opuscules*, 27–33).

7. *Op.* 20 (PG 91, 241C).

saying that Christ "gave himself as a flawless type [τύπον] and pattern [ὑπογραμμόν] to imitate [πρὸς μίμησιν], so that we would look to him as founder of our salvation, and voluntarily [ἑκουσίως] draw close to God, no longer willing [θέλειν] anything apart from what he wills."[8] The dyothelite contention concerns not only Christ's willing, then, but also Christ's salvation of fallen human willing—if Christ had no human will, humans could not hope to have their wills put right by imitatively sharing in his humility and obedience.[9]

In short, then, Maximus proposes that humility is a volitional activity and that it imitates the harmony of Christ's two wills. This is all the more interesting when we recall that, as we plentifully witnessed in the last chapter, Maximus prefaces many anti-monothelite letters with lengthy praise of Christ-like humility. One might sensibly argue, therefore, that, in the Confessor's eyes, imitating Christ's willing—that is, having humility—sets the scene for and enables the believer's grasp of the doctrine of Christ's two harmonious wills. By exhorting his readers to humility in the letter addresses we studied, Maximus positions his dyothelite Christology as sourced, at least in part, by the volitional life of the believer, and specifically by humility—the correspondence of the believer's volition with Christ's.

## Desire and dyothelite Christology

### Opusculum 1: a case study in will, desire, and discernment

Along with humility and its accompanying virtues, the most obvious and enduring volitional vocabulary to be found among Maximus' christological letter introductions is "desire." I will propose in the remainder of this chapter that Maximus thinks that right desiring, along with humility, imitates Christ's volitional life and is a key spiritual source of and condition for understanding dyothelite doctrine. I will assemble my argument first from Opusculum 1, a detailed anti-monothelite letter to Marinus. Let me spell out this argument before substantiating it: in Opusculum 1 Maximus says that the whole process of human "willing" (θέλησις) begins

8. *Pyrr.* (PG 91, 305C–D). Maximus makes exactly the same point at *op. 7* (PG 91, 80D).

9. On the salvation of the human will that Maximus believes only the dyothelite position can affirm, see, e.g. *Pyrh.* (PG 91, 325A). See also, Berthold, "Free Will," 176; Hovorun, "Maximus, a Cautious Neo-Chalcedonian," 119.

with a natural "desire" or "appetite" (ὄρεξις); when this appetite draws towards God, its natural object, Maximus calls it πόθος, another word meaning "desire"; Christ exemplified this state of willing, with his natural human appetite completely drawn by God and aligned to the divine will; *Opusculum* 1 and, we will see further on, a host of other dyothelite letters begin with Maximus praising his recipients for their divinely oriented desiring (often πόθος); therefore, according to our prior conclusions about the Confessor's praise rhetoric, in *Opusculum* 1 Maximus posits Christ-like desire as the proper condition for comprehending Christ's pattern of willing—a human will totally allied to the divine will.

I want to preface this argument by briefly pointing out, using *Opusculum* 1, that Maximus freely and happily associates different and unclearly linked conversations that bear upon the issue of willing. At the end of *Opusculum* 1's praise address, Maximus says that, through the "orthopraxis [κατορθώσει] of virtue" and resulting "grasp of divine dogmas," Marinus has become aware of "some people's inaccurate proposals about 'wills' [θελημάτων]." Intriguingly, Maximus is not simply referring to monothelitism. Rather, he refers to three different inaccuracies, which he will refute in turn in the letter: the claim that all willing terminology means the same thing, differing in name alone; the claim that in the eschaton of deification "there shall be one will of God and of the saints"; and thirdly, "and because of this" (καὶ διὰ τοῦτο), the monothelite claim that Christ has one will.[10] There is clearly a serious connection in Maximus' mind between all these different conversations about "wills." A mistaken conviction about wills in one context leads to or arises from mistakes elsewhere.[11] Perhaps Maximus thinks that these three mistakes are linked progressively, beginning with the first and culminating in the third. What is indubitable is that Maximus thinks the monothelite mistake of affirming that Christ had one will arises "because of *this*," and "this," while it might refer to both prior errors, certainly refers to the second error of eschatological monothelitism: affirming one will of God and the saints. In other words, there is a link in Maximus' mind between the deified willing of Christ and the deified willing of the saints. This link finds further confirmation in the fact that in this *Opusculum*[12] Maximus clarifies

10. *Op.* 1 (PG 91, 12A–B).

11. Larchet notices this connection: "The *Opusculum* [1] is directed at those who attribute one will to Christ by confusing notions that should be distinguished regarding wills" ("Introduction," in Ponsoye, *Opuscules*, 86).

12. *Op.* 1 (PG 91, 33A–36A).

his earlier statement from *Difficulty* 7 that there will be one "activity" (ἐνέργεια) among God and the saints,[13] and he does so for a sole explicit reason: so that "no one will suspect from these words that I declared one activity of Christ."[14] This tells us clearly that in Maximus' mind, and presumably in the mind of Marinus and his other inquisitive contemporaries too, there is a freedom of association when it comes to themes of willing, and a special link between convictions about deified willing and about Christ's willing. In this light, when, in the passages to come, Maximus describes a believer's volitional and desirous union with God, the reader, with Maximus, can keep Christ's deified volitional union with God at the front of their mind. As we will see, the latter is in fact the archetype of the former, exemplifying and enabling it.

Much scholarship on the will in Maximus has noted the Confessor's clarity that will is a matter of desire.[15] Specifically, in *Opusculum* 1 Maximus is very clear that the "natural will [θέλημα . . . φυσικόν], that is to say, the faculty of willing [θέλησιν]" (the two terms are synonymous) is simply a name for the "desirous" or "appetitive drive [δύναμιν . . . ὀρεκτικήν] for what is according to nature."[16] Maximus reinforces the same point elsewhere.[17] For example, at the beginning of *Opusculum* 3 he clarifies that Christ's human will is, like every other human will, a "natural appetite" (φυσικὴν . . . ὄρεξιν).[18] In the Aristotelian tradition, "appetite" (ὄρεξις) is the source of movement that belongs to all animals,[19] all that is "living"; but by "natural will" Maximus refers specially to this basic appetite as it exists in "rational" creatures: not only is "the will [θέλημα] a natural and living appetite [ὄρεξιν]" but "willing [θέλησις] is a simple appetite [ἁπλῆ τις ὄρεξις], *rational* and living."[20] Since Gauthier's article

13. *Ambig.* 7 (DOML 28, 90–91, and see n. 16).

14. *Op.* 1 (PG 91, 36A).

15. In an article that founded much of the discussion on Maximus' understanding of volition, Gauthier attends in detail to the relationship of appetite and will in Maximus and in the philosophy that influenced him: "Saint Maxime," 51–100; see especially 57–79.

16. *Op.* 1 (PG 91, 12C).

17. See e.g. *Pyrr.* (PG 91, 293B–C and 317C).

18. *Op.* 3 (PG 91, 45C). Maximus is also clear on this point at *op.* 1 (PG 91, 29C).

19. On ὄρεξις as a faculty shared by humans and non-rational animals, see Nemesius, *nat. hom.* 33 (Morani, *Nemesii Emeseni*, 99–100); and Aristotle, *de an.* 432A–434A.

20. *Op.* 1 (PG 91, 13A).

in 1954, on "Saint Maxime le Confesseur et la psychologie de l'acte humain," commentators have been aware that in *Opusculum* 1 Maximus
takes many of his definitions of volition terminology from Nemesius of
Emesa, who in turn was mediating the accounts of human action given
by Aristotle and the Stoics.[21] But as Gauthier warned, "Maximus does not
repeat Nemesius."[22] For one, he sabotages Nemesius' teaching on appetite. Maximus ignores Nemesius' placement of appetite *after* choice and
deliberation, and instead, in a way more faithful to Aristotle, sets it at the
foundation of the volitional process.[23] At the same time, Maximus talks
about "appetite" with a synonymous language of natural "will" (θέλησις)
alien to Nemesius (and Aristotle), and which he probably invented himself.[24] This all goes to show how keen Maximus is to reject any account of
human volition that downgrades desire to anything less than inaugural.

In the first *Opusculum*, Maximus begins his justification of why
the saints and God do not share a single will by outlining his Nemesius-
inspired model of the workings of human willing. Again, Maximus says,
will is a "rational appetite" (λογικὴ ὄρεξις). Most of the time this appetite
involves itself with the diverse "options available to us" (τῶν ἐφ᾽ ἡμίν).[25]
And with this begins the volitional process that ends in choice and action, which earlier in the letter Maximus called gnome (γνώμη).[26] First,
appetite issues in a "wish" (βούλησις), which "is not simply the natural
will [i.e. the raw appetite] but the *kind* [ποιάν] of will, that is to say, the
will as it regards some particular thing [περί τινος]."[27] Again, these are
definitive features of gnomic will.[28] From the wish there follows an order
of "seeking," "consideration," "deliberation," "judgement," "choice," and
finally the "triggering" and "carrying out" of an action.[29] Such is the nor-

21. Namely, *nat. hom* 33 (Morani, *Nemesii Emeseni*, 99–101). Gauthier, "Saint
Maxime."

22. Gauthier, "Saint Maxime," 72.

23. Gauthier, "Saint Maxime," 68–71.

24. As Madden convincingly argued: "The Authenticity of Early Definitions,"
61–79.

25. *Op.* 1 (PG 91, 24B).

26. *Op.* 1 (PG 91, 17C).

27. *Op.* 1 (PG 91, 21D).

28. *Pyrr.* (PG 91, 308C); *op.* 3 (PG 91, 45C). See McFarland, "The Theology of the
Will," 521.

29. *Op.* 1 (PG 91, 21D–24A). For a more detailed summary and philosophical
background of the concatenation of stages in gnomic willing that Maximus lays out in
this passage and elsewhere, see Blowers, *Maximus the Confessor*, 159–61.

mal or gnomic activity of the will, as it navigates the uncertainty, change, and choice of "options laid before us" (τῶν ἀμφιβόλων . . . ὡς ἐφ᾽ ἡμῖν). But, Maximus asks, what about "when there are no options" (οὐκ ἔστι τὰ ἀμφίβολα), or when options become needless for freedom, "when, that is, Truth itself is shown visibly in all things" in the future deified union of the saints with God?[30] In his answer, the Confessor argues that because this Truth or union with God is the natural end of natural and rational desire, choice is rendered unnecessary.[31] All that remains is the will's unwavering natural trajectory of desire towards God. Maximus then argues that because humans will this end in diverse "modes," that is, with different intensities of desire, there can be no single will among the saints let alone between the saints and God, even if the *object* of their will, deification, is the same. But what is most interesting about Maximus' answer is the shift in desire language that takes place. Let us look at his answer in full:

> [In this situation] choice is not moved by the intervening pro-
> cesses [i.e. wishing, seeking, considering, deliberating, etc.] that
> deal with the options available to us, seeing as there are no oppo-
> site courses for judgement to distinguish between, from which
> to choose the better over the worse. So, if . . . there is no choice,
> with every option among existing things removed, then the ac-
> tivating desire [ὄρεξις] will be solely intellectual and, in this way,
> will be for those things that are desirable [ὀρεκτικοῖς] by nature.
> It is seized only by the mystical enjoyment [ἀπολαύσεως] of
> what is desirable [ὀρεκτοῦ] by nature, towards which it moves
> through the things that have been enumerated. The surfeit of this
> movement is the extension to infinity [ἡ ἐπ᾽ ἄπειρον ἐπίτασις] of
> this desire [ὀρέξεως] for what is enjoyed [ἀπολαυόντων]. Each
> person marvelously partakes of this as much as he has longed
> for [ἐπόθησε] it, in an unmediated mixture with that which is
> itself naturally longed for [αὐτὸ τὸ φύσει ποθούμενον]. Now if
> one partakes of this longed for object [τοῦ ποθουμένου] to the
> extent that he longed for [ἐπόθησε] it, then the will [θέλησις] of
> all is shown to be one according to its natural principle, but dif-
> ferent according to the mode of movement. If the will of all men

30. *Op.* 1 (PG 91, 24B–C).

31. On this point, see McFarland, "The Theology of the Will," 520–53. On God as the object of natural human willing, see Hovorun's summary: for Maximus, "no volitional impulse and action of a human being could be opposite to the will of God, if it functioned in accordance with nature (κατὰ φύσιν). . . Only what is against nature (παρὰ φύσιν) interferes with the will of God" (Hovorun, "Maximus, a Cautious Neo-Chalcedonian," 119).

is not one according to its mode of movement, then, on account
of every mode, the will between God and the saved will absolutely not be one, as some hold, even if the salvation of the saved
is the one *object* of will [τὸ θεληθέν] for God and the worthy.[32]

This new object, "Truth itself," is so natural that it surpasses the fit-
fulness of choice. Instead, Maximus elaborates, it brings sheer and "mystical enjoyment," of a kind that extends the reach of desire "to infinity." And
as he talks like this, as the natural will becomes afflicted and enamored
with the discovery of the infinite and blissful truth of its natural object,
so does the Confessor's volitional vocabulary suddenly shift from ὄρεξις,
"desire" or "appetite," to πόθος, which also means "desire" but holds a
connotation of hurt—loss, lack, regret—so I have translated it "longing"
above. From this passage we can conclude that, for Maximus, "longing"
is a piece of volitional vocabulary that describes a special movement of
the natural will or natural appetite: namely, its undistracted turning away
from "choice" and choice's ambiguities, and towards union with God, its
natural object.[33] Elsewhere in Maximus' corpus, too, πόθος almost always
belongs to the height of spiritual achievement, accompanying the mind's
movement beyond the fleeting realities of the sensible world and towards
encounter with and knowledge of God. But as we will see in a moment,
there is small chance of pinning down a strict definition of πόθος, since
Maximus is not strict with his vocabulary of desire. As we will discover
shortly, he can happily employ a stimulating array of "desire" words to
paint a single picture. In this passage, however, πόθος is the dominant
language.

Importantly, this is not the first time πόθος features in this letter. We
find it (along with the closely linked term ἔφεσις) in the praise address,
which, perhaps unsurprisingly by now, prefigures the coming content of
the letter. The praise address encapsulates the will's desirous movement
towards union with God with just the same language (πόθος, ἀπειρία,
ἀπόλαυσις) that we have just seen Maximus use later in the letter to de-
pict the union (though not union of will) of God and the saints:

Together with virtue and knowledge the white-hot longing
[πόθος] for God enters in, which stretches out the movement

32. *Op.* 1 (PG 91, 24B–25A).

33. Maximus had already suggested, in *qu. Thal.* 30 (CCSG 7, 219), written around
ten years earlier, that "divine longing" (θεῖος πόθος) is just the thing that arises when
one is drawn beyond "choice" (προαίρεσις).

of your longing [ποθοῦντος] to infinity [ἀπειρίᾳ], and which, by your unbounded object of longing [τοῦ ποθουμένου], unbinds your desire [ἔφεσιν], whose end is God himself, the fulfilment of longing [πόθου] for those who are worthy, as himself the very enjoyment [ἀπόλαυσις] of good things. This enjoyment falls within no sort of conception whatsoever, and its principle knows only what is grasped by experience and clearly beyond conceiving—union.[34]

To draw Marinus into sympathy for and understanding of his letter's subject-matter, Maximus begins his letter by praising him and rhetorically incorporating him into the mystery of this subject-matter, that is, the deified willing of the saints with God: Marinus, Maximus says, possesses πόθος, "longing," the activity of will characteristic of deified life, and this longing looses him into "infinity"[35] and "enjoyment."

How would this introduction prepare Marinus for comprehending the willing of *Christ*, not just of the saints, which is the other crucial subject of this letter? To tackle this question let us first recall how, in the next paragraph of the introductory address, Maximus demonstrated his freedom of association between different issues of willing, and sees a special link between the question of deified willing or desiring and of Christ's willing. Secondly, if we read the final section of the letter, which is on Christ's wills, the exact nature of this link becomes apparent. Namely, Maximus says that the deified willing of the saints, which in the address he has praised Marinus for attaining, *imitates* and follows after Christ's deified human willing:

> For the human will of God [in Christ] is not moved by choice, as it is with us, distinguishing opposite courses through council and judgement. So it is not considered naturally prone to choice's fitfulness, but rather it undoubtedly took its existence from the union with God the Word, while truly possessing a naturally appetitive will [τὴν κατ᾽ ὄρεξιν φυσικὴν . . . θέλησιν] with its stable movement. Or put even better, it possessed the unmoving rest in God of the purest existence, entirely deified by God the Word.[36]

34. *Op.* 1 (PG 91, 9A).

35. On the theme of infinite desire in Maximus and its root in Gregory of Nyssa, see Dalmais, "Les lignes essentielles," 194; Blowers, "Maximus the Confessor, Gregory of Nyssa," 153–55; Blowers, "The Dialectics and Therapeutics," 431–34.

36. *Op.* 1 (PG 91, 32A).

Relinquishing the burden of choice, empowering the stable course of natural desire, harmony with God's will, deification; as we have seen already
in the same *Opususclum*, these are all features of deified human willing
in which the saints and Marinus share. But at once, Maximus makes clear
in this passage, these salvific shapes of desire belong primarily and foundationally to *Christ's* perfect, deified human willing. The deified willing
of the saints is an imitation and sharing of Christ's willing. Accordingly,
in the praise address, after picturing Marinus as a saint with his will approaching deification, Maximus continues to praise him by saying that
his willing imitates Christ the Word:

> This is why life has become in you a face of the Word, and the
> Word the nature of life, truly outlining the new man according
> to Christ. This new man bears in exact imitation the image and
> the likeness of God the Creator . . .[37]

Through the movement of his natural will and longing, Marinus unites
himself with God, just as Christ does by *his* human will, and as a consequence of this, Marinus' life comes to imitate the life of Christ. We can see
now that the familiar pattern of knowing-by-likeness animates Maximus'
christological method here. Divinely oriented human willing or desiring
imitates and shares in Christ's human willing, and Maximus therefore
rhetorically recommends it to Marinus as the spiritual condition for
grasping the claim of dyothelite Christology—that Christ possessed a
human will completely oriented to the divine will.

### Maximus' many words for "desire"

A number of Maximus' other dyothelite letters include praise addresses
that similarly exhibit desire as an activity that can come to imitate Christ.
Before moving to them it is worth highlighting that Maximus' many
terms for "desire" are flexible and interrelated. Consider the following
astonishing passage:

> Every mind . . . possesses the rational faculty [τὴν λογικὴν
> δύναμιν], from which knowledgeable faith is naturally begot-
> ten . . . And it possesses the desirous faculty [τὴν ἐπιθυμητικὴν
> δύναμιν], according to which the divine love [ἡ θεία . . . ἀγάπη]
> is established, and through which the mind voluntarily nails
> itself to the longing [πόθῳ] for unmixed divinity, possessing

37. *Op.* 1 (PG 91, 9A–12A).

the unfailing desire [ἔφεσιν] for the longed-for object [τοῦ ποθουμένου]. And it possesses the irascible faculty [τὴν θυμικὴν δύναμιν], by which it cleaves fast to divine peace, turning the movement of desire [ἐπιθυμίας] towards the divine *eros* [τὸν θεῖον ἔρωτα].[38]

Here Maximus outlines the composition of the mind, and he is probably following Nemesius' endorsement of Plato's tripartite theory of the soul.[39] The mind has three faculties or drives—one "rational" and two non-rational, the "desirous" and the "irascible"—all three of which Maximus thinks can be divinely oriented. He characterizes the activity of these last two faculties with a baffling selection of terms for love and desire. There are a number of other places in Maximus' writings where we find a similarly dense and excited mixture of desire terms.[40] Maximus feels free to throw all of his desire words together, with little obvious precision, and this is surely because he is aware of the shared ultimate object of all kinds of desire. Perhaps, even, the convocation of these words intends to incite in the reader a feeling for the overwhelming effect of desire's divine object. Maximus' "desire" terms are, then, often interchangeable. For example, he occasionally calls the natural will a "desire [ἔφεσις] for what is natural," instead of the usual vocabulary of "natural appetite [ὄρεξις]."[41] Or, in *Difficulty* 7, he describes the desire that motivates and moves creatures using the words ἔφεσις, ὄρεξις, and ἔρως, without any clear distinction between them.[42] Sometimes, however, Maximus unfolds different desire terms in orders of relation. For instance, ὄρεξις flourishes in πόθος in *Opusculum* 1, and elsewhere ἔφεσις precedes and anticipates πόθος.[43] As this suggests, for Maximus the word πόθος normally indicates the highest, most divine kind of desiring available to humans (but both ἔφεσις[44] and ἔρως[45] can also dwell this lofty position). In sum, all

38. *Qu. Thal.* 49 (CCSG 7, 355).

39. Nemesius, *nat. hom.* 14–16 (Morani, *Nemesii Emeseni*, 71–75). For more on Maximus' use of this trichotomy, along with a detailed account of its background, see Thunberg, *Microcosm and Mediator*, 174–95.

40. See e.g. *qu. Thal.* 65 (CCSG 22, 293), and *or. dom.* (CCSG 23, 58).

41. *Op.* 14 (PG 91, 153B); *op.* 26 (PG 91, 280A).

42. *Ambig.* 7.7 (DOML 28, 82–83).

43. *Qu. Thal.* 29 (CCSG 7, 213); *qu. Thal.* 49 (CCSG 7, 353); *myst. prol.* (CCSG 69, 7). See also the mysterious isolated words, ἔφεσις καὶ πόθος θεοῦ, preserved amongst the manuscript wreckage at the beginning of *qu. dub.* 1 (CCSG 10, 3).

44. *Op.* 4 (PG 91, 56D).

45. *Ambig.* 48.2 (DOML 29, 212–13).

kinds of desire are related for Maximus; one expression of desire entails or implies others. Consequently, his vocabulary of desire is flexible but can follow traceable orders.[46]

When it comes to Christology and the divine desire at work in the incarnation, the same is true. Towards the beginning of *Opusculum* 3, Maximus argues that the fathers "considered there to be in Christ not a gnomic appetite [ὄρεξιν] belonging to some particular man but a natural appetite belonging to the flesh intellectually animated by an intellect's movements, possessing the faculty of desire [ἐφέσεως] for what is natural, naturally moved and stamped by the Word for the fulfilment of the economy." They "wisely called it 'will,'" Maximus clarifies, "without which there could be no human nature."[47] As he does elsewhere, Maximus uses ὄρεξις and ἔφεσις interchangeably, and both refer to the basic driving force that belongs to every natural human will, and thus that belongs to the natural human will in Christ. As well as recognizing the desire at work in Christ's human will, Maximus is not afraid to speak of leases of divine desire, God the Word's own desire, active in the incarnation. In the introduction to one christological letter, for example, Maximus praises Stephen his recipient for imitating "God the Word who is beyond infinity, and who displayed the height of his own uncircumscribable glory by emptying himself for us, because he longed so much more [τοσοῦτον . . . ἐπιποθέστερον] to transform us that he conformed himself in flesh to what is lowlier."[48] Before there is need to speak of the will and desire of the human Jesus, Maximus says that the incarnation occurs at all as the fallout of God's own "longing" (πόθος). In *Difficulty* 5, Maximus makes the same claim more clearly: "Out of His infinite longing [ἀπείρω . . . πόθῳ] for human beings, He [the Word] has become truly and according to nature the very thing for which He longed [τὸ ποθούμενον]."[49] In

---

46. For a useful recent discussion of desire in Maximus that, following Maximus himself, does not over-categorize or set apart his many different "desire" words, see Blowers, *Maximus the Confessor*, 258–71. One distinction that Blowers does offer is the following: ὄρεξις is a "faculty" of desire whereas ἔφεσις and πόθος describe the "activity" of desire "after a targeted goal" (262). This is often a helpful distinction, but does not hold up against at least two facts. First, as I have mentioned, Maximus sometimes uses ἔφεσις in place of ὄρεξις. Secondly, he employs the adjective ὀρεκτός—"desired" or, literally, "appetized-over"—which suggests he understood ὄρεξις not only as a "faculty" but as a "targeted" activity (e.g. *Op.* 1 [PG 91, 24B–25A] and *cap. theol.* 2.86 [PG 90, 1165B]).

47. *Op.* 3 (PG 91, 45C–D).

48. *Op.* 15 (PG 91, 156C).

49. *Ambig.* 5.4 (DOML 28, 34–35, including trans.).

short, Maximus follows Dionysius' boldness in ascribing "desire" to God himself. For Maximus, however, it seems that πόθος is the substitute for Dionysius' ἔρος—indeed, it is interesting and perhaps not coincidental that, at the beginning and the end of the *Mystagogy*, Maximus recommends "longing" (πόθος) to his readers as the appropriate motivation out of which to approach Dionysius' teachings.[50] Whatever Maximus' exact thoughts on God's desire, we can be certain from these passages that "longing" (πόθος), again, is consistently the highest, most divine kind of desire, characterized by "infinity." For example, we saw at the beginning of *Opusculum* 1 that πόθος draws human minds towards divine "infinity" (ἀπειρία),[51] and in the excerpts above it is itself "infinite" and characterizes God's descent from "beyond infinity" (ὑπεράπειρος) into humanity: longing is the energy not only behind human deification but behind God's incarnation too.

To parse these findings: Maximus musters a dizzying selection of "desire" terms and he considers at least three of them apt for naming the driving forces behind the incarnate life of the Word: ὄρεξις, ἔφεσις, and πόθος, the first two of which can describe Christ's human willing, the last the divine willing, or the activity of the divine Word.

### Desire and dyothelite Christology in Maximus' letters

With this in mind, let us move on to some other praise addresses. In the early christological letter, the *Second Letter to Thomas*, Maximus includes in his praise address a paean to Thomas' desire: "laboring only for that insatiable desire [ἀπληστίαν] for deifying knowledge, you possess an ever-moving desire [ἔφεσιν], whose satisfaction fathers in you more longing [πόθου], paradoxically increasing your appetite [ὄρεξιν] in participation."[52] As Maximus praises Thomas, preparing him for the christological content of the letter, he outlines a concatenation of deifying movements of desire growing out of Thomas' ascetic endeavor. Maximus imagines Thomas' divinely oriented desiring to be a felicitous condition for grasping the mystery of the incarnation. But more interestingly, Maximus encourages just those conditions of desire—ὄρεξις, ἔφεσις, and

50. *Myst.* prol. (CCSG 69, 7), where Maximus also uses the synonym ἔφεσις; *myst.* 24 (CCSG 69, 71), where Maximus also uses the word ἐπιθυμία.

51. *Op.* 1 (PG 91, 9A).

52. *Ep. sec.* prol. (CCSG 48, 38).

πόθος—that we have seen him elsewhere attribute to the incarnate Word. Divinely directed desiring conforms one's mind and life to Christ's, in other words, and thereby grants a visceral comprehension of the mystery of the incarnation.

When we see this same rhetorical pattern at play in the anti-mono-thelite letters, we can specify this claim: for Maximus, divinely directed desiring conforms one's willing or desiring to Christ's, and thereby fits the mind to understand and accept the dyothelite position through likeness to the reality it points to. I have already shown that this is the case in *Opusculum* 1, and there are a number of other letters in which Maximus primes his readers for grasping the mystery of Christ's wills by praising their desire. As we saw in the last chapter, Maximus opens *Opusculum* 4, a letter on Christ's wills, by praising his recipient George for being cap-tivated "with divine desire" (ἐφέσει θεία).[53] Or again, in *Opusculum* 8 on Christ's wills, during the praise address which we translated in the previous chapter, Maximus says that Nikandros attains that which is "by nature desirable [ἐφετοῦ],"[54] and with this attainment has the power to reform Maximus' own volition: Christ-like Nikandros dissuades Maxi-mus from "gnomically" (γνωμικῶς), "deliberately" (ἐμπροθέτως), and "actively" (δι' ἐνεργείας) separating himself from Christ, and instead kindles "desire" (ἔφεσις) in him.[55] Clearly, Maximus paints Nikandros as an exemplar and pioneer of a Christ-like, gnome-free human will, and rhetorically sets himself up in contrasting comparison as one plagued with a disordered gnomic will. In all of this, Maximus aims to stimulate Nikandros into grasping the mystery of Christ's two wills—a human will in complete deified accord with the divine will—by making him aware of his own achievements of Christ-like human willing.

As a last example, we can take the typical threefold praise introduc-tion found in *Opusculum* 16, to Theodore:

> [PREAMBLE:] Some have thought that shapes and forms sys-tematically make up stability and the cosmos. Such is what lazy people, out of their ignorance of what is hidden, suppose fits the appearance of things. But with you, holy Father, who have already brought your thinking over to uninterrupted life, with you that virtue prevails that is simple and unsystematic, rising above every form and shape towards beauty and refuge. This

53. *Op.* 4 (PG 91, 56D).
54. *Op.* 8 (PG 91, 89D).
55. *Op.* 8 (PG 91, 92B).

virtue beautifies what is invisible in you, as well as what appears to all, as far as you preferred sure and insatiable longing [πόθον] over the unravelling world. Or rather, properly speaking, it shows a person to be assimilated and like to God, as far as it has displayed his condition to be in every way unlike and estranged from matter and all the things to do with it. [DEEDS:] In this way, you remain unassailed by evil deeds. For naturally you undergo nothing at the hands of evil deeds, having undergone good things and become completely swayed by them, and having received the fulfilment of longing [πόθου], the final achievement of what you desire [τοῦ ποθουμένου], and a rest from movement in ever-moving stillness. And with this, the death that ruled over nature from of old completely disappears and nature is no longer broken by it through transgression. For you no longer stand on what tosses and turns, thanks to the prevailing grace of the Spirit. Under this grace you endure in prayers and accomplish its paths with understanding, actively demonstrating how great are the royal and divine paths for those who wish to walk straight along the unswerving path of pious belief. You mark out the forks in these paths, making clear the sorrows threatened by some routes and the holy rewards promised by others, so that with both fear and desire [πόθῳ] you might lead on wanderers towards perfection in God. [COMPARISON:] I marvel at your achievement and rightly praise your wisdom; or rather, being struck by your vigor in both of these respects, I glorify God who gives you your strength and wisdom, and I beseech you to use these same methods for those who fall short in their understanding, and to do so without being wearied. For this virtue knows no weariness, working all good things until you instill the mind of Christ and are trained to "examine the depths of the Spirit" [1 Cor 2:10], who uses visible things to trace out the wisdom and power that has been spoken in a mystery, and reveal it to those like you who have attached themselves to him and consider nothing more valuable than life together with him. But since you have grasped this preeminent and perfect virtue, which shines like a promotion and seal—which virtue is, I say, *humility*—you deemed it worthy to inquire of me, your slave and student, whether the definition of natural will that the venerable monk gave was good or bad . . .[56]

Maximus lauds Theodore at length for the journey that his plenitude of "insatiable longing [πόθος]" is taking him on. This longing springs,

56. *Op.* 16 (PG 91, 184D–185C).

moreover, from a certain unidentified "virtue." Eventually, Maximus reveals that this virtue, governing Theodore's activity and funding his desire, is nothing other than Christ-like "humility," which Theodore displays in condescending to seek advice from Maximus the lowly "slave." As we have seen, Maximus understands "humility" to be an activity of will that imitates Christ, or as he puts it here, it "instills the mind of Christ." Consequently, as Theodore embraces humility his will takes on the shape of Christ, descending to help those who "fall short," those like Maximus the "slave," and a special kind of desiring takes hold of him, "longing" (πόθος), which makes him utterly "assimilated to" and "like" (ὅμοιος) God. This tallies with what we have already learnt about "longing." For Maximus, "longing" is the kind of desire that takes a human will into the volitional life of Christ: into the divinely-aligned, deified will known first by Jesus and then the saints, and into God the Word's own will to become incarnate. In this letter, and in the other introductions where we have seen Maximus ascribe "longing" (πόθος) or "divine" desire to his human recipients, Maximus rhetorically places his addressee right in the middle of the deifying interaction and harmony of human and divine willing at work in the incarnation. This is the place the believer must seek out, Maximus implies, in their striving for clarity in christological truth, especially on the topic of Christ's willing. This is the place wherefrom "deep calls out to deep," and wherefrom the desire of Theodore, and Maximus' other interlocutors, reaches out to grasp the dyothelite mystery—such, at least, is what the praise rhetoric shows that Maximus hoped for and intended.

## Conclusion

In this chapter, we sought to explore what activities of imitation Maximus recommended for discerning dyothelite Christology. We began by noting that humility, a key christological virtue explored in the previous chapter, is in fact a virtue of *will*, that brings believers close to the mystery of Christ's two wills by aligning their volitional life with his. Then our attention was caught by the presence of emphatic "desire" language in the praise addresses of Maximus' dyothelite letters. I argued that we had here another example of Maximus' likeness epistemology at work. We found that there was a match between Maximus' teaching on Christ's human will, in *Opusculum* 1 for example, and the way he typically portrays the desire of his addressees. The states of desire that Maximus praises his readers for achieving mirror Christ's own deified willing, as Maximus describes it in his dyothelite letters—a human will completely harmonized and enrapt with the divine will. From this we pieced together a pattern of doctrinal discernment that Maximus repeatedly encouraged his readers to follow in order to feel their way into the mystery of Christ's two wills. This pattern sees would-be christologians humbly shaping their desiring after Christ's desiring, thus finding themselves present with the reality they seek to know.

# Conclusion

## *"Christology from within"*

In summarizing the findings of this study we can return to how it began, with "a problem with Maximus the Confessor." In the introduction, I put forward the following problematic question: how does Maximus' oeuvre hold together comfortably when his early and late writings apparently work on two drastically disparate models of knowledge-management, one ascetic, the other dogmatic? The body of our study has labored to show a facet of Maximus' approach to knowledge, a facet I have called his "likeness epistemology," that acts as a long thread tying together his most incongruent writings and characterizing them, offering a solution to our "problem."

It is worth briefly recalling how I went about this. In the first chapter we identified an epistemological theme entering Christian discourse in second- and third-century Alexandria (a theme summarized throughout the study with Aristotle's phrase, "like is known by like"). The second chapter identified some familiar and novel ways that Maximus played with this theme in his early works, and then, in the third chapter, we asked *why* likeness, or imitation, holds any epistemological facility at all in Maximus' outlook. The short answer was that likeness to God, for Maximus, is a form of deification or "tropological" identity to God; and more specifically, Maximus argued that this deification occurs "in proportion" to humans' likeness to God. In parallel, we also discovered that the same was true in the believer's relationship with Christ: for Maximus, when a believer imitates Christ, one can truly say that Christ is present there, "incarnate" in the believer, again "in proportion" to the kind of Christ-likeness the believer enacts. The remaining three chapters moved on to the previously unnoticed rhetorical tactics at work in many of Maximus' letters, and together put forward the following fundamental claim: that the praise addresses in these letters show up a model of discernment in which imitating the objects of doctrine proves the key to understanding and accepting them, whether the object is the mystery of divine love, the incarnation, or Christ's two natural wills.

In answer to our opening "problem," then, we have found that an epistemological ideal variously propounded in Maximus' early works— that "like is known by like"—is traceably active in his late works and patterns them; in this way his epistemological approach throughout his corpus is coherent. The early works give the theory: imitation is the key to knowledge of divine things. And in the late christological works we find the practice: the ideal of imitation stands guard at the beginning of Maximus' texts, enabling and managing the flow of communication and knowledge in matters of christological doctrine.

If we have solved our "problem," and have discovered that Maximus' late christological letters are resourced by his early ascetic theory that imitation leads to knowledge, the last thing I want to do is find a final summarizing label, or image, for Maximus' christological method. Perhaps we could label it a "practical Christology," or "ascetic Christology": how people act in relation to Christ shapes how people know Christ. Or maybe we could go a bit further. We saw in Chapter 3 that Maximus not only made the practical or phenomenological claim that imitation brings knowledge but, more deeply and foundationally, he made clear his trust in a theological reality: that imitation brings an "incarnate" intimacy with God and Christ. For Maximus, how people act in relation to Christ shapes how Christ dwells in people. Polycarp Sherwood offhandedly comes at our "problem" when, in a footnote to his translation of Maximus' *Ascetic Life*, he suggests the following deep link running between the Confessor's spirituality and dogmatic Christology: "The fact of the indwelling of Christ is dear to Maximus . . . It is perhaps the christological conflicts that have contributed to this emphasis."[1] From the conclusions of this study we can clarify Sherwood's connection by turning it on its head: it is Maximus' early emphasis on the indwelling of Christ, Christ's "incarnation" in the believer, that lays the ground and method for his later engagement in christological conflict. In early works like *Difficulties* 47 and 48, we found Maximus notionally portraying Christ present, incarnate, amidst those who imitate him. And then in his later christological letters we saw

1. ACW 21, 266, n. 237.

Maximus encouraging his listeners to step into this very same encounter, to imitate Christ, find him present within them, and only then to engage in christological reflection. In this sense, the real "manager" of knowledge is not a standard of imitation, but God. Maximus' christological method is not only "practical" or "ascetic" but "theological."

With this in mind, perhaps we could characterize Maximus' Christology with a phrase coined by a modern theologian, Mark McIntosh, to summarize the Christology of Hans Urs von Balthasar (one of Maximus' great interpreters). From all that has been argued in this study, we might conclude that Maximus propounded a "Christology from within." McIntosh describes von Balthasar's Christology as follows:

> [I]t is not a standard Christology "from above"; that is, its center is not really the eternal life of the divine Logos. Nor is it a Christology "from below," focusing on the critical examination of Jesus' earthly sayings or ministry or sociocultural milieu. Rather von Balthasar develops a Christology from within, an analysis of Christ from the perspective of those women and men who have mystically entered *within* the life of Christ.[2]

For Maximus, something essentially similar is the case, and perhaps it is not surprising that von Balthasar's Christology should take shape like this, steeped as he was in Maximus' thought. The Confessor believes that the lines of christological orthodoxy are traced seminally and diversely from "within" the life and practice of those who imitate Christ, and who find Christ incarnate "within" them. Maximus' christological method is to point out these lines and shapes in his listeners, designing a space in them for the incarnate Christ to come in and teach them about himself.

2. McIntosh, *Christology from Within*, 2.

# Bibliography

Alexander, Patrick H., et al., eds. *The SBL handbook of Style: For Ancient Near Eastern, Biblical, and Early Christian Studies*. Peabody, MA: Hendrickson, 1999.

Allen, Pauline. "Life and Times of Maximus the Confessor." In *The Oxford Handbook of Maximus the Confessor*, edited by Pauline Allen and Bronwen Neil, 3–18. Oxford: Oxford University Press, 2015.

———, and Bronwen Neil, eds. and trans. *Maximus the Confessor and His Companions: Documents from Exile*. Oxford Early Christian Texts. Oxford: Oxford University Press, 2002.

———. "Prolegomena to a Study of the Letter-Bearer in Christian Antiquity." *Studia Patristica* 62 (2013) 481–91.

———, trans. *Severus of Antioch*. Early Church Fathers. London: Routledge, 2004.

———, ed. and trans. *Sophronius of Jerusalem and Seventh-Century Heresy: The Synodical Letter and Other Documents*. Oxford Early Christian Texts. Oxford: Oxford University Press, 2009.

Aquino, Frederick D. "Maximus the Confessor." In *The Spiritual Senses: Perceiving God in Western Christianity*, edited by Paul L. Gavrilyuk and Sarah Coakley, 104–20. Cambridge: Cambridge University Press, 2011.

———. "The Synthetic Unity of Virtue and Epistemic Goods in Maximus the Confessor." *Studies in Christian Ethics* 26 (2013) 378–90.

Ashwin-Siejkowski, Piotr. *Clement of Alexandria: A Project of Christian Perfection*. London: T. & T. Clark, 2008.

Athanassiadi, Polymnia. *La Lutte pour l'orthodoxie dans le platonisme tardif: De Numénius à Damascius*. Paris: Les Belles Lettres, 2006.

Ayres, Lewis. "Christology as Contemplative Practice: Understanding the Union of Natures in Augustine's *Letter 137*." In *In the Shadow of the Incarnation: Essays on Jesus Christ in the Early Church in Honor of Brian E. Daley, S.J.*, edited by Peter William Martens, 190–211. Notre Dame, IN: University of Notre Dame Press, 2008.

———. "Irenaeus vs. the Valentinians: Toward a Rethinking of Patristic Exegetical Origins." *Journal of Early Christian Studies* 23 (2015) 153–87.

———. *Nicaea and Its Legacy: An Approach to Fourth-Century Trinitarian Theology*. Oxford: Oxford University Press, 2004.

———. "'There's Fire in That Rain': On Reading the Letter and Reading Allegorically." *Modern Theology* 28 (2012) 616–34.

Babbitt, Frank Cole, trans. *Plutarch. Moralia, Volume V: Isis and Osiris. The E at Delphi. The Oracles at Delphi No Longer Given in Verse. The Obsolescence of Oracles.* Loeb Classical Library 306. Cambridge: Harvard University Press, 1936.

Baehrens, Wilhelm Adolf, ed. *Origenes Werke, Band 8: Homilien zu Samuel I, zum Hohelied und zu den Propheten.* Griechischen christlichen schriftsteller 33. Berlin: De Gruyter, 1925.

Balthasar, Hans Urs von. *Cosmic Liturgy: The Universe according to Maximus the Confessor.* Translated by Brian E. Daley. San Francisco: Ignatius, 2003.

Banev, Krastu. *Theophilus of Alexandria and the First Origenist Controversy: Rhetoric and Power.* Oxford Early Christian Studies. Oxford: Oxford University Press, 2015.

Bathrellos, Demetrios. *The Byzantine Christ: Person, Nature, and Will in the Christology of St Maximus the Confessor.* Oxford: Oxford University Press, 2004.

———. "Passions, Ascesis, and the Virtues." In *The Oxford Handbook of Maximus the Confessor,* edited by Pauline Allen and Bronwen Neil, 287–306. Oxford: Oxford University Press, 2015.

Beeley, Christopher A. *Gregory of Nazianzus on the Trinity and the Knowledge of God: In Your Light We Shall See Light.* Oxford Studies in Historical Theology. Oxford: Oxford University Press, 2008.

Benevich, Grigory. "God's Logoi and Human Personhood in St Maximus the Confessor." *Studi sull'Oriente Cristiano* 13 (2009) 137–52.

———, "John Philoponus and Maximus the Confessor at the Crossroads of Philosophical and Theological Thought in Late Antiquity." *Scrinium* 7–8 (2011) 102–30.

———. "Maximus the Confessor's Polemics against Anti-Origenism: *Epistulae* 6 and 7 as a Context for the *Ambigua Ad Iohannem.*" *Revue d'histoire ecclésiastique* 104 (2009) 5–15.

Bernardi, Jean, ed. and trans. *Grégoire de Nazianze. Discours 4–5. Contre Julien.* Sources Chrétiennes 309. Paris: Cerf, 1983.

Berthold, George C. "Aspects of the Will in Maximus the Confessor." *Studia Patristica* 48 (2010) 65–69.

———. "The Cappadocian Roots of Maximus the Confessor." In *Maximus Confessor: actes du Symposium sur Maxime le Confesseur, Fribourg, 2–5 Septembre 1980,* edited by Felix Heinzer and Christoph Schönborn, 51–59. Fribourg: Éditions universitaires, 1982.

———. "Free Will as a Partner of Nature: Maximus the Confessor on the *Our Father.*" *Studia Patristica* 51 (2011) 173–19.

———, trans. *Maximus Confessor: Selected Writings.* New York: Paulist, 1985.

Binns, John, *Ascetics and Ambassadors of Christ: The Monasteries of Palestine, 314–631.* Oxford Early Christian Studies. Oxford: Clarendon, 1994.

Blanc, Cécile, ed. and trans. *Origène. Commentaire sur saint Jean, tome I (livres I–V).* Sources Chrétiennes 120. Paris: Cerf, 1966.

———, ed. and trans. *Origène. Commentaire sur saint Jean, tome III (livre XIII).* Sources Chrétiennes 222. Paris: Cerf, 1975.

———, ed. and trans. *Origène. Commentaire sur saint Jean, tome IV (livres XIX et XX).* Sources Chrétiennes 290. Paris: Cerf, 1982.

———, ed. and trans. *Origène. Commentaire sur saint Jean, tome V (livres XXVIII et XXXII).* Sources Chrétiennes 385. Paris: Cerf, 1992.

Blowers, Paul M. "Aligning and Reorienting the Passible Self: Maximus the Confessor's Virtue Ethics." *Studies in Christian Ethics* 26 (2013) 333–50.

———. "Bodily Inequality, Material Chaos, and the Ethics of Equalization in Maximus the Confessor." *Studia Patristica* 42 (2006) 51–56.

———. "The Dialectics and Therapeutics of Desire in Maximus the Confessor." *Vigiliae Christianae* 65 (2011) 425–51.

———. *Exegesis and Spiritual Pedagogy in Maximus the Confessor: An Investigation of the* Quaestiones Ad Thalassium. Notre Dame, IN: University of Notre Dame Press, 1991.

———. "Interpreting Scripture." In *The Cambridge History of Christianity, Vol. 2: Constantine to C. 600,* edited by Augustine Casiday and Frederick W. Norris, 618–36. Cambridge: Cambridge University Press, 2007.

———. "The Logology of Maximus the Confessor in His Criticism of Origenism." In *Origeniana Quinta: Historica, Text and Method, Biblica, Philosophica, Theologica, Origenism and Later Developments: Papers of the 5th International Origen Congress, Boston College, 14–18 August 1989,* edited by Robert J. Daly, 570–76. Leuven: Peeters, 1992.

———. "Maximus the Confessor and John of Damascus on Gnomic Will (*gnōmē*) in Christ: Clarity and Ambiguity." *Union Seminary Quarterly Review* 63 (2012) 44–50.

———, "Maximus the Confessor, Gregory of Nyssa, and the Concept of 'Perpetual Progress.'" *Vigiliae Christianae* (1992) 151–71.

———. *Maximus the Confessor: Jesus Christ and the Transfiguration of the World.* Christian Theology in Context. Oxford: Oxford University Press, 2016.

———, and Robert Louis Wilken, trans. *On the Cosmic Mystery of Jesus Christ: Selected Writings from St. Maximus the Confessor.* St. Vladimir's Seminary Press "Popular Patristics" Series 25. Crestwood, NY: St. Vladimir's Seminary, 2003.

———. "On the 'Play' of Divine Providence in Gregory Nazianzen and Maximus the Confessor." In *Re-Reading Gregory of Nazianzus: Essays on History, Theology, and Culture,* edited by Christopher W. Beeley, 199–217. Washington, DC: Catholic University of America Press, 2012.

———. "The Passion of Jesus Christ in Maximus the Confessor: A Reconsideration." *Studia Patristica* 37 (2001) 361–77.

———. "The World in the Mirror of Holy Scripture: Maximus the Confessor's Short Hermeneutical Treatise in *Ambiguum Ad Joannem 37.*" In *In Dominico eloquio—In Lordly Eloquence: Essays on Patristic Exegesis in Honor of Robert Louis Wilken,* edited by Paul M. Blowers et al., 408–26. Grand Rapids: Eerdmans, 2002.

Blumenthal, H. J. *Aristotle and Neoplatonism in Late Antiquity: Interpretations of the De Anima.* London: Duckworth, 1996.

Bondi, Roberta C. *Three Monophysite Christologies: Severus of Antioch, Philoxenus of Mabbug and Jacob of Sarug.* Oxford Theological Monographs. London: Oxford University Press, 1976.

Booth, Phil. *Crisis of Empire: Doctrine and Dissent at the End of Late Antiquity.* Transformation of the Classical Heritage 52. Berkeley: University of California Press, 2014.

Borgen, Peder. *Philo of Alexandria: An Exegete for His Time.* Supplements to Novum Testamentum 86. Leiden: Brill, 1997.

Borret, Marcel, ed. *Origène. Contre Celse, tome I (livres I et II)*. Sources Chrétiennes 132. Paris: Cerf, 1967.

———, ed. and trans. *Origène. Homélies sur le Lévitique (I–VII), tome I*. Sources Chrétiennes 286. Paris: Cerf, 1981

———, ed. and trans. *Origène. Homélies sur le Lévitique (VIII–XVI), tome II*. Sources Chrétiennes 287. Paris: Cerf, 1982.

———, ed. and trans. *Origène. Homélies sur l'Exode*. Sources Chrétiennes 321. Paris: Cerf, 1985.

Boudignon, Christian. "Maxime le Confesseur était-il constantinopolitain?" In *Philomathestatos: Studies in Greek and Byzantine Texts Presented to Jacques Noret for his Sixty-fifth Birthday*, edited by Bart Janssens et al., 11–43. Leuven: Peeters, 2004.

———, ed. *Maximi Confessor. Mystagogia*. Corpus Christianorum, series graeca 69. Turnhout: Brepols, 2011.

———. "Le pouvoir de l'anathème, ou Maxime le Confesseur et les moines palestiniens du VIIe siècle." In *Foundations of Power and Conflicts of Authority in Late-Antique Monasticism: Proceedings of the International Seminar, Turin, December 2–4, 2004*, edited by A. Camplani and G. Filoramo, 245–74. Leuven: Peeters, 2007.

Boys-Stones, George. "The Stoics' Two Types of Allegory." In *Metaphor, Allegory, and the Classical Tradition: Ancient Thought and Modern Revisions*, edited by George Boys-Stones, 189–216. Oxford: Oxford University Press, 2003.

Bracke, Raphael, et al. "Some Aspects of the Manuscript Tradition of the *Ambigua* of Maximus the Confessor." In *Maximus Confessor: actes du Symposium sur Maxime le Confesseur, Fribourg, 2–5 Septembre 1980*, edited by Felix Heinzer and Christoph Schönborn, 97–109. Fribourg: Éditions universitaires, 1982.

———. "Two Fragments of a Greek Manuscript Containing a Corpus Maximianum: Mss. Genavensis Graecus 360 and Leidensis Scaligeranus 33." *The Patristic and Byzantine Review* 4 (1985) 110–14.

Bradshaw, David. "The Logoi of Beings in Greek Patristic Thought." In *Toward an Ecology of Transfiguration: Orthodox Christian Perspectives on Environment, Nature, and Creation*, edited by John Chryssavgis and Bruce V. Foltz, 9–22. New York: Fordham University Press, 2013.

———. "St Maximus the Confessor on the Will." In *Knowing the Purpose of Creation through the Resurrection*, edited by Maxim Vasiljević, 143–57. Alhambra, CA: Sebastian, 2013.

Bremmer, Jan. "How Old Is the Ideal of Holiness (Of Mind) in the Epidaurian Temple Inscription and the Hippocratic Oath?" *Zeitschrift Für Papyrologie Und Epigraphik* 141 (2002) 106–8.

Bringel, Pauline, ed. *Sophronius of Jerusalem. Panégyrique des saints Cyr et Jean*. Patrologia Orientalis 51. Turnhout: Brepols, 2008.

Brisson, Luc. *How Philosophers Saved Myths: Allegorical Interpretation and Classical Mythology*. Chicago: University of Chicago Press, 2008.

Broadie, Sarah, ed., and Christopher Rowe, trans. *Aristotle. Nicomachean Ethics*. Oxford: Oxford University Press, 2002.

Bruce, Barbara J., trans., and Cynthia White, ed. *Origen. Homilies on Joshua*. Fathers of the Church 105. Washington, DC: Catholic University of America Press, 2002.

Bryan, Jenny. *Likeness and Likelihood in the Presocratics and Plato*. Cambridge Classical Studies. Cambridge: Cambridge University Press, 2012.

Bucur, Bogdan G. "Matt. 17:1–9 as a Vision of a Vision: A Neglected Strand in the Patristic Reception of the Transfiguration Account." *Neotestamentica* (2010) 15–30.

Buffière, Félix. *Les mythes d'Homère et la pensée grecque*. Collection d'Études anciennes 11. Paris: Les Belles Lettres, 1956.

Burnyeat, Myles. "ΕΙΚΩΣ ΜΥΘΟΣ." *Rhizai* 2 (2005) 143–65.

Busse, Adolfus, and Maximilianus Wallies, eds. *Ammonius in Aristotelis Categorias commentarium*. Commentaria in Aristotelem Graeca 4.4. Berlin: De Gruyter, 1895.

Butterworth, George William, *Origen on First Principles: Being Koetschau's Text of the De Principiis*. Gloucester, MA: Peter Smith, 1973.

Cameron, Averil. "Ascetic Closure and the End of Antiquity." In *Asceticism*, edited by Vincent L. Wimbush and Richard Valantasis, 147–61. New York: Oxford University Press, 1995.

———. "Byzantium and the Past in the Seventh Century: The Search for Redefinition." In *Changing Cultures in Early Byzantium*, 250–76. Aldershot, UK: Variorum, 1996.

———. *Christianity and the Rhetoric of Empire: The Development of Christian Discourse*. Berkeley: University of California Press, 1991.

———. "Disputations, Polemical Literature and the Formation of Opinion in the Early Byzantine Period." In *Changing Cultures in Early Byzantium*, 91–108. Aldershot, UK: Variorum, 1996.

———. "Thinking with Byzantium." *Transactions of the Royal Historical Society* 21 (1939) 39–57.

Canart, Paul "La deuxième Lettre à Thomas de saint Maxime le Confesseur, introduction, texte critique et traduction." *Byzantion* 34 (1964) 415–45.

Carabine, Deirdre. "A Dark Cloud: Hellenistic Influences on the Scriptural Exegesis of Clement of Alexandria and the Pseudo-Dionysius." In *Scriptural Interpretation in the Fathers*, edited by Thomas Finan and Vincent Twomey, 61–74. Dublin: Four Courts, 1995.

Chadwick, Henry. "John Moschus and His Friend Sophronius the Sophist." *Journal of Theological Studies* 25 (1974) 385–418.

———, trans. *Origen. Contra Celsum*. Cambridge: Cambridge University Press, 1980.

Cherniss, Harold. *Aristotle's Criticism of Presocratic Philosophy*. Baltimore: Johns Hopkins, 1935.

———. "Galen and Posidonius' Theory of Vision." *The American Journal of Philology* 54 (1933) 154–61.

Chiaradonna, Riccardo. "Plotinus' Account of the Cognitive Powers of the Soul: Sense Perception and Discursive Thought." *Topoi* 31 (2012) 191–207.

Choufrine, Arkadi. *Gnosis, Theophany, Theosis: Studies in Clement of Alexandria's Appropriation of His Background*. New York: Lang, 2002.

Clark, Elizabeth Ann. *The Origenist Controversy: The Cultural Construction of an Early Christian Debate*. Princeton, NJ: Princeton University Press, 1992.

Coakley, Sarah. "'Mingling' in Gregory of Nyssa's Christology: A Reconsideration." In *Who Is Jesus Christ for Us Today? Pathways to Contemporary Christology*, edited by Andreas Schuele and Günter Thomas, 72–84. Louisville, KY: Westminster/John Knox, 2009.

———. "Prayer, Politics and the Trinity: Vying Models of Authority in Third–Fourth-Century Debates on Prayer and 'Orthodoxy.'" *Scottish Journal of Theology* 66 (2013) 379–99.

Cohen, S. Marc, and Gareth B. Matthews, trans. *Ammonius Hermiae. On Aristotle Categories*. Ancient Commentators on Aristotle. London: Duckworth, 1991.

Cohn, Leopold, ed. *Philonis Alexandrini. De specialibus legibus (I–IV). De virtutibus. De fortitudine. De humanitate. De paenitentia. De nobilitate. De praemiis et poenis. De exsecrationibus*. Philonis Alexandrini opera quae supersunt 5. Berlin: De Gruyter, 1963.

———, and Siegfried Reiter, eds. *Philonis Alexandrini. Quod omnis probus liber sit. De vita contemplativa. De aeternitate mundi. In Flaccum. Legatio ad Gaium*. Philonis Alexandrini opera quae supersunt 6. Berlin: De Gruyter, 1963.

Constas, Nicholas, ed. and trans. *On Difficulties in the Church Fathers: The Ambigua, Volume I*. Dumbarton Oaks Medieval Library 28. Cambridge: Harvard University Press, 2014.

———. *On Difficulties in the Church Fathers: The Ambigua, Volume II*. Dumbarton Oaks Medieval Library 29. Cambridge: Harvard University Press, 2014.

Cooper, Adam G. *The Body in St Maximus the Confessor: Holy Flesh, Wholly Deified*. Oxford: Oxford University Press, 2005.

———. "Christ as Teacher of Theology: Praying the Our Father with Origen and Maximus." In *Origeniana Octava: Origen and the Alexandrian tradition: Papers of the 8th International Origen Congress, Pisa, 27–31 August 2001*, edited by Lorenzo Perrone, 1053–59. Leuven: Peeters, 2003.

Cooper, John M., and D. S. Hutchinson, eds. *Plato: Complete Works*. Indianapolis: Hackett, 1997.

Courtine, Jean-François. *Inventio analogiae: Métaphysique et ontothéologie*. Paris: Vrin, 2005.

Crouzel, Henri. "Faut-il voir trois personnages en Grégoire le Thaumaturge?" *Gregorianum* 60 (1979) 287–319.

———, ed. and trans. *Grégoire le Thaumaturge, Origène. Remerciements à Origène et Lettre d'Origène à Grégoire*. Sources Chrétiennes 148. Paris: Cerf, 1969.

———, F. Fournier, and P. Périchon, eds. and trans. *Origène. Homélies sur saint Luc*. Sources Chrétiennes 87. Paris: Cerf, 1962.

———, and Manlio Simonetti, eds. and trans. *Origène. Traité des principes, tome III (livres III et IV)*. Sources Chrétiennes 268. Paris: Cerf, 1980.

———. *Théologie de l'image de Dieu chez Origène*. Paris: Aubier, 1956.

Cunningham, Mary, and Pauline Allen. *Preacher and Audience: Studies in Early Christian and Byzantine Homiletics*. Leiden: Brill, 1998.

Daley, Brian E., trans. *Gregory of Nazianzus*. The Early Church Fathers. London: Routledge, 2006.

———. "Making a Human Will Divine." In *Orthodox Readings of Augustine*, edited by George E. Demacopoulos and Aristotle Papanikolaou, 101–26. Crestwood, NY: St. Vladimir's Seminary, 2008.

———. "Nature and the 'Mode of Union': Late Patristic Models for the Personal Unity of Christ." In *The Incarnation: An Interdisciplinary Symposium on the Incarnation of the Son of God*, edited by Stephen T. Davis et al., 164–96. Oxford: Oxford University Press, 2004.

———. "The Origenism of Leontius of Byzantium." *Journal of Theological Studies* 27 (1976) 333–69.

———. "Origen's *De Principiis*: A Guide to the Principles of Christian Scriptural Interpretation." In *Nova et Vetera: Patristic Studies in Honor of Thomas Patrick Halton*, edited by John Petruccione, 3–21. Washington, DC: Catholic University of America Press, 1998.

———. "What Did 'Origenism' Mean in the Sixth Century?" In *Origeniana Sexta: Origène et la bible: Actes du Colloquium Origenianum Sextum, Chantilly, 30 Août– 3 Septembre 1993*, edited by Gilles Dorival and Alain Le Boulluec, 627–38. Leuven: Leuven University Press, 1995.

Dalmais, Irénée Henri. "La doctrine ascétique de S. Maxime le Confesseur d'après le *Liber Asceticus*." *Irénikon* 26 (1953) 17–39.

———. "L'innovation des natures d'après S. Maxime le Confesseur (à propos d'*Ambiguum* 42)." *Studia Patristica* 15 (1984) 285–90.

———. "Les lignes essentielles de la vie spirituelle selon S. Maxime le Confesseur." *Studia Patristica* 18 (1989) 191–96.

———. "La manifestation du Logos dans l'homme et dans l'Église: Typologie anthropologique et typologie écclesiale d'après *Qu. Thal.* 60 et la *Mystagogie*." In *Maximus Confessor: actes du Symposium sur Maxime le Confesseur, Fribourg, 2–5 Septembre 1980*, edited by Felix Heinzer and Christoph Schönborn, 13–25. Fribourg: Éditions universitaires, 1982.

———. "Mystère liturgique et divinisation dans la Mystagogie de saint Maxime le Confesseur." In *Epektasis: melanges patristiques offerts au Cardinal Jean Danielou*, edited by Jacques Fontaine and Charles Kannengiesser, 55–62. Paris: Editions Beauchesne, 1972.

———. "La théorie des 'logoi' des créatures chez S. Maxime le confesseur." *Revue des Sciences philosophiques et théologiques* 36 (1952) 244–49.

———. "Le Vocabulaire des activités intellectuelles, volontaires, et spirituelles dans l'anthropologie de S. Maxime le Confesseur." In *Melanges offerts à M. D. Chenu, maître en theologie*, 189–202. Paris: Librairie Philosophique, 1967.

Daniélou, Jean. "Aux sources de l'ésotérisme judéo-chrétien." *Archivio di Filosofia* 2–3 (1960) 39–46.

———. *Message évangélique et culture hellénistique aux IIe et IIIe siècles*. Tournai: Desclée, 1961.

Davis, Janet B. "Hermogenes of Tarsus." In *Classical Rhetorics and Rhetoricians: Critical Studies and Sources*, edited by Michelle Ballif and Michael G. Moran, 194–202. Westport, CT: Praeger, 2005.

Dawson, David, *Allegorical Readers and Cultural Revision in Ancient Alexandria*. Berkeley: University of California Press, 1992.

———. *Christian Figural Reading and the Fashioning of Identity*. Berkeley: University of California Press, 2002.

de Andia, Ysabel. "Transfiguration et théologie négative chez Maxime le Confesseur et Denys l'Aréopagite." In *Denys l'Aréopagite et sa postérité en Orient et en Occident*, edited by Ysabel de Andia, 293–328. Paris: Institut d'Études Augustiniennes, 1997.

Declerck, José, ed. *Maximi Confessoris. Quaestiones et dubia*. Corpus Christianorum, series graeca 10. Turnhout: Brepols, 1982.

Deferrari, Roy J., trans. *Basil. Letters, Volume III: Letters 186–248*. Loeb Classical Library 243. Cambridge: Harvard University Press, 1930.

————, trans. *Basil. Letters, Volume IV: Letters 249–368. On Greek Literature.* Loeb Classical Library 270. Cambridge: Harvard University Press, 1934.

De Lacy, Phillip, ed. and trans. *Galen. On the Doctrines of Hippocrates and Plato*, vol. 2. Berlin: Akademie Verlag, 2005.

————. "Stoic Views of Poetry." *The American Journal of Philology* 69 (1948) 241–71.

De Lange, Nicholas. *Origen and the Jews: Studies in Jewish-Christian Relations in Third-Century Palestine.* Cambridge: Cambridge University Press, 1976.

de Libera, Alain. "Les sources gréco-arabes de la théorie médiévale de l'analogie de l'être." *Les Études philosophiques* 3/4 (1989) 319–45.

De Lubac, Henri, *Medieval Exegesis. Vol. 2: The Four Senses of Scripture.* Grand Rapids: Eerdmans, 1998.

Dennis, George. "The Byzantines as Revealed in Their Letters." In *Gonimos: Neoplatonic and Byzantine Studies Presented to Leendert G. Westerink at 75*, edited by John M. Duffy and John Peradotto, 155–65. Buffalo, NY: Arethusa, 1988.

Descourtieux, Patrick, ed. and trans. *Clément d'Alexandrie. Les Stromates. Stromate VI.* Sources Chrétiennes 446. Paris: Cerf, 1999.

des Places, Édouard, ed. and trans. *Numenius of Apamea. Fragments.* Paris: Les Belles Lettres, 1973.

Detienne, Marcel. *Homère, Hésiode et Pythagore: Poésie et philosophie dans le pythagorisme ancien.* Bruxelles, Berchem: Latomus, Revue d'Études latines, 1962.

Devreesse, Robert. "L'église d'Afrique durant l'occupation byzantine." *Mélanges d'archéologie et d'histoire* 57 (1940) 143–66.

Dillon, John M. "Protreptic Epistolography, Hellenic and Christian." *Studia Patristica* 62 (2013) 29–40.

Disdier, M.-Th. "Les fondements dogmatiques de la spiritualité de saint Maxime le Confesseur." *Échos d'Orient* 29 (1930) 296–313.

Dively Lauro, Elizabeth Ann. *The Soul and Spirit of Scripture within Origen's Exegesis.* The Bible in Ancient Christianity 3. Leiden: Brill Academic, 2005.

Dolna, Bernhard. "The Hidden and Revealed Torah in Philo and Qumran." In *Qumran Legal Texts between the Hebrew Bible and Its Interpretation*, 91–107. Leuven: Peeters, 2011.

Doutreleau, Louis, ed. and trans. *Origène. Homélies sur la Genèse.* Sources Chrétiennes 7. Paris: Cerf, 1976.

————, ed. *Origène. Homélies sur les Nombres, III: Homélies XX–XXVIII.* Sources Chrétiennes 461. Paris: Cerf, 2001.

Downing, K. Kenneth, et al., eds. *Gregorii Nysseni. Opera dogmatica minora, In illud; Tunc et ipse filius.* Gregorii Nysseni Opera 3/2. Leiden: Brill, 1987.

Droge, Arthur J. "Homeric Exegesis among the Gnostics." *Studia Patristica* 19 (1989) 313–21.

Dubois, Jean-Daniel. "L'exégèse des gnostiques et l'histoire du canon des Écritures." In *Les règles de l'interprétation*, edited by Michel Tardieu, 89–97. Paris: Cerf, 1987.

Dunderberg, Ismo. *Beyond Gnosticism: Myth, Lifestyle, and Society in the School of Valentinus.* New York: Columbia University Press, 2008.

Ehrman, Bart D., ed. and trans. *The Apostolic Fathers, Volume II: Epistle of Barnabas. Papias and Quadratus. Epistle to Diognetus. The Shepherd of Hermas.* Loeb Classical Library 25. Cambridge: Harvard University Press, 2003.

————. "Heracleon, Origen, and the Text of the Fourth Gospel." *Vigiliae Christianae* 47 (1993) 105–18.

Emilsson, Eyjólfur K. *Plotinus on Sense-Perception: A Philosophical Study*. Cambridge: Cambridge University Press, 1988.

Felten, Joseph, ed. *Nicolai Progymnasmata*. Rhetores Graeci 11. Leipzig: In aedibus B. G. Teubneri, 1913.

Festugière, André Jean. *Contemplation et vie contemplative selon Platon*. Paris: Vrin, 1936.

Finkelberg, Aryeh. "'Like by Like' and Two Reflections of Reality in Parmenides." *Hermes* 114 (1986) 405–12.

Fortin, Ernest L. "Clement and the Esoteric Tradition." *Studia Patristica* 9 (1996) 41–56.

Gallay, Paul, ed. and trans. *Grégoire de Nazianze. Discours 27–31: Discours théologiques*. Sources Chrétiennes 250. Paris: Cerf, 1978.

———, ed. and trans. *Grégoire de Nazianze. Lettres théologiques*. Sources Chrétiennes 208. Paris: Cerf, 1974.

———, ed. and trans. *Saint Grégoire de Nazianze. Lettres*, vol. 1. Paris: Les Belles Lettres, 1964.

———, ed. and trans. *Saint Grégoire de Nazianze. Lettres*, vol. 2. Paris: Les Belles Lettres, 1967.

Gauthier, R. A. "Saint Maxime le Confesseur et la psychologie de l'acte humain." *Recherches de Théologie et Philosophie Médiévales* 21 (1954) 51–100.

Gersh, Stephen. *From Iamblichus to Eriugena: An Investigation of the Prehistory and Evolution of the Pseudo-Dionysian Tradition*. Leiden: Brill, 1978.

Gibson, Craig A. "The Agenda of Libanius' Hypotheses to Demosthenes." *Greek, Roman, and Byzantine Studies* 40 (1999) 171–202.

Grabar, André. "Plotin et les origenes de l'esthétique medieval." *Cahiers archéologiques* 1 (1945) 15–34.

Graeser, Andreas. *Plotinus and the Stoics: A Preliminary Study*. Philosophia Antiqua 22. Leiden: Brill, 1972.

Grant, Robert M. "Paul, Galen, and Origen." *The Journal of Theological Studies* 34 (1983) 533–36.

Greer, Rowan A., trans. *Origen*. Classics of Western Spirituality. New York: Paulist, 1979.

Grumel, Venance. "L'Union hypostatique et la comparaison de l'âme et du corps chez Léonce de Byzance et saint Maxime le Confesseur." *Échos d'Orient* 25 (1926) 393–406.

Guiu, Adrian. "Christology and Philosophical Culture in Maximus the Confessor's *Ambiguum* 41." *Studia Patristica* 48 (2010) 111–16.

Guthrie, Kenneth Sylvan. *Numenius of Apamea, the Father of Neo-Platonism: Works, Biography, Message, Sources, and Influence*. London: Bell & Sons, 1917.

Hadot, Ilsetraut. "Les introductions aux commentaires exégétiques chez les auteurs néoplatoniciens et les auteurs chrétiens." In *Les Règles de l'interprétation*, edited by Michel Tardieu, 99–119. Paris: Cerf, 1987.

Hadot, Pierre. *Philosophy as a Way of Life: Spiritual Exercises from Socrates to Foucault*, edited by Arnold Davidson. Oxford: Blackwell, 1995.

———. "Théologie, exégèse, révélation, écriture, dans la philosophie grecque." In *Les Règles de l'interprétation*, edited by Michel Tardieu, 13–34. Paris: Cerf, 1987.

Hägg, Henny Fiskå. *Clement of Alexandria and the Beginnings of Christian Apophaticism*. Oxford Early Christian Studies. Oxford: Oxford University Press, 2006.

Hahm, David E. "Early Hellenistic Theories of Vision and the Perception of Color." In *Studies in Perception*, edited by P. K. Machamer and R. Turnbull, 60–95. Columbus, OH: Ohio State University Press, 1978.

Haldon, John F. *Byzantium in the Seventh Century: The Transformation of a Culture*. Cambridge: Cambridge University Press, 1997.

———. "Ideology and the Byzantine State in the Seventh Century: The 'Trial' of Maximus the Confessor." In *From Late Antiquity to Early Byzantium: Proceedings of the Byzantinological Symposium in the 16th International Eirene Conference*, edited by Vladimír Vavřínek, 87–92. Prague: Academia, 1985.

Hall, Christopher A., ed., and Thomas P. Scheck, trans. *Origen. Homilies on Numbers*. Ancient Christian Texts. Downers Grove, IL: IVP Academic, 2009.

Hammond Bammel, Caroline P., ed., and L. Brésard., trans. *Origène. Commentaire de l'Épître aux Romains, tome I (livres I–II)*. Sources Chrétiennes 532. Paris: Cerf, 2009.

———, et al., eds. *Origène. Commentaire sur l'Épître aux Romains, tome IV (livres IX–X)*. Sources Chrétiennes 555. Paris: Cerf, 2012.

Hanson, Richard P. C. *Allegory and Event: A Study of the Sources and Significance of Origen's Interpretation of Scripture*. London: SCM, 1959.

Harl, Marguerite, trans. *Clément d'Alexandrie. Le Pédagogue, livre I*. Sources Chrétiennes 208. Paris: Cerf, 1960.

———. "Origène et les interprétations patristiques grecques de l'obscurité biblique." *Vigiliae Christianae* 36 (1982) 334–71.

———. "Pointes antignostiques d'Origène; le questionnement impie des écritures." In *Studies in Gnosticism and Hellenistic Religions: Presented to Gilles Quispel on the Occasion of His 65th Birthday*, edited by Roelof van den Broek and M. J. Vermaseren, 205–17. Leiden: Brill, 1981.

Harrington, Michael. "What Are the 'Hypothetical Logoi' of Dionysian Mystical Theology?" *Studia Patristica* 48 (2010) 177–82.

Hatlie, Peter. "Redeeming Byzantine Epistolography." *Byzantine and Modern Greek Studies* 20 (1996) 213–48.

Hausherr, Irénée. "Dogme et spiritualité orientale." *Revue d'ascétique et de mystique* 23 (1947) 3–37.

———. "L'imitation de Jésus-Christ dans la spiritualité byzantine." In *Études de spiritualité orientale*, 217–45. Roma: Pontificium Institutum Studiorum Orientalium, 1969.

Hayduck, Michael, ed. *Ioannis Philoponi in Aristotelis de anima libros commentaria*. Commentaria in Aristotelem Graeca 15. Berlin: De Gruyter, 1897.

Head, Peter M. "Letter Carriers in the Ancient Jewish Epistolary Material." In *Jewish and Christian Scripture as Artifact and Canon*, edited by Craig A. Evans, 203–19. London: T. & T. Clark, 2009.

———. "Named Letter-Carriers among the Oxyrhynchus Papyri." *Journal for the Study of the New Testament* 31 (2009) 279–99.

Heath, Malcolm. *Menander: A Rhetor in Context*. Oxford: Oxford University Press, 2004.

———. "Theon and the History of the Progymnasmata." *Greek, Roman and Byzantine Studies* 43 (2002) 129–60.

Heil, Günter, ed., and Maurice de Gandillac, trans. *Denys l'Aréopagite (Pseudo-). La Hiérarchie celeste*. Sources Chrétiennes 58. Paris: Cerf, 1958.

Heine, Ronald E., trans. *Origen. Commentary on the Gospel according to John, Books 1–10.* Fathers of the Church 80. Washington, DC: Catholic University of America Press, 1989.

———, trans. *Origen. Commentary on the Gospel according to John, Books 13–32.* Fathers of the Church 89. Washington, DC: Catholic University of America Press, 1993.

———, trans. *Origen. Homilies on Genesis and Exodus.* Fathers of the Church 71. Washington, DC: Catholic University of America Press, 1982.

Helmreich, Georg, ed. *Galeni De Usu Partium Libri XVII,* vol. 1. Leipzig: in aedibus B. G. Teubneri, 1907.

Henry, René, trans. *Photius I. Bibliothèque, Tome III (Codices 186–222).* Paris: Les Belles Lettres, 1962.

Hofer, Andrew. *Christ in the Life and Teaching of Gregory of Nazianzus.* Oxford Early Christian Studies. Oxford: Oxford University Press, 2013.

Holmes, Michael W., trans. *The Apostolic Fathers in English.* Grand Rapids: Baker Academic, 2006.

Hornblower, Simon, and Antony Spawforth, eds. *The Oxford Classical Dictionary,* 3rd ed. Oxford: Oxford University Press, 2003.

Hovorun, Cyril. "Maximus, a Cautious Neo-Chalcedonian." In *The Oxford Handbook of Maximus the Confessor,* edited by Pauline Allen and Bronwen Neil, 106–24. Oxford: Oxford University Press, 2015.

———. *Will, Action, and Freedom: Christological Controversies in the Seventh Century.* Leiden: Brill, 2008.

Itter, Andrew C. *Esoteric Teaching in the* Stromateis *of Clement of Alexandria.* Supplements to Vigiliae Christianae 97. Leiden: Brill, 2009.

Jaeger, Werner, ed. *Gregorii Nysseni. Contra Eunomium liber III.* Gregorii Nysseni Opera 2. Leiden: Brill, 2002.

Jaeger, Werner, et al., eds. *Gregorii Nysseni. Opera ascetica et Epistulae, Volume 1 Opera ascetica.* Gregorii Nysseni Opera 8/1. Leiden: Brill, 1986.

Jankowiak, Marek, and Phil Booth. "A New Date-List of the Works of Maximus the Confessor." In *The Oxford Handbook of Maximus the Confessor,* edited by Pauline Allen and Bronwen Neil, 19–83. Oxford: Oxford University Press, 2015.

Janssens, Bart. "Does the Combination of Maximus' *Ambigua ad Thomam* and *Ambigua ad Iohannem* Go Back to the Confessor Himself?" *Sacris Eruditi* 42 (2003) 281–86.

———, ed. *Maximus Confessor. Ambigua ad Thomam una cum Epistula secunda ad eundem.* Corpus Christianorum, series graeca 48. Turnhout: Brepols, 2002.

Jauuert, A., ed. and trans. *Origène. Homélies sur Josué.* Sources Chrétiennes 71. Paris: Cerf, 1960.

Kamesar, Adam. "Biblical Interpretation in Philo." In *The Cambridge Companion to Philo,* edited by Adam Kamesar, 65–92. Cambridge: Cambridge University Press, 2009.

Kamtekar, Rachana. "Knowing by Likeness in Empedocles." *Phronesis* 54 (2009) 215–38.

Karlsson, Gustav. "Formelhaftes in Paulusbriefen." *Eranos* 54 (1956) 138–41.

———. *Idéologie et cérémonial dans l'épistolographie byzantine.* Uppsala: Almqvist et Wiksell, 1962.

Kennedy, George A. *Classical Rhetoric and Its Christian and Secular Tradition from Ancient to Modern Times.* London: Croom Helm, 1980.

——. *Greek Rhetoric under Christian Emperors*. Princeton, NJ: Princeton University Press, 1983.

——. *Progymnasmata: Greek Textbooks of Prose Composition and Rhetoric*. Writings from the Greco-Roman World 10. Atlanta: Society of Biblical Literature, 2003.

Klostermann, Erich, ed. *Origenes Werke, Band 10: Origenes Matthäuserklärung I. Die Griechisch erhaltenen Tomoi*. Die Griechischen christlichen schriftsteller 40. Berlin: De Gruyter, 1935.

Knežević, Mikonja. *Maximus the Confessor (580–662): Bibliography*. Belgrade: Institute for Theological Research, 2012.

Koetschau, Paul, ed. *Origenes Werke, Band 2: Buch V–VIII gegen Celsus. Die Schrift vom Gebet*. Die Griechischen christlichen schriftsteller 3. Berlin: De Gruyter, 1903.

——, ed. *Origenes Werke, Band 5: De Principiis*. Griechischen christlichen schriftsteller 22. Berlin: De Gruyter, 1913.

Kosman, Aryeh. *The Activity of Being: An Essay on Aristotle's Ontology*. Cambridge: Harvard University Press, 2013.

Kovacs, Judith L. "Clement of Alexandria and Valentinian Exegesis in the *Excerpts from Theodotus*." *Studia Patristica* 41 (2006) 187–200.

——. "Concealment and Gnostic Exegesis: Clement of Alexandria's Interpretation of the Tabernacle." *Studia Patristica* 31 (1997) 414–37.

——. "Divine Pedagogy and the Gnostic Teacher according to Clement of Alexandria." *Journal of Early Christian Studies* 9 (2001) 3–25.

——. "Echoes of Valentinian Exegesis in Clement of Alexandria and Origen: The Interpretation of 1 Cor 3, 1–3." In *Origeniana Octava: Origen and the Alexandrian tradition: Papers of the 8th International Origen Congress, Pisa, 27–31 August 2001*, edited by Lorenzo Perrone, 317–29. Leuven: Peeters, 2003.

——. "Grace and Works: Clement of Alexandria's Response to Valentinian Exegesis of Paul." In *Ancient Perspectives on Paul*, edited by Tobias Nicklas et al., 191–210. Göttingen: Vandenhoeck & Ruprecht, 2013.

——. "The Language of Grace: Valentinian Reflection on New Testament Imagery." In *Radical Christian Voices and Practice: Essays in Honour of Christopher Rowland*, edited by David B. Gowler and Zoë Bennett, 69–85. Oxford: Oxford University Press, 2012.

——. "A Letter 'Weighty and Powerful': The Importance of 1 Corinthians in the Early Church." *Studia Patristica* 44 (2010) 235–47.

——. "The Revelation to John in Origen's *Commentary on John*: Hearing the Voice of the Seven Thunders." In *Origeniana nona: Origen and the Religious Practice of His Time: Papers of the 9th International Origen Congress, Pécs, Hungary, 29 August–2 September 2005*, edited by G. Heidl and R. Somos, 217–30. Leuven: Peeters, 2009.

——. "Servant of Christ and Steward of the Mysteries of God: The Purpose of a Pauline Letter according to Origen's *Homilies on 1 Corinthians*." In *In Dominico eloquio/In Lordly Eloquence: Essays on Patristic Exegesis in Honor of Robert Louis Wilken*, edited by Paul M. Blowers et al., 147–71. Grand Rapids: Eerdmans, 2002.

Krausmüller, Dirk. "Aristotelianism and the Disintegration of the Late Antique Theological Discourse." In *Interpreting the Bible and Aristotle in Late Antiquity: The Alexandrian Commentary Tradition between Rome and Baghdad*, edited by Josef Lössl and J. W. Watt, 151–64. Farnham, UK: Ashgate, 2011.

Krueger, Derek. *Writing and Holiness: The Practice of Authorship in the Early Christian East*. Philadelphia: University of Pennsylvania Press, 2004.

Kustas, George L. *Studies in Byzantine Rhetoric*. Thessalonikē: Patriarchikon Hidryma Paterikōn, 1973.

Laga, Carl, and Carlos Steel, eds. *Maximus Confessoris, Iohannes Scotus Eriugena. Quaestiones ad Thalassium I. Quaestiones I–LV, una cum latina interpretatione Ioannis Scotti Eriugenae.* Corpus Christianorum, series graeca 7. Turnhout: Brepols, 1980.

———, eds. *Maximus Confessoris, Iohannes Scotus Eriugena. Quaestiones ad Thalassium II. Quaestiones LVI–LXV, una cum latina interpretatione Ioannis Scotti Eriugenae.* Corpus Christianorum, series graeca 22. Turnhout: Brepols, 1990.

Lamberton, Robert, and John J. Keaney. *Homer's Ancient Readers: The Hermeneutics of Greek Epic's Earliest Exegetes.* Princeton: Princeton University Press, 1992.

———. *Homer the Theologian: Neoplatonist Allegorical Reading and the Growth of the Epic Tradition.* Berkeley: University of California Press, 1986.

Lampe, G. W. H., ed. *A Patristic Greek Lexicon.* Oxford: Clarendon, 1961.

Langerbeck, Hermann, ed. *Gregorii Nysseni. In Canticum Canticorum.* Gregorii Nysseni Opera 6. Leiden: Brill, 1986.

Larchet, Jean-Claude. "La conception maximienne des énergies divines et des logoi et la théorie platonicienne des idées." *Philotheos* 4 (2004) 276–83.

———. *La divinisation de l'homme selon saint Maxime le Confesseur.* Paris: Cerf, 1996.

———. "The Mode of Deification." In *The Oxford Handbook of Maximus the Confessor,* edited by Pauline Allen and Bronwen Neil, 341–59. Oxford: Oxford University Press, 2015.

Le Boulluec, Alain, ed., and Pierre Voulet, trans. *Clément d'Alexandrie. Les Stromates. Stromate V, tome I.* Sources Chrétiennes 278. Paris: Cerf, 1981.

———, ed. *Clément d'Alexandrie. Les Stromates. Stromate VII.* Sources Chrétiennes 428. Paris: Cerf, 1997.

———. "De Paul à Origène: continuité ou divergence?" In *Alexandrie antique et chrétienne: Clément et Origène,* edited by Carmelo Giuseppe Conticello, 415–35. Paris: Institut d'Études Augustiniennes, 2006.

Lehoux, Danny. *What Did the Romans Know? An Inquiry into Science and Worldmaking.* Chicago: University of Chicago Press, 2012.

Léthel, François-Marie. *Théologie de l'agonie du Christ: La liberté humaine du Fils de Dieu et son importance sotériologique mises en lumière par saint Maxime le Confesseur.* Paris: Beauchesne, 1979.

Lévy, Antoine. *Le créé et l'incréé: Maxime le confesseur et Thomas d'Aquin: aux sources de la querelle palamienne.* Paris: Vrin, 2006.

———. "Liberté et 'structure profonde' des régimes politiques en Orient byzantin et en Occident latin." *Istina* 56 (2011) 179–206.

Littlewood, A. R. "An Ikon of the Soul: The Byzantine Letter." *Visible Language* 10 (1976) 197–222.

Lollar, Joshua, trans. *Maximus the Confessor. Ambigua to Thomas and Second Letter to Thomas.* Corpus Christianorum in Translation 2. Turnhout: Brepols, 2009.

———. *To See into the Life of Things: The Contemplation of Nature in Maximus the Confessor and His Predecessors.* Monothéismes et Philosophie. Turnhout: Brepols, 2013.

Loman, Janni. "The *Letter of Barnabas* in Early Second Century Egypt." In *The Wisdom of Egypt: Jewish, Early Christian, and Gnostic Essays in Honour of Gerard*

*P. Luttikhuizen*, edited by A. Hilhorst and Geurt Hendrik van Kooten, 247–65. Leiden: Brill, 2005.

Lossky, Vladimir. "La notion des 'Analogies' chez Denys le Pseudo-Areopagite." *Archives d'histoire doctrinale et littéraire du Moyen-âge* 5 (1930) 279–309.

Loudovikos, Nikolaos. *A Eucharistic Ontology: Maximus the Confessor's Eschatological Ontology of Being as Dialogical Reciprocity.* Brookline, MA: Holy Cross Orthodox, 2010.

Louth, Andrew. "Apophatic Theology and the Liturgy in St Maximos the Confessor." *Criterion* 36 (1997) 2–9.

———. "The *Collectio Sabbaitica* and Sixth-Century Origenism." In *Origeniana Octava: Origen and the Alexandrian tradition: Papers of the 8th International Origen Congress, Pisa, 27–31 August 2001,* edited by Lorenzo Perrone, 1167–75. Leuven: Peeters, 2003.

———. "Dogma and Spirituality in St Maximus the Confessor." In *Prayer and Spirituality in the Early Church,* edited by Pauline Allen et al., 197–208. Brisbane: Australian Catholic University, 1998.

———, ed., and G. A. Williamson, trans. *Eusebius. The History of the Church from Christ to Constantine.* London: Penguin, 1989.

———. "From Doctrine of Christ to Icon of Christ: St. Maximus the Confessor on the Transfiguration of Christ." In *In the Shadow of the Incarnation: Essays on Jesus Christ in the Early Church in Honor of Brian E. Daley, S.J.,* edited by Peter Martens, 260–75. Notre Dame, IN: University of Notre Dame Press, 2008.

———. *Maximus the Confessor.* Early Church Fathers. London: Routledge, 1996.

———. "Mysticism." In *A Dictionary of Christian Spirituality,* edited by G. S. Wakefield, 272–74. London: SCM, 1984.

———. *The Origins of the Christian Mystical Tradition: From Plato to Denys.* Oxford: Oxford University Press, 2007.

———. "Recent Research on St Maximus the Confessor: A Survey." *St Vladimir's Theological Quarterly* 42 (1998) 67–84.

———. "The Reception of Dionysius in the Byzantine World: Maximus to Palamas." *Modern Theology* 24 (2008) 585–99.

———. "The Reception of Dionysius up to Maximus the Confessor." *Modern Theology* 24 (2008) 573–83.

———. "St Denys the Areopagite and St Maximus the Confessor: A Question of Influence." *Studia Patristica* 27 (1993) 166–74.

———. "St Gregory the Theologian and St Maximus the Confessor: The Shaping of Tradition." In *The Making and Remaking of Christian Doctrine: Essays in Honour of Maurice Wiles,* edited by Sarah Coakley and David A. Palin, 117–30. Oxford: Clarendon, 1993.

———. "St Maximos' Doctrine of the *logoi* of Creation." *Studia Patristica* 48 (2010) 77–84.

——— "St Maximus the Confessor between East and West." *Studia Patristica* 32 (1997) 332–45.

———. Review of *La Théologie de énergies divines des Origines à Saint Jean Damascène,* by Jean-Claude Larchet. *The Journal of Theological Studies* 62 (2011) 746–48.

———. "Virtue Ethics: St Maximos the Confessor and Aquinas Compared." *Studies in Christian Ethics* 26 (2013) 351–63.

Madden, John. "The Authenticity of Early Definitions of Will (thelēsis)." In *Maximus Confessor: actes du Symposium sur Maxime le Confesseur, Fribourg, 2–5 Septembre 1980*, edited by Felix Heinzer and Christoph Schönborn, 61–79. Fribourg: Éditions universitaires, 1982.

Madden, Nicholas. "Composite Hypostasis in Maximus Confessor." *Studia Patristica* 27 (1993) 175–97.

Malherbe, Abraham J., trans. *Ancient Epistolary Theorists*. Atlanta: Scholars, 1988.

Mansfeld, Jaap. "Aristote et la structure du *De sensibus* de Théophraste." *Phronesis* 41 (1996) 158–88.

Marcovich, Miroslav, ed. *Hippolytus. Refutatio omnium haeresium*. Patristische Texte und Studien 25. Berlin: De Gruyter, 1986.

Markesinis, Basile. "Les extraits de S. Maxime le Confesseur transmis par le Parisinus gr. 854 (13e s.)." *Orientalia Lovaniensia Periodica* 31 (2000) 109–17.

Marrou, Henri Irénée. *A History of Education in Antiquity*. London: Sheed and Ward, 1956.

Martens, Peter William. *Origen and Scripture: The Contours of the Exegetical Life*. Oxford Early Christian Studies. Oxford: Oxford University Press, 2012.

———. "Why Does Origen Introduce the Trinitarian Authorship of Scripture in Book 4 of *Peri Archon*?" *Vigiliae Christianae* 60 (2006) 1–8.

Martijn, M. "The 'Eikōs Mythos' in Proclus' Commentary on the *Timaeus*." In *Reading Plato in Antiquity*, edited by Harold Tarrant and Dirk Baltzly, 151–67. London: Duckworth, 2006.

Mateo-Seco, Lucas Francisco, and Giulio Maspero, eds. *The Brill Dictionary of Gregory of Nyssa*. Leiden: Brill, 2010.

Mathew, Gervase. "The Aesthetic Theories of Gregory of Nyssa." In *Studies in Memory of David Talbot Rice*, edited by Giles Robertson and George Henderson, 217–22. Edinburgh: Edinburgh University Press, 1975.

McEnerney, John, trans. *Cyril of Alexandria. Letters 51–110*. Fathers of the Church 77. Washington, DC: Catholic University of America Press, 1987.

McFarland, Ian A. "Developing an Apophatic Christocentrism: Lessons from Maximus the Confessor." *Theology Today* 60 (2003) 200–214.

———. "Fleshing out Christ: Maximus the Confessor's Christology in Anthropological Perspective." *St Vladimir's Theological Quarterly* 49 (2005) 417–36.

———. "The Theology of the Will." In *The Oxford Handbook of Maximus the Confessor*, edited by Pauline Allen and Bronwen Neil, 516–32. Oxford: Oxford University Press, 2015.

McGuckin, John A. "The Patristic Exegesis of the Transfiguration." *Studia Patristica* 18 (1985) 335–41.

McIntosh, Mark A. *Christology from Within: Spirituality and the Incarnation in Hans Urs von Balthasar*. Studies in Spirituality and Theology 3. Notre Dame, IN: University of Notre Dame Press, 2000.

———. *Discernment and Truth: The Spirituality and Theology of Knowledge*. New York: Crossroad, 2004.

Menzies, Allan, ed. *Ante-Nicene Christian Library: additional volume, containing early Christian works discovered since the completion of the series, and selections from the commentaries of Origen*. Ante-Nicene Christian Library 25. Edinburgh: T. & T. Clark, 1897.

Metzger, Bruce M. *The Canon of the New Testament: Its Origin, Development, and Significance.* Oxford: Clarendon, 1987.

Michelson, David. *The Practical Christology of Philoxenos of Mabbug.* Oxford Early Christian Studies. Oxford: Oxford University Press, 2014.

Migne, Jacques-Paul, ed. *Sancti patris nostri Basilii Caesareae Cappadociae archiepiscopi, opera omnia quae exstant,* vol. 1. Patrologia Graeca 29. Paris: Imprimerie Catholique, Paris, 1857.

———, ed. *Sancti patris nostri Gregorii Episcopi Nysseni, opera omnia,* vol. 1. Patrologia Graeca 44. Paris: Imprimerie Catholique, Paris, 1865.

———, ed. *Sancti patris nostri Gregorii Theologi, vulgo Nazianzeni, Archiepiscopi Constantinopolitani, opera quae exstant omnia,* vols. 1–3 Patrologia Graeca 35–37. Paris: Imprimerie Catholique, Paris, 1862.

———, ed. *Sancti patris nostri Maximi Confessoris, opera omnia,* vols. 1–2. Patrologia Graeca 90–91. Paris: Imprimerie Catholique, Paris, 1865.

———, ed. *S. Dionysii Areopagitae, opera omnia quae exstant* Patrologia Graeca 3. Paris: Imprimerie Catholique, Paris, 1857.

Miquel, Pierre. "La naissance de Dieu dans l'âme." *Revue des sciences religieuses* 35 (1961) 378–406.

——— "Πεῖρα: Contribution à l'étude du vocabulaire de l'expérience religieuse dans l'oeuvre de Maxime le Confesseur." *Studia Patristica* 7 (1966) 355–61.

Molinié, Pierre. "La confession de foi inaugurale dans la *Lettre* 12 de Maxime le Confesseur." *Revue d'études augustiniennes et patristiques* 57 (2011) 325–56.

Mondésert, Claude, introduction, and Marcel Caster, trans., *Clément d'Alexandrie. Les Stromates. Stromate I.* Sources Chrétiennes 30. Paris: Cerf, 1951.

———, ed. and trans. *Clément d'Alexandrie. Les Stromates. Stromate II.* Sources Chrétiennes 38. Paris: Cerf, 1954.

———, trans., and Annewies van den Hoek, ed. *Clément d'Alexandrie. Les Stromates. Stromate IV.* Sources Chrétiennes 463. Paris: Cerf, 2001.

Morani, Moreno, ed. *Nemesii Emeseni De Natura Hominis.* Bibliotheca scriptorum Graecorum et Romanorum Teubneriana. Leipzig: Teubner, 1987.

Moreschini, Claudio, ed., and Paul Gallay, trans. *Grégoire de Nazianze. Discours 32–37.* Sources Chrétiennes 318 Paris: Cerf, 1985.

———. *Grégoire de Nazianze. Discours 38–41.* Sources Chrétiennes 358. Paris: Cerf, 1990.

Mortley, Raoul J. "Ἀναλογία chez Clément d'Alexandrie." *Revue des Études Grecques* 84 (1971) 80–93.

Mossay, Justin, ed. and trans. *Grégoire de Nazianze. Discours. 20–23.* Sources Chrétiennes 270. Paris: Cerf, 1980.

———, ed. and trans. *Grégoire de Nazianze. Discours 24–26.* Sources Chrétiennes 284. Paris: Cerf, 1981.

Mosser, Carl. "Deification: A Truly Ecumenical Concept." *Perspectives: A Journal of Reformed Thought* 30 (2015) 8–14.

———. "The Earliest Patristic Interpretations of Psalm 82, Jewish Antecedents, and the Origin of Christian Deification." *The Journal of Theological Studies* 56 (2005) 30–74.

Mueller, Fridericus, ed. *Gregorii Nysseni. Opera dogmatica minora, Pars 1.* Gregorii Nysseni Opera 3/1. Leiden: Brill, 1958.

Müller, Carl Werner. *Gleiches zu Gleichem: Ein Prinzip frühgriechischen Denkens.* Wiesbaden: Harrassowitz, 1965.

Mullett, Margaret. "The Classical Tradition in the Byzantine Letter." In *Byzantium and the Classical Tradition: University of Birmingham Thirteenth Spring Symposium of Byzantine Studies 1979,* edited by Margaret Mullett and Roger Scott, 75–93. Birmingham, UK: Centre for Byzantine Studies, University of Birmingham, 1981.

———. "The Language of Diplomacy." In *Byzantine Diplomacy: Papers of the Twenty-Fourth Spring Symposium of Byzantine Studies, Cambridge, March 1990,* edited by Jonathan Shepard and Simon Franklin, 203–16. Aldershot, UK: Variorum, 1992.

———. *Letters, Literacy and Literature in Byzantium.* Aldershot, UK: Variorum, 2007.

———. "The Madness of Genre." In *Homo Byzantinus: Papers in Honor of Alexander Kazhdan,* edited by Anthony Cutler and Simon Franklin, 235–43. Washington, DC: Dumbarton Oaks Research Library and Collection, 1992.

———. *Theophylacht of Ochrid: Reading the Letters of a Byzantine Archbishop.* Aldershot, UK: Variorum, 1997.

Musurillo, H., ed., and Victor-Henry Debidour, trans. *Méthode d'Olympe. Le banquet.* Sources Chrétiennes 95. Paris: Cerf, 1963.

Nagy, Gregory. *The Best of the Achaeans: Concepts of the Hero in Archaic Greek Poetry.* Baltimore: Johns Hopkins University Press, 1979.

Nautin, Pierre, ed. and trans. *Didyme d'Alexandrie Sur la Genèse (5–17), tome II: Texte inédit d'après un papyrus de Toura.* Sources Chrétiennes 244. Paris: Cerf, 1978.

———. *Origène: Sa vie et son oeuvre.* Paris: Beauchesne, 1977.

Nichols, J. C. A. *Byzantine Gospel: Maximus the Confessor in Modern Scholarship.* Edinburgh: T. & T. Clark, 1993.

Niehoff, Maren. "A Jewish Critique of Christianity from Second-Century Alexandria: Revisiting the Jew Mentioned in *Contra Celsum*." *Journal of Early Christian Studies* 21 (2013) 151–75.

———. *Jewish Exegesis and Homeric Scholarship in Alexandria.* Cambridge: Cambridge University Press, 2011.

Norris, Frederick W. "The Theologian and Technical Rhetoric: Gregory of Nazianzus and Hermogenes of Tarsus." In *Nova et Vetera: Patristic Studies in Honor of Thomas Patrick Halton,* edited by John Petruccione, 84–95. Washington, DC: Catholic University of America Press, 1998.

Norris, Richard A., trans. *Gregory of Nyssa. Homilies on the Song of Songs.* Writings from the Greco-Roman World. Atlanta: Society of Biblical Literature, 2012.

Obbink, Dirk. "Allegory and Exegesis in the Derveni Papyrus: The Origin of Greek Scholarship." In *Metaphor, Allegory, and the Classical Tradition: Ancient Thought and Modern Revisions,* edited by George R. Boys-Stones, 177–88. Oxford: Oxford University Press, 2003.

Olster, David Michael. *The Politics of Usurpation in the Seventh Century: Rhetoric and Revolution in Byzantium.* Amsterdam: A. M. Hakkert, 1993.

Osborn, Eric. *Clement of Alexandria.* Cambridge: Cambridge University Press, 2005.

Pagels, Elaine H. *The Gnostic Paul: Gnostic Exegesis of the Pauline Letters.* London: Continuum, 1992.

———. *The Johannine Gospel in Gnostic Exegesis: Heracleon's Commentary on John.* Nashville: Abingdon, 1973.

———. "The Valentinian Claim to Esoteric Exegesis of Romans as Basis for Anthropological Theory." *Vigiliae Christianae* 26 (1972) 241–58.

Pasquali, Georgius ed. *Gregorii Nysseni. Opera ascetica et Epistulae, Volume 2 Epistulae.* Gregorii Nysseni Opera 8/2. Leiden: Brill, 1959.

Pearson, Birger A. "Biblical Exegesis in Gnostic Literature." In *Armenian and Biblical Studies*, edited by Michael Stone, 70–80. Jerusalem: St James, 1976.

Pépin, Jean. "Remarques sur la théorie de l'exégèse allégorique chez Philon." In *Philon d'Alexandrie: Lyon, 11–15 September 1966*, 131–67. Paris: Éditions du centre national de la recherche scientifique, 1967.

———. *La tradition de l'allégorie, de Philon d'Alexandrie à Dante.* Paris: Études Augustiniennes, 1987.

Perl, Eric David. "Metaphysics and Christology in Maximus Confessor and Eriugena." In *Eriugena: East and West: Papers of the Eighth International Colloquium of the Society for the Promotion of Eriugenian Studies, Chicago and Notre Dame, 18–20 October 1991*, edited by Bernard McGinn and Willemien Otten, 253–70. Notre Dame, IN: University of Notre Dame Press, 1994.

Pernot, Laurent. *Rhetoric in Antiquity.* Washington, DC: Catholic University of America Press, 2005.

———. *La rhétorique de l'éloge dans le monde gréco-romain*, books 1 and 2. Paris: Institut d'Études Augustiniennes, 1993.

Plested, Marcus. *The Macarian Legacy: The Place of Macarius-Symeon in the Eastern Christian Tradition.* Oxford: Oxford University Press, 2004.

Ponsoye, Emmanuel, trans. *Maxime le Confesseur. Lettres.* Sagesses chrétiennes. Paris: Cerf, 1998.

———, trans. *Maxime le Confesseur. Opuscules théologiques et polémiques.* Sagesses chrétiennes. Paris: Cerf, 1998.

Portaru, Marius. "Classical and Philosophical Influences: Aristotle and Platonism." In *The Oxford Handbook of Maximus the Confessor*, edited by Pauline Allen and Bronwen Neil, 127–48. Oxford: Oxford University Press, 2015.

———. "Gradual Participation according to St Maximus the Confessor." *Studia Patristica* 68 (2013) 281–93.

———. "The Vocabulary of Participation in the Works of Saint Maximus the Confessor." *Via lui Nabot / Naboth's Vineyard—studia theologica recentiora*, edited by Octavian Gordon and Alexandru Mihăilă, 295–317. Cluj-Napoca, Romania: Presa Universitară Clujeană, 2012.

Poster, Carol. "A Conversation Halved: Epistolary Theory in Graeco-Roman Antiquity." In *Letter-Writing Manuals and Instruction from Antiquity to the Present: Historical and Bibliographic Studies*, edited by Carol Poster and Linda C. Mitchell, 21–51. Columbia, SC: University of South Carolina Press, 2007.

———. "The Economy of Letter-Writing in Graeco-Roman Antiquity." In *Rhetorical Argumentation in Biblical Texts: Essays from the Lund 2000 Conference*, edited by Anders Eriksson et al., 114–26. Harrisburg, PA: Trinity, 2002.

Prassas, Despina D., trans. *St. Maximus the Confessor's Questions and Doubts.* DeKalb, Ill.: Northern Illinois University Press, 2010.

Preger, Theodor. *Inscriptiones Graecae Metricae: Ex Scriptoribus Praeter Anthologiam Collectae.* Leipzig: In Aedibus B. G. Teubneri, 1891.

Preuschen, Erwin, ed. *Origenes Werke, Band 4: Der Johanneskommentar.* Griechischen christlichen schriftsteller 10. Berlin: De Gruyter, 1903.

Rabe, Hugo, ed. *Aphthonii Progymnasmata.* Rhetores Graeci 10. Leipzig: In aedibus B. G. Teubneri, 1926.

————, ed. *Hermogenis Opera*. Rhetores Graeci 6. Leipzig: In aedibus B. G. Teubneri, 1913.

Rackham, H., trans. *Aristotle. Athenian Constitution. Eudemian Ethics. Virtues and Vices*. Loeb Classical Library 285. Cambridge: Harvard University Press, 1935.

Ramelli, Illaria L. E. "Origen and the Stoic Allegorical Tradition: Continuity and Innovation." *Invigilata Lucernis* 28 (2006) 195–225.

————. "Philo as Origen's Declared Model: Allegorical and Historical Exegesis of Scripture." *Studies in Christian-Jewish Relations* 7 (2012) 1–17.

Ramsbotham, A. "The Commentary of Origen on the Epistle to the Romans." *Journal of Theological Studies* 13 (1912) 209–24, 357–68.

Remes, Pauliina, *Neoplatonism*. Berkeley: University of California Press, 2008.

Renczes, Philipp Gabriel. *Agir de Dieu et la liberté de l'homme: Recherches sur l'anthopologie théologique de Saint Maxime le Confesseur*. Paris: Cerf, 2003.

Rondeau, M.-J. "Le commentaire sur les Psaumes d'Evagre le Pontique." *Orientalia Christiana Periodica* 26 (1960) 329–48.

Roosen, Bram, and Peter van Deun. "Les collections de définitions philosophico-théologiques appartenant à la tradition de Maxime le Confesseur." In *Philosophie et sciences à Byzance de 1204 à 1453: Les textes, les doctrines et leur transmission: Actes de la Table Ronde organisée au XXe Congrès International d'Études Byzantines, Paris, 2001*, edited by Michel Cacouros and Marie-Hélène Congourdeau, 53–76. Leuven: Peeters, 2006.

Roueché, Mossman. "Byzantine Philosophical Texts of the Seventh Century." *Jahrbuch Der österreichischen Byzantinistik* 23 (1974) 61–76.

————. "A Middle Byzantine Handbook of Logical Terminology." *Jahrbuch Der österreichischen Byzantinistik* 29 (1980) 71–98.

Rousseau, Adelin, ed. and trans. *Irénée de Lyon. Contre les hérésies, livre I, tome II*. Sources Chrétiennes 264. Paris: Cerf, 1979.

————, and Louis Doutreleau, eds. and trans. *Irénée de Lyon. Contre les hérésies, livre II, tome II*. Sources Chrétiennes 294. Paris: Cerf, 1982.

————, and Louis. Doutreleau, ed. and trans. *Irénée de Lyon. Contre les hérésies, livre III, tome II*. Sources Chrétiennes 211. Paris: Cerf, 1974.

————, ed. and trans. *Irénée de Lyon. Contre les hérésies, livre IV, tome II*. Sources Chrétiennes 100. Paris: Cerf, 1965.

Russell, David, and Nigel Wilson, eds. and trans. *Menander Rhetor*. Oxford: Clarendon, 1981.

Russell, Donald A., and David Konstan, trans. *Heraclitus: Homeric Problems*. Leiden: Brill, 2005.

Russell, Norman. *The Doctrine of Deification in the Greek Patristic Tradition*. Oxford Early Christian Studies. Oxford: Oxford University Press, 2006.

Salés, Joshua. "Divine Incarnation through the Virtues: The Central Soteriological Role of Maximos the Confessor's Aretology." *St Vladimir's Theological Quarterly* 58 (2014) 159–76.

Sandmel, Samuel. *Philo's Place in Judaism: A Study of Conceptions of Abraham in Jewish Literature*. New York: Ktav,1971.

Schaff, Philip, and Henry Wace, eds. *Gregory of Nyssa: Dogmatic Treatises, Etc*. Nicene and Post-Nicene Fathers 5. Peabody, MA: Hendrickson, 1994.

Schamp, Jacques. "Maxime le Confesseur et Photios: À propos d'une édition récente des Questions à Thalassius." *Revue belge de Philologie et d'Histoire* 60 (1982) 163–76.

Schäublin, Christoph. "Homerum Ex Homero." *Museum Helveticum* 34 (1977) 221–27.

Schneider, Artur. "Der Gedanke der Erkenntnis des Gleichen durch Gleiches in antiker und patristischer Zeit." In *Abhandlungen zur Geschichte der Philosophie des Mittelalters: Festgabe für Clemens Baeumker zum 70 Geburtstag*, edited by F. Ehrle, 65–76. Münster: Aschendorff, 1923.

Schwartz, Eduard, ed. *Collectio Vaticana 120–139*. Acta conciliorum oecumenicorum 1.1.4. Berlin: De Gruyter, 1927.

Sedley, David. "Empedocles' Theory of Vision and Theophrastus' *De Sensibus*." In *Theophrastus: His Psychological, Doxographical, and Scientific Writings*, edited by William W. Fortenbaugh and Dimitri Gutas, 20–31. New Brunswick, NJ: Transaction, 1992.

———. "The Ideal of Godlikeness." In *Plato 2: Ethics, Politics, Religion, and the Soul*, edited by G. Fine, 309–28. Oxford: Oxford University Press, 1999.

Shepard, Jonathan. *The Cambridge History of the Byzantine Empire c. 500–1492*. Cambridge: Cambridge University Press, 2008.

Sherwood, Polycarp. *An Annotated Date-List of the Works of Maximus the Confessor*. Rome: "Orbis Catholicus," Herder, 1952.

———, trans. *Maximus the Confessor. The Ascetic Life; The Four Centuries on Charity*. Ancient Christian Writers 21. New York: Newman, 1978.

Siegel, Rudolph E. *Galen on Sense Perception: His Doctrines, Observations and Experiments on Vision, Hearing, Smell, Taste, Touch, Pain, and Their Historical Sources*. Basel: Karger, 1970.

Silvas, Anna, trans. *Gregory of Nyssa: The Letters*. Supplèments to Vigiliae Christianae 83. Leiden: Brill, 2007.

Siorvanes, Lucas. *Proclus: Neo-Platonic Philosophy and Science*. Edinburgh: Edinburgh University Press, 1996.

Squire, A. K. "The Idea of the Soul as Virgin and Mother in Maximus the Confessor." *Studia Patristica* 8 (1966) 456–61.

Steel, Carlos G. "Le jeu du Verbe: À propos de Maxime, *Amb Ad Ioh* LXVII." In *Philohistôr: Miscellanea in Honorem Caroli Laga Septuagenarii*, edited by Peter Van Deun and Antoon Shoors, 281–93. Louvain: Peeters, 1994.

Stefaniw, Blossom. *Mind, Text, and Commentary: Noetic Exegesis in Origen of Alexandria, Didymus the Blind, and Evagrius Ponticus*. Frankfurt am Main: Lang, 2010.

Steven, Luke. "Mixture, Beauty, and the Incarnation in Gregory's *In Canticum Canticorum*." In *Gregory of Nyssa: In Canticum Canticorum: Analytical and Supporting Studies. Proceedings of the 13th International Colloquium on Gregory of Nyssa (Rome, 17–20 September 2014)*, edited by Giulio Maspero et al., 508–16. Leiden: Brill, 2018.

Stowers, Stanley K. *Letter-Writing in Greco-Roman Antiquity*. Philadelphia: Westminster, 1989.

Stratton, George Malcolm, ed. and trans. *Theophrastus and the Greek Physiological Psychology before Aristotle*. London: Allen & Unwin, 1917.

Stroumsa, Guy G. "Clement, Origen, and Jewish Esoteric Traditions." In *Origeniana Sexta: Origène et la bible: Actes du Colloquium Origenianum Sextum, Chantilly, 30 Août–3 Septembre 1993*, edited by Gilles Dorival and Alain Le Boulluec, 53–70. Leuven: Leuven University Press, 1995.

————. *Hidden Wisdom: Esoteric Traditions and the Roots of Christian Mysticism.* Leiden: Brill, 1996.

Struck, Peter. *Birth of the Symbol: Ancient Readers at the Limits of Their Texts.* Princeton, NJ: Princeton University Press, 2004.

Thomassen, Einar. *The Spiritual Seed: The Church of the Valentinians.* Leiden: Brill, 2008.

Thomson, Robert W., ed. and trans. *Athanasius. Contra Gentes; and, De Incarnatione.* Oxford Early Christian Texts. Oxford: Clarendon, 1971.

Thunberg, Lars. *Man and the Cosmos: The Vision of St. Maximus the Confessor.* Crestwood, NY: St. Vladimir's Seminary, 1985.

————. *Microcosm and Mediator: The Theological Anthropology of Maximus the Confessor.* 2nd ed. Chicago: Open Court, 1995.

————. "Symbol and Mystery in St. Maximus the Confessor." In *Maximus Confessor: actes du Symposium sur Maxime le Confesseur, Fribourg, 2–5 Septembre 1980,* edited by Felix Heinzer and Christoph Schönborn, 285–308. Fribourg: Éditions universitaires, 1982.

Tollefsen, Torstein. *The Christocentric Cosmology of St Maximus the Confessor.* Oxford Early Christian Studies. Oxford: Oxford University Press, 2008.

Torjesen, Karen Jo. "'Body,' 'Soul,' and 'Spirit' in Origen's Theory of Exegesis." *Anglican Theological Review* (1985) 17–30.

————. *Hermeneutical Procedure and Theological Method in Origen's Exegesis.* Berlin: De Gruyter, 1986.

————. "Pedagogical Soteriology from Clement to Origen." In *Origeniana quarta: die Referate des 4. Internationalen Origenskongresses (Innsbruck, 2.-6. September 1985),* edited by Lothar Lies, 370–78. Innsbruck: Tyrolia-Verlag, 1987.

Törönen, Melchisedec. *Union and Distinction in the Thought of St. Maximus the Confessor.* Oxford Early Christian Studies. Oxford: Oxford University Press, 2007.

Torrance, Iain R. *Christology after Chalcedon: Severus of Antioch and Sergius the Monophysite.* Norwich: Canterbury, 1988.

Trigg, Joseph W. "Divine Deception and the Truthfulness of Scripture." In *Origen of Alexandria: His World and His Legacy,* edited by Charles Kannengiesser and William L. Peterson, 147–64. Notre Dame, IN: University of Notre Dame Press, 1988.

————. "God's Marvelous *Oikonomia*: Reflections of Origen's Understanding of Divine and Human Pedagogy in the Address Ascribed to Gregory Thaumaturgus." *Journal of Early Christian Studies* 9 (2001) 27–52.

————. "Knowing God in the *Theological Orations* of Gregory of Nazianzus: The Heritage of Origen." In *God in Early Christian Thought: Essays in Memory of Lloyd G. Patterson,* edited by Andrew B. McGowan et al., 83–104. Leiden: Brill, 2009.

————. *Origen.* The Early Church Fathers. London: Routledge, 1998.

Tsantsanoglou, Kyriakos, et al., eds. and trans. *The Derveni Papyrus.* Firenze: Leo S. Olschki, 2006.

Tsakiridou, Cornelia A. *Icons in Time, Persons in Eternity: Orthodox Theology and the Aesthetics of the Christian Image.* Farnham, UK: Ashgate, 2013.

Unger, Dominic J. "Christ Jesus, Centre and Final Scope of All Creation according to St. Maximus Confessor." *Franciscan Studies* (1949) 50–62.

————, trans. *Irenaeus of Lyon. Against the Heresies, Book 1.* Ancient Christian Writers 55. New York: Paulist, 1992.

van den Hoek, Annewies. "Assessing Philo's Legacy in Christian Alexandria." In *Shem in the Tents of Japhet: Essays on the Encounter of Judaism and Hellenism*, edited by James L. Kugel, 223–39. Leiden: Brill, 2002.

———. "The 'Catechetical' School of Early Christian Alexandria and its Philonic Heritage." *Harvard Theological Review* 90 (1997) 59–87.

———. *Clement of Alexandria and His Use of Philo in the* Stromateis: *An Early Christian Reshaping of a Jewish Model*. Leiden: Brill, 1988.

———. "How Alexandrian Was Clement of Alexandria? Reflections on Clement and His Alexandrian Background." *Heythrop Journal* 31 (1990) 179–94.

———. "Philo and Origen: A Descriptive Catalogue of Their Relationship." *The Studia Philonica Annual* 12 (2000) 44–121.

van der Eijk, Philip J., trans. *John Philoponus. On Aristotle's On the Soul 1.1–2*. Ancient Commentators on Aristotle. Ithaca, N.Y.: Cornell University Press, 2005.

van der Horst, Pieter Willem, trans. *Chaeremon, Egyptian Priest and Stoic Philosopher: The Fragments Collected and Translated with Explanatory Notes*. Leiden: Brill, 1984.

Van Deun, Peter, ed. *Maximi Confessor. Liber asceticus*, Corpus Christianorum, series graeca 40. Turnhout: Brepols, 2000.

———, ed. *Maximus Confessor. Opuscula exegetica duo Expositio in Psalmum LIX. Expositio orationis dominicae*. Corpus Christianorum, series graeca 23. Turnhout: Brepols, 1991.

———. "Maximus the Confessor's Use of Literary Genres." In *The Oxford Handbook of Maximus the Confessor*, edited by Pauline Allen and Bronwen Neil, 274–86. Oxford: Oxford University Press, 2015.

———. "L'Unionum definitiones (CPG 7697, 18) attribué à Maxime le Confesseur: étude et édition du traité." *Revue des études byzantines* 58 (2000) 123–47.

Vinson, Martha, trans. *Gregory of Nazianzus. Select Orations*. Fathers of the Church 107. Washington, DC: Catholic University of America Press, 2004.

Völker, Walther. *Maximus Confessor als Meister des geistlichen Lebens*. Wiesbaden: Steiner, 1965.

Watts, Edward Jay. *City and School in Late Antique Athens and Alexandria*. Berkeley: University of California Press, 2006.

Webb, Ruth. "Praise and Persuasion: Argumentation and Audience Response in Epideictic Oratory." In *Rhetoric in Byzantium: Papers from the Thirty-Fifth Spring Symposium of Byzantine Studies, Exeter College, University of Oxford, March 2001*, edited by Elizabeth Jeffreys, 127–35. Aldershot, UK: Ashgate, 2003.

Wessel, Susan. "The Reception of Greek Science in Gregory of Nyssa's *De Hominis Opificio*." *Vigiliae Christianae* 63 (2009) 24–46.

West, Martin L. "Hocus-Pocus in East and West: Theogeny, Ritual, and the Tradition of Esoteric Commentary." In *Studies on the Derveni Papyrus*, edited by André Laks and Glenn W. Most, 81–90. Oxford: Clarendon, 1997.

Whitby, Mary. *The Propaganda of Power: The Role of Panegyric in Late Antiquity*. Leiden: Brill, 1998.

Wilken, Robert L. "Alexandria: A School for Training in Virtue." In *Schools of Thought in the Christian Tradition*, edited by Patrick Henry, 15–30. Philadelphia: Fortress, 1984.

————. "Maximus the Confessor on the Affections in Historical Perspective." In *Asceticism*, edited by Vincent L. Wimbush and Richard Valantasis, 412–23. Oxford: Oxford University Press, 1995.

Williams, Frederick J., and Lionel R. Wickham, trans. *Gregory Nazianzen. On God and Christ: The Five Theological Orations and Two Letters to Cledonius*. St. Vladimir's Seminary Press "Popular Patristics" Series 23. Crestwood, NY: St. Vladimir's Seminary, 2002.

Williams, Rowan. "Augustine's Christology: Its Spirituality and Rhetoric." In *In the Shadow of the Incarnation: Essays on Jesus Christ in the Early Church in Honor of Brian E. Daley, S.J.*, edited by Peter William Martens, 176–89. Notre Dame, IN: University of Notre Dame Press, 2008.

————. "Origen: Between Orthodoxy and Heresy." In *Origeniana Septima: Origenes in den Auseinandersetzungen des 4. Jahrhunderts*, edited by W. A. Bienert and U. Kühneweg, 3–14. Leuven: Leuven University Press, 1999.

Winston, David. trans. *Philo of Alexandria. The Contemplative Life, the Giants, and Selections*. Classics of Western Spirituality. London: SPCK, 1981.

Wood, Simon P., trans. *Clement of Alexandria. Christ the Educator*. Fathers of the Church 23. Washington, DC: Catholic University of America Press, 1954.

Wooten, Cecil W. trans. *Hermogenes' On Types of Style*. Chapel Hill, NC: The University of North Carolina Press, 1987.

Wright, M. R. ed. *Empedocles: The Extant Fragments*. New Haven, CT: Yale University Press, 1981.

Wright, William M. "The Literal Sense of Scripture according to Henri de Lubac: Insights from Patristic Exegesis of the Transfiguration." *Modern Theology* 28 (2012) 252–77.

Yeago, David S. "Jesus of Nazareth and Cosmic Redemption: The Relevance of St Maximus the Confessor." *Modern Theology* 12 (1996) 163–93.

Young, Frances M. *Biblical Exegesis and the Formation of Christian Culture*. Cambridge: Cambridge University Press, 1997.

————. "*Paideia* and the Myth of Static Dogma." *The Making and Remaking of Christian Doctrine: Essays in Honour of Maurice Wiles*, edited by Sarah Coakley and David A. Palin, 265–83. Oxford: Clarendon, 1993.

———— "Panegyric and the Bible." *Studia Patristica* 25 (1993) 194–208.

————. "The Rhetorical Schools and Their Influence on Patristic Exegesis." In *Making of Orthodoxy*, edited by Rowan Williams, 182–99. Cambridge: Cambridge University Press, 1989.

# Index

# Index

mixture, 66–67, 137–40, 161–62,
    180
monothelitism and monoenergism,
    2, 117, 124, 128, 131, 134,
    136, 142, 155, 164–66,
    175–77
*Mystagogia*, 81, 82
"mystery", 25n51, 51–54, 150–51,
    156–60
nature, *see* "essence" (*ousia*) and
    "nature" *(physis), and see*
    dyophysitism (two natures
    of Christ)
Nemesius of Emesa, 19n33, 58,
    178n19, 179, 184
Neoplatonism, 18, 31–33, 36, 90–91
Numenius of Apamea, 35–36
*Opuscula*, 112, 124–25, 152–53,
    164–70, 176–89
Origen, 12–14, 21–22, 25–26,
    34–36, 38–42, 44–47, 53–55,
    64, 91–93
Paul (apostle), 14n4, 40, 42–43,
    46–47, 62, 89, 91–94, 96,
    98–100, 104–5, 143
Philo, 19, 33–34
Plato and Platonism, 15–17, 19–20,
    26–30, 33, 35–36, 42–43, 53,
    90, 184
Plutarch, 25n51, 30
"practice" (*praxis*), ascetical, 62, 65,
    95, 103, 105, 157, 162, 167
prayer, 126–28, 153–56
Proclus, 32, 90
*Questions and Doubts*, 81, 83, 94
*Questions to Thalassius*, 81, 95, 135,
    139
rhetoric, 3–4, 111–48
    as argumentative strategy,
        124–25
    epistolary, 112, 116–18, 129–32
    of comparison, 121–22, 126–28,
        137–38, 141, 143–44, 148,
        162–67, 169, 187–88
    of praise, 111–16, 119, 121–32,
        135–38, 140–42, 144–48,
        151–52, 156–57, 161–71,
        173–77, 181–83, 185–90

polemical, 135–36, 140, 142, 164
*progymnasmata* textbooks of,
    121, 125–26
*Second Letter to Thomas*, 132–45,
    148, 161, 186–87
Sergius (Patriarch of
    Constantinople), 128,
    131–32
Stoicism, 27n62, 29–30, 34–35, 140,
    179
Theodosius (bishop of Caesarea
    Bithynia), 149–50, 172
Theophilus of Alexandria, 124, 126,
    128
Theophrastus, 16–17
*tropos* ("mode") of being, *see logos/
    tropos* ("principle"/"mode")
    distinction
Valentinianism, 34, 38–40
virtue, 49–50, 53, 69, 73, 81, 86,
    95–96, 99, 103–4, 106–7,
    121, 129, 136–37, 152, 157,
    162, 169, 187–89
    *see also* knowledge, through
        virtue
will, 172–90
    *see also* Jesus Christ, will(s) of